RECENT DEVELOPMENTS IN
TRINITARIAN THEOLOGY

RECENT DEVELOPMENTS IN TRINITARIAN THEOLOGY

AN INTERNATIONAL SYMPOSIUM

CHRISTOPHE CHALAMET AND MARC VIAL, EDITORS

Fortress Press
Minneapolis

RECENT DEVELOPMENTS IN TRINITARIAN THEOLOGY

An International Symposium

Scripture quotations are from the New Revised Standard Version Bible, copyright © 1989 by the Division of Christian Education of the National Council of the Churches of Christ in the USA. Used by permission. All rights reserved.

Cover image: *Supper at Emmaus*, Caravaggio, Pinacoteca di Brera/The Bridgeman Art Library

Cover design: Laurie Ingram

Library of Congress Cataloging-in-Publication Data is available

Print ISBN: 978-1-4514-7040-6

eBook ISBN: 978-1-4514-8748-0

The paper used in this publication meets the minimum requirements of American National Standard for Information Sciences — Permanence of Paper for Printed Library Materials, ANSI Z329.48-1984.

Manufactured in the U.S.A.

This book was produced using PressBooks.com, and PDF rendering was done by PrinceXML.

CONTENTS

Introduction   1
Christophe Chalamet and Marc Vial

1. Where Do We Stand in Trinitarian Theology?   9
Resources, Revisions, and Reappraisals
Christoph Schwöbel

2. Trinity, Tradition, and Politics   73
Karen Kilby

3. The Necessity for *Theologia*   87
Thinking the Immanent Trinity in Orthodox Theology
Aristotle Papanikolaou

4. The Trinity and the World Religions   107
Perils and Promise
Gavin D'Costa

5. Colin Gunton on the Trinity and the Divine Attributes   127
Marc Vial

6. God's "Liveliness" in Robert W. Jenson's Trinitarian Thought   141
Christophe Chalamet

7. Social Trinity   153
Theological Doctrine as a Foundation for Metaphysics
Mathias Hassenfratz-Coffinet

List of Contributors   167
Index   169

Introduction

Christophe Chalamet and Marc Vial

> When people seek to know God, and bend their minds according to the capacity of human weakness to the understanding of the Trinity; learning, as they must, by experience, the wearisome difficulties of the task, whether from the sight itself of the mind striving to gaze upon light unapproachable, or, indeed, from the manifold and various modes of speech employed in the sacred writings (wherein, as it seems to me, the mind is nothing else but roughly exercised, in order that it may find sweetness when glorified by the grace of Christ); such people, I say, when they have dispelled every ambiguity, and arrived at something certain, ought of all others most easily to make allowance for those who err in the investigation of so deep a secret.
>
> —Augustine of Hippo, *On the Trinity*, Preface to Book 2.[1]

The doctrine of the Trinity has been enjoying a striking "revival" for several decades. Any eighteenth- or nineteenth-century theologian would probably be astonished if she or he could witness all of the recent publications on this topic. Things looked very different back then. According to Immanuel Kant,

> . . . [the] doctrine of the Trinity, taken literally, has *no practical relevance at all*, even if we think we understand it; and it is even more clearly irrelevant if we realize that it transcends all our concepts. Whether we are to worship three or ten persons in the Divinity makes no difference: the pupil will implicitly accept one as readily as the other because he has no concept at all of a number of persons in one God (*hypostases*), and still more so because this distinction can make no difference in his rules of conduct. On the other hand, if we read a moral meaning into this article of faith (as I have tried to do in *Religion within the Limits* etc.), it would no longer contain an inconsequential belief but an intelligible one that refers to our moral vocation.[2]

---

1. *Nicene and Post-Nicene Fathers of the Christian Church*, ed. Philip Schaff, trans. Arthur West Haddan and William G. T. Shedd (Edinburgh/Grand Rapids: T&T Clark/Eerdmans, 1993), 3:37 (trans. rev.).

Theological doctrines that have no implications for the conduct of our lives have become irrelevant, according to Kant. In order to salvage a theological theme such as the Trinity, one would have to show how it pertains to the moral life, to practical reason. As Friedrich Schleiermacher famously wrote, "this doctrine itself, as ecclesiastically framed, is not an immediate utterance concerning the Christian self-consciousness, but only a combination of several such utterances."[3] The most important nineteenth-century thinker on the Trinity was arguably G. W. F. Hegel, who was not a professional theologian, *stricto sensu*, but a philosopher. Yet Hegel had a deeper sense for the importance of trinitarian thought than most theologians of his time. He criticized August Tholuck, a well-known Pietist theologian and professor at the University of Halle who had published a historical study on early trinitarian constructs, for his lack of real understanding of what is at stake and what comes to expression in trinitarian theology:

> Does not the eminent Christian knowledge of God as the Triune merit a completely different respect than merely to ascribe it to an externally historical process? Throughout your essay I could neither feel nor find a trace of your own sensibility for this doctrine. I am a Lutheran, and through philosophy I am all the more confirmed in Lutheranism. I will not permit myself to be satisfied with external historical explanation when it comes to such basic doctrines. There is a higher spirit there than merely that of such human tradition. It is an outrage to me to see these things explained in a way comparable to the lineage and dissemination of silk manufacture, cherry growing, the pox and so forth.[4]

2. Immanuel Kant, *The Conflict of the Faculties (Der Streit der Fakultäten)*, trans. Mary J. Gregor (Lincoln: University of Nebraska Press, 1979), 65–67.

3. Friedrich Schleiermacher, *The Christian Faith*, trans. H. R. Mackintosh and J. S. Stewart (Edinburgh: T&T Clark, 1989), 738 (§170). Does such a sentence, and the locating of trinitarian doctrine as a sort of "appendix" (Claude Welch), represent a marginalization of trinitarian doctrine? No, according to Paul J. DeHart, in his insightful article: "*Ter mundus accipit infinitum.* The Dogmatic Coordinates of Schleiermacher's Trinitarian Treatise," *Neue Zeitschrift für systematische Theologie und Religionsphilosophie* 52 (2010): 17–39.

4. "Verdient die hohe christliche Erkenntnis von Gott als dem Dreieinigen nicht eine ganz andere Ehrfurcht, als sie nur so einem äusserlich historischen Gange zuzuschreiben? In Ihrer ganzen Schrift habe ich keine Spur eines eigenen Sinns für diese Lehre fühlen und finden können. Ich bin ein Lutheraner und durch Philosophie ebenso ganz im Luthertum befestigt. Ich lasse mich nicht über solche Grundlehre mit äusserlich historischer Erklärungsweise abspeisen. Es ist ein höherer Geist darin, als nur solcher menschlichen Tradition. Mir ist es ein Greuel, dergleichen auf eine Weise erklärt zu sehen, wie etwa die

Hegel took issue with a purely descriptive study of trinitarian doctrine, as if such doctrine could be reduced to a mere "human tradition." What mattered to him was the "higher spirit" that comes to expression in it. Even a deeply committed, pastoral Christian theologian such as Tholuck had been unable to become personally involved in the subject matter he had researched. And so it is not through theologians, but through a major figure in German idealist philosophy, that the doctrine of the Trinity was actualized in the nineteenth century, before a few theologians reappropriated it later in the same century (e.g., Isaak August Dorner) and much more broadly in the twentieth century.

The twentieth century can be seen as the century of a rediscovery of trinitarian thought in at least two ways. First, one might interpret this twentieth-century rediscovery as following a vaguely trinitarian pattern. Around the turn of the century, a specific kind of theological liberalism, represented by Adolf Harnack, focused on *God*; in this reading Jesus does *not* belong in the gospel he proclaimed. After World War I, starting in the 1920s and 1930s, a *christocentric* approach dominated the theological landscape, led by Karl Barth and his friends. It was only in the latter part of the century that a renewed interest in the *Holy Spirit* became noticeable, through a flood of publications. And so, in a kind of Joachimite interpretation of twentieth-century Christian theology, one may discern a trinitarian pattern: it all began with "God," continued with a christological concentration ("the Son"), and ended with a strong pneumatological accent ("the Spirit").[5]

This Joachimite reading may be a little too neat to be fully convincing (liberal theology prior to World War I, for instance, was already often christocentric), but it seems to contain a grain of truth. But the weaknesses of this reading leads us to the second reason for this twentieth-century rediscovery of trinitarian thought. Despite their christocentric emphases, both Karl Barth and Karl Rahner displayed a decisive trinitarian impetus—since the 1930s in Barth's case, a little later for Rahner—that had a tremendous influence on (and beyond) their own respective churches—Reformed and Roman Catholic. Barth, in particular, was not simply a "christocentric" theologian. Rather, he wished

Abstammung und Verbreitung des Seidenbaues, der Kirschen, der Pocken u. s. f. erklärt wird." Letter to August Tholuck, July 3, 1826, in Rolf Flechsig, ed., *Briefe von und an Hegel*, 4 vol., ed. Johannes Hoffmeister (Hamburg: F. Meiner, 1961), 4:29. Quoted in Eberhard Jüngel, *God as The Mystery of the World: On the Foundation of the Theology of the Crucified One in the Dispute between Theism and Atheism*, trans. Darrell Guder (Grand Rapids: Eerdmans, 1983), 90 (trans. rev.).

5. See Martin Leiner, "Der trinitarische Rhythmus der Theologiegeschichte im 20. Jahrhundert. Ein Vorschlag zur Strukturierung der Theologiegeschichte und seine Konsequenzen," *Theologische Zeitschrift* 56 (2000): 264–97.

to be seen as a trinitarian theologian, namely someone who focuses on the Son as the Father's Son who is active in and beyond the Christian community through the Spirit. This full commitment to trinitarian theology is true also of the following generation of thinkers, such as Jürgen Moltmann, Wolfhart Pannenberg, and Eberhard Jüngel. Many of the contemporary theologians who write about the Trinity are, in one way or another, indebted to these thinkers, even as they move beyond them or combine various elements from several of them.

The principal aim of the present volume is to highlight and to evaluate some of the main discussions about trinitarian theology within the contemporary anglophone theological literature, in particular as regards three main questions:

1. THE ECONOMIC AND IMMANENT TRINITY

How should one articulate the relation between God's immanent trinitarian life (what the Greek Fathers called *theologia*) and the "economy," namely the history of God's act in relation to the world? The debate is never likely to be resolved between, on the one hand, those who wish to preserve a difference between God in God's own life and God's act *ad extra* (toward what is not God), and, on the other hand, those who, without collapsing the two, see a decisive correspondence or even unity between the two. Karl Rahner's well-known basic axiom—"The 'economic' Trinity is the 'immanent' Trinity and the 'immanent' Trinity is the 'economic' Trinity"[6]—is an important guideline for the latter group of theologians. The former group is keen to preserve God's freedom not only *for* the world but also *from* the world, and so questions the adequacy of Rahner's axiom, especially of the second part, in which he identifies the immanent Trinity with the economic Trinity.[7] This book postulates that talk of a "unity" and "correspondence" between God's life and God's action toward the world is warranted, without collapsing the two's unity or identity. Both defenders and critics of the idea of a unity between the immanent and the economic Trinity can find support in Barth's *Kirchliche Dogmatik*. Barth, in his

---

6. Karl Rahner, *The Trinity*, trans. Joseph Donceel (New York: Crossroad-Herder, 1997 [1970]), 22; "Der dreifaltige Gott als transzendenter Urgrund der Heilsgeschichte," in *Die Heilsgeschichte vor Christus*, in *Mysterium Salutis* (Einsiedeln: Benziger, 1967), 2:328.

7. Paul D. Molnar, *Divine Freedom and the Doctrine of the Immanent Trinity* (Edinburgh: T&T Clark, 2003), but also Yves Congar, *I Believe in the Holy Spirit*, trans. David Smith (New York: Seabury, 1983), 3:13; and John Zizioulas, "The Doctrine of the Trinity Today: Suggestions for an Ecumenical Study," in Alasdair Heron, ed., *The Forgotten Trinity* (London: British Council of Churches/CCBI, 1991), 3:23.

way of thinking about the immanent and the economic Trinity, operated with an axiom similar to Rahner's, as can be seen in his discussion of the question of the Spirit's procession from the Father *and* from the Son (the contentious doctrine of the *filioque*, which contributed to the schism in 1054, and which Barth endorses).[8]

More than two decades ago already, Catherine LaCugna argued that trinitarian doctrine should never have been severed from God's relation to us and therefore from human existence, from practical life. The separation of the *ad intra* (God's own life) from the *ad extra* (God's action toward the world) had been disastrous, rendering the Trinity vacuous, without existential import, when in fact the doctrine of the Trinity calls for a "form of life appropriate to God's economy."[9] In part thanks to LaCugna, one notices a very important emphasis, in recent publications, on the relevance of the Trinity for the Christian and for human life, far from any theoretical speculation or abstraction about the idea of God or God "in Godself," independent of God's act toward creation. If one follows a decisive insight found in Reformation theology, this can still be a very fruitful orientation for today's constructive trinitarian reflection. Such reflection, as LaCugna and others have argued, is rooted in practice: baptism in the name of the Father, the Son, and the Holy Spirit; the Eucharist as a celebration of "the loving God who comes to us in Jesus Christ by the power of the Holy Spirit"[10]; and liturgy. But it is also orientated toward practice (doxology, or praise of God), as it leads to a communal and individual commitment to the reality God creates and sustains out of love, namely all of creation, and particularly the least among us.[11] The emphasis of this practical dimension finds an echo in the present volume, especially in Karen

8. ". . . . we have consistently followed the rule, which we regard as basic, that statements about the divine modes of being 'antecedently in themselves' cannot be different in content from those that are to be made about their reality in revelation." Karl Barth, *Church Dogmatics* I/1, trans. G. W. Bromiley (London/New York: T&T Clark, 2004), 479; *Kirchliche Dogmatik* I/1 (Zollikon: Verlag der evangelischen Buchhandlung, 1932), 503.

9. Catherine Mowry LaCugna, *God for Us: The Trinity and Christian Life* (New York: HarperCollins, 1991), 381. For a fairly recent appreciation of LaCugna's work, see Elizabeth T. Groppe, "Catherine Mowry LaCugna's Contribution to Trinitarian Theology," *Theological Studies* 63 (2002): 730–63. LaCugna's work has received critical acclaim for its breadth and vision, but it has been criticized for certain inaccuracies in the detail of her interpretation of several theologians (chs. 2–3 and 5–6 of her book tackle the Cappadocians, Augustine, Aquinas, and Gregory Palamas).

10. LaCugna, *God for Us*, 405.

11. The sixth part of Gilles Emery and Matthew Levering, ed., *The Oxford Handbook of the Trinity* (New York: Oxford University Press, 2011), is notably devoted to "The Trinity and Christian Life" (455–543). It includes essays on the Trinity in liturgy and preaching, the Trinity and moral life, the

Kilby's essay, whose conclusion sketches the main lines of what could be called a "political trinitarian theology."

2. Social Trinitarianism

How should the relations within the Trinity be conceived, and what kind of inferences may one draw from these relations? Many questions need to be addressed here. Whereas the Greek Fathers strongly defended the "monarchy" of the Father, or the idea that the Father is the "sole cause" (*mia aitia*) of the begotten Son and the Spirit who proceeds from the Father, recent proposals, often with an eye toward human relations, have emphasized the "perichoretic" aspect, namely the "interpenetration" of the three divine persons or identities. "Social trinitarianism" is one of the major offshoots of the recent trinitarian renewal. This interpretation, which is often associated with differing proposals from Jürgen Moltmann, Leonardo Boff, and others (such as Miroslav Volf, who wrote his dissertation under Moltmann's guidance), is not afraid of emphasizing the community of the three persons in their relation, and of using this as a model for social relations between human beings in the world. Egalitarian concerns are obvious here, and stand in opposition to hierarchical models that emphasize the obedience and subordination of the Son to the Father and thus the monarchy of the Father. Such a (more or less) direct application of trinitarian elements to the social field (from "social Trinity" to "social theory") has been criticized, especially for epistemological reasons, by Karen Kilby, as well as by others.[12]

3. Persons and Identity

What is the most adequate language for thinking about the three who comprise God's triune identity? One finds a striking agreement between Barth and Rahner on this specific question. Barth suggests the word *Seinsweisen*, or "modes of being," which should not be interpreted in any "modalist" sense, as if God were *in turn* Father, Son, and Spirit, or as if God merely *appears*—to human minds—as Father, Son, and Spirit (Barth's unfortunate way of speaking about a triple "repetition" in God led to further modalist misinterpretations).[13] As

---

Trinity and politics. Sarah Coakley's *God, Sexuality and the Self: An Essay 'On the Trinity'* (Cambridge: Cambridge University Press, 2013) seems to be moving in similar directions.

12. See Karen Kilby, "Perichoresis and Projection: Problems with Social Doctrines of the Trinity," *New Blackfriars* 81 (2000): 432–45.

13. In a recently published handbook, Barth's position, as well as Rahner's, is still labeled "the neo-modal Trinity" model. See Richard J. Plantinga, Thomas R. Thompson, and Matthew D. Lundberg, *An*

Augustine wrote, "What therefore remains, except that we confess that these terms sprang from the necessity of speaking, when copious reasoning was required against the devices or errors of the heretics?"[14]

Those who wish to maintain the relative adequacy of the word *person* are confronted by another difficulty: one sees fairly easily how the Father and his Son are "persons," but the matter is quite different when one turns to the Holy Spirit. In the Augustinian–Latin tradition especially, the Spirit is often interpreted as the "bond of love" (*vinculum caritatis*) between the Father and the Son. As many have noted, the Spirit's "personal" dimension seems to be very weak when compared with the two persons it brings into mutual relation. The reader will find echoes of this discussion in chapters 5 and 6, which are devoted to two advocates who plead the cause of the Holy Spirit's "personality": Robert W. Jenson, and one of his most brilliant doctoral students, Colin E. Gunton.

One of the questions the present volume seeks to address is whether the quality of the works produced in recent years on the Trinity is on a par with the quantity of studies. By what criteria may one reach the beginning of an answer to that question? If one wants to avoid rushing into effusive praise for this renewal and wishes to ask evaluative/qualitative questions beyond the simple acknowledgment of the quantity of books and articles, then one may want to reflect on the "measure" to be used when reflecting on the soundness of all these trinitarian proposals. Several contributions to the volume give an indirect answer to that question, sometimes in relation to a specific theological topic or school of thought. One essay, however, addresses the question directly and offers criteria for an evaluation of the contemporary contributions to trinitarian theology: the opening chapter by Christoph Schwöbel.

* * *

Almost all of the essays collected in this volume were presented at a one-day conference that the editors organized at the University of Strasbourg, France, on February 5, 2013. The first aim of the conference was to introduce current anglophone trinitarian proposals to a francophone audience. The

---

Introduction to Christian Theology (Cambridge: Cambridge University Press, 2010), 135–37. The Cappadocian Fathers themselves wrote of the divine persons' "modes of being" (*tròpoi tès uparxeós*), obviously not in a modalist perspective, but in order to point out the irreducible distinctiveness of each person; cf. esp. Basil of Caesarea, *De Spiritu Sancto* 18,46 (152b), as well as *Homil.* 24,6 (PG 31,613a), and *Letter* 235,2, in *Saint Basile. Lettres*, ed. Yves Courtonne (Paris: Les Belles Lettres, 1966), III:48,8. See already, but in a different (anthropological) sense, Gregory of Nyssa, *Contra Eunomium* I,15 (548a).

14. Augustine, *On the Trinity*, VII,4,9; ed. Schaff, p. 110; see also V,9,10 and VII,6,11–12.

intention was to let some of the main Christian traditions (Roman Catholic, Orthodox, and Protestant) come to expression and to show the variety of issues raised by trinitarian theology nowadays, not only in terms of topics (such as those listed above), but also in terms of currents (see Mathias Hassenfratz's contribution on process theology) and of disciplines (see Gavin D'Costa's paper on the relevance of the Trinity for the theology of religions). One of the topics that was not treated in Strasbourg, but which deserves attention, is the current feminist interpretation of trinitarian theology.[15]

There is something artificial in limiting the scope to the anglophone world. Clearly, these anglophone theologians are often well versed in (and influenced by) the major twentieth-century works first produced by German and German-speaking thinkers. In the case of Orthodox theology, as Aristotle Papanikolaou shows in his essay, one can only speak of an anglophone reception of Orthodox theologians who write in languages other than English. However, it seemed to the editors that it would be useful to offer something like a snapshot of some of the contemporary Anglo-Saxon contributions to the contemporary trinitarian debates and that such a picture, primarily intended for francophone readers, might also interest an anglophone readership.

---

15. For a recent contribution, see, e.g., Hannah Bacon, "Thinking the Trinity as Resource for Feminist Theology Today?," *Cross Currents* 62, no. 4 (2012): 442–64, as well as her monograph *What's Right with the Trinity? Conversations in Feminist Theology* (Aldershot, UK: Ashgate, 2009).

Where Do We Stand in Trinitarian Theology?

Resources, Revisions, and Reappraisals

Christoph Schwöbel

THE "RENAISSANCE OF TRINITARIAN THEOLOGY"—REVISITED

TRINITARIAN THEOLOGY TODAY

Twenty years ago, I wrote a brief introduction to a volume of essays entitled *Trinitarian Theology Today: Essays on Divine Being and Act*, under the heading "The Renaissance of Trinitarian Theology: Reasons, Problems and Tasks."[1] The book is a collection of papers, originally delivered at the first international conference of the Research Institute in Systematic Theology, King's College London, in 1990. Apart from giving a brief overview of the papers published in the volume, the introduction was intended as a kind of interim report on the new interest that had been given to the doctrine of the Trinity and its significance for the task of Christian theology at the end of the twentieth century. While noting the tremendous variety of approaches to the doctrine of the Trinity and the fact that the increased engagement with the doctrine of the Trinity is not restricted to one discipline of theology but somehow embraces all theological disciplines and the whole project of Christian theology in relation to its cultural settings, the introduction tried to point to a number of factors

---

1. Christoph Schwöbel, "The Renaissance of Trinitarian Theology: Reasons, Problems and Tasks," in idem, ed., *Trinitarian Theology Today: Essays on Divine Being and Act* (Edinburgh: T&T Clark, 1995), 1–30.

and motives that had contributed to the increased interest in the doctrine of the Trinity.

The first of these factors mentioned is the encounter of Western theology with the traditions of Eastern Orthodoxy in ecumenical conversations. These encounters have not only confronted Western theology with the significance that Eastern theology has ascribed to the doctrine of the Trinity, but also have pointed to effects this focus on the Trinity has for the practice of worship and for views of community organization in the church in the wider society. Apart from the notorious question of the *filioque* that once led to schism between Eastern and Western Christianity, there is also the issue of the personhood of the Holy Spirit, which Eastern theology raised as a problematic aspect of Western traditions. Encountering another tradition in ecumenical conversations not only leads to discovering the riches and problems of the other tradition but also encourages the critical engagement with one's own tradition and its history as it is reflected in the eyes of the other. It is in this context that the question of the differences and similarities between both traditions arises. Is it correct to see decisive differences between both traditions with regard to the doctrine of the Trinity, although they both profess the Nicene-Constantinopolitan creed? If so, where would these differences then be located—in doctrine, in forms of church order, or in the practice of Christian worship? How should one assess the influence of complex historical and cultural factors?

The second of the factors mentioned for the new interest in trinitarian theology draws attention to the charge that the doctrine of the Trinity has been marginalized, as Karl Rahner so memorably diagnosed. Is it true that the distinction between the dogmatic treatises *De Deo uno* and *De Deo trino* indicates that the doctrine of the Trinity had become largely irrelevant for Western theology, relegated to spheres of abstract speculation and the liturgy? Is Rahner's diagnosis correct that this marginalization, which has the effect that many Christians have a monotheist faith, lacking a distinctive Christian trinitarian profile, is connected to a separation of the inner processions and the economic missions of the Trinity? Do we find here the reason that the immanent and economic Trinity were not seen as constitutively related so that matters of biblical exegesis and questions of dogmatic reflection are pursued as independent exercises, despite all Protestant protestations that doctrine should be based on Scripture alone? If the diagnosis is correct, will Rahner's therapy, expressed in the slogan "the immanent Trinity *is* the economic Trinity, and the economic Trinity *is* the immanent Trinity," bring the desired recovery, restoring the doctrine of the Trinity to the center of the Christian faith?

The third group of factors mentioned in my 1995 introduction refers to the relationship between philosophical theism and its modern twin, philosophical atheism, and a trinitarian doctrine of God. It is noted that the philosophical debate on the existence of God and the coherence of theism have, at least sometimes, ignored the Christian confession that God is triune. Conversely, trinitarian theologies, it seems, have at least sometimes ignored the thorny questions of how confessing God the Father, Son, and Holy Spirit shapes the views of divine essence and existence, of the divine attributes and their relationship to divine agency. Twenty years ago, systematic theologians and philosophical theologians moved in different circles of thought and exchange. The new interest in trinitarian theology, however, has motivated the analysis of questions of the doctrine of God in the *confinium* of Christian doctrinal theology and philosophical theology, so that the doctrine of the Trinity is now a focus of lively debate in philosophical theology.

The fourth group of factors points to the connections between the understanding of God and the understanding of human persons and human society, especially in the way both come together in the understanding of the church. The temptation to draw easy correlations between a unipersonal image of God and authoritarian structures in church and society and contrast them to a trinitarian view of God and a correlative view of church and society, where personal particularity and social community are respected and celebrated, is criticized in the 1995 introduction: "It would be theologically disastrous if one criticized the projection of certain views of the divine nature on the order of human society for its alienating effects and then proceeded by projecting a view of desirable human relationships on the divine being."[2] Nevertheless, in spite of this criticism of a way of doing trinitarian theology, it is acknowledged that, because theology always has social effects, although they may be quite indirect and mediated in various ways, the question of the relationship of our images of the divine and our view of social relationships has to be analyzed. Does it matter for our engagement in the social world whether our theology is trinitarian or not?

The question of how this new interest in trinitarian theology should be interpreted already played a role twenty years ago. Is it a revolution moving theological thinking forward into new areas of theological exploration, or a restoration of an already established doctrine, a return to conciliar orthodoxy? Clearly, both elements played a role in the engagement with the Trinity. On the one hand, it was a new development if one considered the established forms

---

2. Ibid., 11.

of theological thought in the time immediately before the renewal of trinitarian interests. On the other hand, this step forward beyond the fashionable theologies of the time consisted in taking seriously the developments in the history of doctrine that had played a formative role in establishing Christian orthodoxy. At the time, it seemed that the metaphor of renaissance or revival captured most accurately the spirit of the new way of doing theology. Theologians employed this metaphor well aware that trinitarian theology was never completely dead, although it may not have had a high point on the theological agendas. And, of course, that there had been quite a number of previous revivals, for instance the conscious turn to trinitarian thinking in the systems of German idealism over against the deistic and theistic reductions of the doctrine of God during the Enlightenment. The interesting question, however, is not whether the metaphor is appropriate but whether the renewed interest in trinitarian theology has produced productive and significant theological developments.

THE FORGOTTEN TRINITY

The papers from the aforementioned conference are, of course, only a small detail of a much larger picture of the development of trinitarian theology. Academic theological conferences do not occur in a vacuum, and their topics do not grow out of academic interest alone. Many more factors influencing this development would have to be taken into account.[3] For the British setting, one particular event needs to be mentioned. The immediate context of the revival of interest in the doctrine of the Trinity was very much influenced by a Study Commission of the British Council of Churches on "Trinitarian Doctrine Today," which met between November 1983 and May 1988. With Costa Carras and James B. Torrance as their joint chairs, the study commission published a report under the evocative title *The Forgotten Trinity*, a selection of papers with the same title, and a study guide for local churches.[4] The impact of these three pieces should not be underestimated. The report was intended not only to offer trinitarian reorientation in matters of church doctrine on God, but to reshape the life of the churches from a trinitarian perspective.

---

3. The story is told more fully by Stanley J. Grenz, *Rediscovering the Triune God: The Trinity in Contemporary Theology* (Minneapolis: Fortress Press, 2004).

4. *The Forgotten Trinity: 1. The Report of the BCC Study Commission on Trinitarian Doctrine Today* (London: British Council of Churches [BCC], 1989); *The Forgotten Trinity: 2. A Study Guide on Issues Contained in the Report of the BCC Study Commission on Trinitarian Doctrine Today* (London: BCC, 1989); Alasdair I. C. Heron, ed., *The Forgotten Trinity: A Selection of Papers Presented to the BCC Study Commission on Trinitarian Doctrine Today* (London: BCC/CCBI, 1991).

This can most clearly be seen in the study guide, which relates the Trinity to worship, Scripture, tradition, our relationship with God, human relationships, and society. The renaissance of trinitarian theology was from the beginning much more than a new theological orientation. As the work of the BCC Study Commission makes quite clear, it was aimed at reshaping the life of the church in its liturgical, doctrinal, and ethical dimensions.

What are the crucial questions that give direction to such a reshaping as envisaged by the BCC Study Commission? It is still useful today to turn to the seminal paper John Zizioulas presented to the commission, delineating its task and defining its agenda.[5] Zizioulas agrees with the view of Barth and Rahner that the doctrine of the Trinity has become marginalized in the church, both East and West, not only in matters of doctrine, but also with regard to the devotional life of Christians. Does it make a difference whether a prayer is addressed to the Father, as in eucharistic prayers, or to the Son, or to the Spirit, as in other services? The sensibility for the question has, in Zizioulas's view, disappeared in both Eastern and Western churches. Does the doctrine of Trinity have anything to say to the question of personal identity, relationality, and communion, or is that left to sociology or psychology because it is felt that there is nothing distinctive that Christian theology has to contribute? Is there a place for the Trinity in the views of the institution and constitution of the church, or is the foundation of the church understood exclusively along christological lines, so that the shape of ecclesial community is dependent on the historic episcopate and the question of apostolic succession? And what is distinctive about Christian views of monotheism in dialogue with other religions? Is there a trinitarian notion of the one God that is different from arithmetical singularity and embraces a notion of relational unity?

The answers to these questions revolve for Zizioulas around three decisive issues. The first focuses on the relation between God and the world as it is expressed in the relationship between the immanent and the economic Trinity. Is there a distinction between the economic and the immanent Trinity which can safeguard against the kind of ontological monism that would make the being of God and the being of the world intrinsically bound up, at the expense of being unable to speak of the freedom of God? Is it right to identify the order of knowing God in the divine economy with the ontological question of God's being? Zizioulas emphatically denies Rahner's identification of the economic and the immanent Trinity:

---

5. John Zizioulas, "The Doctrine of the Trinity Today: Suggestions for an Ecumenical Study," in Heron, ed., *The Forgotten Trinity*, 19–32.

> If God *is* Trinity, he must also be outside the Economy. If he cannot be *known* as Trinity except through and in the Economy this should not lead us to construct our Trinitarian doctrine simply on the basis of the Economy. Without an apophatic theology, which would allow us to go beyond the economic Trinity, and to draw a sharp distinction between ontology and epistemology—something that classical Greek thought as well as Western philosophy have been unable to do—or between *being* and *revelation*, God and the world become an unbreakable unity and God's transcendence is at stake.[6]

The second big issue that Zizoulas identifies, and which has shaped the discussion of trinitarian theology ever since, concerns God's being in Godself. How are threeness and oneness related in God? For Zizioulas, the possible answers to this question boil down to a choice between what he calls "the Augustinian tradition" and "that of the Greek Fathers." If we start from the oneness of God in the sense of the divine *ousia* shared by Father, Son, and Spirit, we cannot logically give primacy to the threeness in God. The Trinity will always remain logically and ontologically secondary: "what is shared is prior to what shares in it."[7] This, however, has far-reaching consequences for the understanding of God and of humanity. Starting from the oneness of God would commit us, Zizioulas insists, to a view that three persons necessarily share in the one divine *ousia*, which, in turn, removes all freedom from the being of God. God is necessarily self-existent, in Zizioulas's words: "The dead ousianic tautology of something existing because it exists."[8] For Zizioulas, the only alternative consists in starting from the Father, the one God, who is the free ground of the being of the Son and the Spirit. This would both give a distinctively Christian view of monotheism, grounded in the freedom of God, and make divine freedom the ground of all created personhood, of who human persons are destined to be in their eschatological participation in the personal communion of the triune God. The choice, according to Zizioulas, is this:

> If God's existence is determined by the necessity of his *ousia*, if he is . . . a necessary being, 'being itself' . . . etc., then all existence is bound by necessity. On the other hand, if God's existence is not bound by a ousianic tautology but is caused by a free person, then there is hope also for the creature which by definition *is* faced by the priority of

6. Ibid., 23–24.

7. Ibid., 25.

8. Ibid.

substance, of 'given realities', to be free from these 'givens' to acquire God's way of being in what the Greek Fathers called *theosis*. 'Theosis' is meaningless apart from the liberation of man from the priority of substance over against the person.[9]

Seeing the person of the Father as the free "cause" of the Trinity would also present a solution to the challenging problems of the division between East and West over the *filioque* clause. It would allow for the view that the Son has a mediating function in the procession of the Spirit (*ek patros di'hyiou*) without claiming that the Son is in any sense the cause of the Spirit's procession—a view that the East regards as a relapse into pagan polytheism by claiming two generating principles in the Godhead. The solution that Zizioulas offers in his account of the metaphysics of trinitarian personhood, however, has the price of putting the blame on Augustine, not only for excluding freedom from the being of God but also for the subsequent developments of deism and atheism in the West.[10]

The third big issue that Zizioulas put on the agenda of the Study Commission concerns the relationship between the doctrine of the Trinity and ecclesiology. His programmatic call for revision of the traditional ecclesiologies is phrased as an invitation: "Let our doctrine of the Trinity suggest our ways of structuring the Church and celebrating the Eucharist."[11] This call for a trinitarian reformation of the understanding and structures of the church concerns all Christian churches, according to Zizioulas, so that he can say with clear echoes of Galatians 3:28: "on this point there is neither Orthodox, nor Protestant nor Roman Catholic."[12] What does this ecumenical trinitarian re-formation consist in? If the church is to be "a sign and a reflection of God's way of being in creation," Zizioulas argues, it must be understood and structured in a trinitarian way. The christological institution of the church must be supplemented by an account of its pneumatological constitution in order

9. Ibid.

10. Zizioulas suggests in a footnote: "We venture to suggest that the entire issue of Deism and Atheism, culminating in the question whether God exists or does not exist, an issue that has prevailed in modern Western thought particularly since the Enlightenment, derives from the fact that ever since Augustine the West has tended to understand God primarily as substance or *divinitas*. This kind of theology has not only made God a competitive and often antagonistic being in relation to man and the world, thus leading to various forms of atheistic secularisation and humanism, but has also made the question of *how* God exists, i.e. the subject of the Trinity, irrelevant or secondary to modern Western man." Ibid., 31.

11. Ibid., 28.

12. Ibid.

to reflect "the *epicletical* character of Ecclesiology,"[13] which becomes especially apparent in the Eucharist, where the words of the institution and the invocation of the Spirit are both needed in order for the Eucharist—and the church—"to be what it is." Zizioulas calls for a "pneumatologically conditioned ontology whereby nothing exists by itself and in itself, but only as a result of free communion which is precisely the essence of the Trinitarian doctrine in its application to the being of God in himself."[14]

In order to understand what trinitarian theology is today in its various forms and in order to assess the criticisms that have been leveled against it, it is necessary to keep this provocative impetus in mind and consider the challenges that were in this way offered to established ways of doing theology. Has the renaissance of trinitarian theology really led to a new liveliness of theological exchange, and has the original impetus been vindicated by mature theological reflection? Has the renaissance of trinitarian theology helped to recover the sense of authentic Christian doctrine, which could claim to be orthodox by reflecting the spirit of right teaching, or has it led theology astray in such a way that it has deviated from the path of correct teaching?

THE MAIN QUESTIONS OF TRINITARIAN THEOLOGY

The challenge of trinitarian theology to established ways of theological thinking has one main emphasis. The doctrine of the Trinity is not to be regarded as a specialized subsection of the Christian doctrine of God, but it functions as the framework for doing Christian theology. It is the point from where the whole of Christian teaching finds its integration.[15] The claims go even further than this: without a trinitarian understanding of God, the central Christian practices, Christian worship, the celebration of baptism and the Eucharist, and the Christian life in the church and society lose their specific profile. The point is well captured by Robert Jenson who, in his contribution to *Trinitarian Theology Today* bearing the title "What Is the Point of Trinitarian Theology?," insists that one can only say what the point of trinitarian theology is, if one has already understood that trinitarian theology *is* the point: "All that can be said about the point that Trinitarian theology *has*, will be false unless we simultaneously think the point that Trinitarian theology *is*."[16] The crucial question is, therefore, How is the doctrine of the Trinity to be understood so

---

13. Ibid.

14. Ibid.

15. See Christoph Schwöbel, "Trinitätslehre als Rahmentheorie des christlichen Glaubens," in idem, *Gott in Beziehung. Studien zur Dogmatik* (Tübingen: Mohr Siebeck, 2002), 24–51.

that trinitarian theology can fulfill this function? This question can be answered by a number of simple theses, pointing to the central questions trinitarian theology has to ask with regard to the doctrine of the Trinity.

The doctrine of the Trinity expresses the answer of the Christian faith to the question: "Who is God?"

The question of the identity of God is central to the Christian faith. A Christian act of worship begins with invocation of God, the Father, the Son, and the Holy Spirit, and it concludes with the Aaronic blessing (Num. 6:24-26), which, in its Christian interpretation, is the blessing in the name of the Father, the Son, and the Holy Spirit. Confessing the Father, the Son, and the Spirit in the creed is the answer of the Christian faith to the proclamation of the Gospel in word and sacraments. The importance attached to the question of the identity of the God who is addressed in Christian worship mirrors the significance that is given to God's identity in the biblical witnesses. In the Hebrew Bible, everything seems to revolve around the question of the true identity of God. Worshiping the true God is at the center of Israel's faith in all its different stages, different forms, and in its different settings. Therefore, idolatry, turning away from the true God, or mistaking someone or something else for God, is at the root of all evil that occurs in Israel's history. Knowing God's identity is only possible where God makes Godself known. Therefore, God's self-identification is the core of the question of God's identity.

God's self-identification has two main forms, which can be combined in many ways. God identifies Godself through revealing God's name and through God's acts in history. The name of God remains mysterious and shall not be used in vain, so that the Tetragrammaton is pronounced with the punctuation for "the Lord." The name of God is indirectly referenced and often an identifying description is added. Calling on the name of God and identifying God by definite descriptions are therefore closely related. The logic of God's self-identification follows this pattern: "A identifies himself to B as A (proper name) or as x (definite description) with the purpose Y." The God who identifies Godself with God's proper name also identifies Godself as God in this way as the "One who alone is to be worshiped." Whatever "x" is (e.g., the one "who brought you out of the land of Egypt, out of the house of slavery"; Exod. 20:2), it is exclusively instantiated by "A" who identifies himself in this way. The self-identification of God and God's self-interpretation through God's words and acts are intrinsically connected.

16. Robert W. Jenson, "The Point of Trinitarian Theology," in Schwöbel, ed., *Trinitarian Theology Today*, 43.

This self-identification of her God also defines the identity of Israel, as, for instance, the covenant formula (e.g., Jer. 30:22) demonstrates. While God's self-identification implies a commitment on the side of God, a promise for the future, it also implies an obligation for Israel. The promissory character of God's identification contains in this way an obligatory imperative, which comprises the whole of Israel's existence, both personal and social. Turning away from God is therefore always accompanied by the loss of identity on the part of Israel. On the other hand, the connection between God's self-identification and self-interpretation also means that Israel, both communally and personally, can turn to God as the one who brought liberation in the past. Knowing God's identity on the basis of God's self-identification is therefore the foundation for the life of worship, for addressing God, for praising, petitioning, and giving thanks to God. The understanding of God, the "theology," so to speak, is implied and enacted in the acts of relating to God on the basis of God's relating to God's people.

The witnesses of the New Testament presuppose Israel's experience of the self-identification of God and coordinate the experience of God in Jesus and in the Spirit with Israel's experiences of God. The Easter experience of the vindication of Jesus' witness to God in his life and death prompts the first Christian communities to see in Jesus a new self-identification of God that does not cancel Israel's experiences of God's self-identification but opens Israel's relationship with her God to all people who believe in Jesus. The Easter experience therefore inaugurates for the first Christian communities a view of their life as an ongoing communion with the risen Lord, even in the absence of the personal experience of Jesus in the flesh as a person they could encounter like other persons, through celebrating the Lord's Supper and preaching and hearing the gospel of Christ. This communion is understood as being exclusively constituted by God. The name for this new presence of God, which connects the Christian communities with Jesus and through him with the God of Israel, is the "Spirit," as the early Christian communities said in adapting one of Israel's ways of speaking about the presence of God in action.

In the New Testament, we can see how the integration of the new ways of the presence of God led to a "prototrinitarian grammar" of talking about God.[17] By understanding Jesus as "the Son" and the God of Israel as "the Father," and by interpreting God's presence with the community of believers as "the Spirit," the

---

17. I have tried to develop the thesis that there is in the New Testament writings an underlying "proto-trinitarian depth structure" which can be expressed in a grammar in my paper on "Christology and Trinitarian Thought," in *Trinitarian Theology Today*, 112–46. This thesis is further developed in "The Trinity between Athens and Jerusalem," *Journal of Reformed Theology* 3 (2009): 22–41.

Christian community was enabled to integrate its experience of God through Christ and in the Spirit. It is important to note the distinctive features of this way of talking about God, of addressing God, and of pronouncing the blessing of God to the community of believers. The one God is not simply replaced by Jesus, but Jesus and God are seen in a relationship that does not cancel the unity of God, but nevertheless introduces an element of differentiation in relationship. In confessing Jesus as the Lord, one confesses no other God than the one God of Israel, but one confesses this God in a new way in which God has become present, although this "new way" is eternally part of the being of God. Similarly, the experience of the Spirit is really the experience of the one God, but in a way that is different from God's history with Israel and God's presence in Jesus, but at the same time related to both in such a way that this difference is part of God's being from eternity.

The doctrine of the Trinity is to be understood as the way in which the Christian church could make sense of her experience of God. It is the way in which the church could express in doctrinal form what shaped her experience of God and her worship. In the early church, the doctrine of the Trinity is not a problem that somehow arose from the encounter with Hellenistic philosophy. It is a solution to the problem of how one should express the genuine Christian experience of God by discourse about the Father, the Son, and the Spirit. In this way it becomes the criterion of what one should regard as genuinely Christian in all discourse about God and in relating to God. The doctrine of the Trinity allows Christians to explain what it means when they respond to the question "Who is God?" by professing the Father, the Son, and the Holy Spirit. Trinitarian theology is therefore a way of doing theology that consistently pays attention to the triune identity of God in every aspect of Christian teaching, Christian worship, and Christian living.

Starting with the question "Who is God?" is a common feature among many, otherwise rather diverse, approaches to the doctrine of the Trinity in modern trinitarian theology. Karl Barth had already indicated that the priority of the question "Who?" points to the distinguishing feature of the doctrine of the Trinity as that which discloses the particular Christian character of the doctrine of God.[18] Robert Jenson has programmatically presented his doctrine of God as a treatise on the *triune identity*.[19] And John Zizioulas develops his approach by unfolding an "ontology of Personhood" starting with the "Who?"

18. Karl Barth, *Church Dogmatics I/1: The Doctrine of the Word of God* (London: T&T Clark, 2004), 297–305.

19. Robert W. Jenson, "The Triune God," in Carl E. Braaten and Robert W. Jenson, eds., *Christian Dogmatics*, vol. 1 (Philadelphia: Fortress Press, 1984), 79–193.

question.[20] This has a number of important implications. Rather than starting with the question "What is God?" and all the qualifications of an epistemological and ontological kind that are necessary in order to deal with that question, the "Who?" question leads immediately to the issue of God's identification and identity. This can take the form of establishing the doctrine of the Trinity as the systematic link between the doctrine of revelation and the doctrine of God (Barth), of developing the link from the identification of God to the temporal structure of the church's experience of God (Jenson), or of systematically presenting an ontology of personhood that gives full weight to the significance of personal particularity (Zizioulas). In all the different cases it assumes that for the practices of the church's proclamation of the triune God and for addressing God in worship, the question of God's identity must take priority. The "What?" question is in this way dealt with in a specific form: "What" can be said about the essence of the God whose identity is expressed by invoking the name of the Father, the Son, and the Spirit? This, however, requires that one can say something about the way in which the triune God relates to creation on the basis of the relationship that God is as Father, Son, and Spirit.

However, this does not mean to identify God's self-identification with God's identity *simpliciter*. There is a sense in which God remains transcendent to God's self-identification in history. This is precisely the element of the "self" in God's self-identification. God is who God is in how God relates to creation, but how God relates to creation in time is eternally rooted in how God is in the immanent relations of the eternal Trinity. God's self-identification is the self-manifestation of God as God is constituted in the eternal Trinity. This is what radically distinguishes God from everything that is not God and which can only be expressed by discourse about God's freedom. Only if God freely relates to the world is it excluded that God is somehow constituted by God's relations to the world, which would deny the gratuitous freedom in which God creates *ex nihilo*. This can only be expressed by relating the "Who?" question more precisely to "How?" questions of how God is in relation to the world and how God is the eternal relations of the three persons in the one divine essence.

The doctrine of the Trinity is the attempt at providing a doctrinal answer to the question "How is God?" in relation to the being of the world and in relation to God's own being.

---

20. See John Zizioulas, "On Being a Person: Towards an Ontology of Personhood," in Christoph Schwöbel and Colin E. Gunton, eds., *Persons, Divine and Human* (Edinburgh: T&T Clark, 1991), 33–46.

In Christian confessions of faith, the triune God, Father, Son, and Holy Spirit, is confessed as the creator, reconciler, and consummator of the world, that is, of everything that is not God. It is the one God, whose identity is expressed in the triune name, who is believed to be the origin, end, and meaning of everything there is. Already in the New Testament we find the beginnings of the attempt to state clearly that the creator of the world and the reconciler of the world is the one God, by talking about the mediation of creation in Christ (Col. 1:15–20). This gained an enormous significance over against all Gnostic tendencies to separate the imperfect creator of an imperfect creation from the redeemer who liberates from the imperfections of the created order. If one follows this line of thought through its different stages in the early debates on the Christian understanding of God, one arrives at the view that everything in the divine economy must be understood as a triune act. This has two implications. First, no act in the divine economy is to be ascribed to the Father, the Son, or the Spirit alone. Rather, the Trinity is the agent of all God's acts in the divine economy. The way in which the Father, Son, and Spirit are involved in this trinitarian action is not identical. The Son becomes incarnate, but not the Father or the Spirit, although the Father and Spirit are involved in the act of the incarnation of the Son. Every act of God in the divine economy appears as a unitary, but internally differentiated, act.

The second implication of that view is that the different acts of God in relation to the world are related through their one triune agent. Understanding this agent as triune as the Father, the Son, and the Spirit points from the start to the interconnectedness of divine action in the divine economy, and so to the trinitarian "dimensionality" in everything that God does. Creation in this way is not just the bringing into existence of something that did not exist before. It is much more than that, because it is the realization of God's will to be in communion with what God creates and so points to its future fulfillment. Viewed from a trinitarian perspective, creation has its purpose and its end in God's fully actualized communion with what God is not. Reconciliation is therefore, in one important respect, God's way of being faithful to God's original decision to be in communion with God's creation, in spite of the rebellion of human creatures against their creator. Interpreting the God who acts in the divine economy consistently as the triune God is therefore a way of expressing the unity of the divine economy while allowing for the differences and relations involved at different stages of the divine economy. The notion of a history of salvation which includes the dramatic events that the biblical story narrates, appears in this way as dependent on the notion of the triune God as the agent of this history, who gives this history, in spite of all its narrative differentiations, its unity and plot.

Yet, this is not the whole story or, rather, the story of God's ways with the world is not all that needs to be said. This way of explaining trinitarian discourse about God can demonstrate that the divine economy has its origin and end, its unity and its dramatic differentiation, in the identity of the triune God. As such, it shows how trinitarian discourse structures the way the story is told and gives a particular matrix to Christian beliefs about God's relationship to the world. However, it has one difficulty. Is God how God is because of God's relationship to the world as creator, reconciler, and consummator of everything that is not God? If that were the case, then God and the world would be mutually constitutive. The whole thrust of the early development of Christian doctrine goes against such a conclusion, and in this way maintains one of the most decisive insights of the faith of Israel. God is not dependent on the world as the world is dependent on God. God is the sovereign Lord over all, and therefore "how God is" cannot be defined in an exclusive sense by God's relationship to the world. It must be defined by how God is in the relations of Father, Son, and Spirit. The development of the doctrine of creation from nothing, which intends to explain the sovereign freedom of God in creating the world, and the differentiation of the way "how" God is in the Trinity (that is, in the immanent relations) from the relations of the triune God to what is not God (in the economic relations) belong together. This explains why the creation of the world and the generation of the Son are so emphatically distinguished.

Negatively, this implies that we cannot simply "read off" the inner constitution of the trinitarian being of God from the way the triune God acts in the divine economy. Positively, this implies that the divine economy must be interpreted as the *self-manifestation* of the triunity of God. There remains a difference that maintains the distinction between epistemology and ontology, between believing and the beatific vision, between the *lumen gratiae* that illumines our faith and the *lumen gloriae* that will disclose the fullness of the glory of the triune God in communion with God's reconciled creation. There is, therefore, space for a qualified apophaticism at this point. It points to the way in which the triune God himself must bridge, and has bridged, the gap that must be maintained at this point.

Far from weakening the link between the immanent Trinity and the economic Trinity, however, acknowledging this distinction strengthens that link. If God and the world cannot be seen as mutually constitutive, and if therefore the world must be seen as God's free creation *ex nihilo*, without any preconditions, and if this structure is maintained in every aspect of God's relating to what is not God, then God's relationship to the world is based on God's freedom in a radical sense. There is then no prior metaphysical link between God and the world. That God creates by the Word has often been seen as an expression of God's freedom in creation by distinguishing creation by the Word of God sharply from any form of emanation from the divine. Everything that God does in the world is thus an expression of divine freedom. The divine economy is therefore in a specific sense the free self-manifestation of the triune God. How God is in relation to the world is a manifestation of God's self-determination. Everything that occurs in the world, including the created self-determination of human persons, is therefore to be seen in the horizon of God's self-determination. This includes God's self-determination to let God's self-determination be shaped by the different states of the world, the freedom to let God's self-determination be determined by what happens in the world.

Now, if *how* God relates to the world is determined not only by the freedom of God's will, which remains external to God's being, but by the freedom of *how* God *is* in the Trinity, this will change the view of the relationship between the divine economy and the immanent Trinity. If God's freedom to relate to what is not God is related to the freedom-in-relationship that God is in God's being, this excludes that God's will could be arbitrary and locates God's will in the freedom that God *is*. If the Word through which God relates to the world is rooted in the Word that "was in the beginning, and was with God, and . . . was God" (John 1:1), the response to the Word of God in faith cannot only be a response to God's will but involves a relationship to God as God is in God's being. We have in this way a strong "relational joint" between how God is in relation to the world and how God is in the inner relations.

This, however, involves choices in the interpretation of the doctrine of the Trinity. If the *homoousios* is simply taken to mean that Father, Son, and Spirit instantiate the same divine essence three times over, without rooting how God is in relation to the world in how God is in God's own being, one has effectively made the doctrine of the Trinity meaningless for understanding the divine economy. If one takes the *homoousios to patri* of the Nicene-Constantinopolitan creed seriously, one will have a view of the Trinity where the *homoousios* is understood in such a way as to make the eternal relations between the persons of the Trinity meaningful for the divine economy. God's freedom is then not to be understood as the freedom of an abstract substance or of an absolute subject, three times over in the Father, the Son, and the Spirit, but as freedom-in-relationship, as freedom-in-communion, which liberates human persons to be free in relationship to the triune God who is freedom. This seems to be crucial for understanding God as love, as the Christian tradition has consistently emphasized on the basis of 1 John 4. It seems that not only the Cappadocians, but also Augustine and the majority of the Western theologians of the Trinity, have in their different reconstructions of the doctrine maintained that how God is in God's own being is relevant to the way in which God is in relation to the being of the world.

Starting from the "Who?" question in trinitarian theology inevitably involves the theologian in the discussion of the "How?" questions, both with regard to the relation of the triune God to creation and with regard to the relations in the divine being itself. It is therefore not surprising that many recent approaches to trinitarian theology have given the question of relation a high priority. It is one of the most significant discoveries of the classical disputes of trinitarian doctrine in the early church that the straightforward application of a received philosophical conceptuality to the doctrine of God leads into difficulties. If the three in God are understood in the sense of three substances sharing one attribute, namely divinity, we are in a tritheistic scheme that can neither do justice to the emphasis on the oneness and uniqueness of God, which Christianity inherited from the Hebrew Scriptures, nor can it distinguish the Christian understanding of God sufficiently from pagan forms of religiosity in its cultural contexts. When only one of the three in the divine Trinity has the divine substance in the full sense and the other two in a lesser sense, it might seem at first that the requirement of the unique transcendence of God can be met, but at the expense of having two demigods, all too familiar in the religious world of the Mediterranean in late antiquity. The astonishing demythologizing effect that Nicaea had by claiming that the Son of God was both fully human and fully divine would have been lost. The alternative of speaking of one divine substance and three modes of appearance, the modalist proposal, denies the eternity of the three in God and turns the conversation and interaction between the three—so central to the New Testament witness—into a charade.

Even such a simplified picture of some of the problems confronting trinitarian reflection can quickly demonstrate that trinitarian theology must in some sense engage in revisionary metaphysics and that for this kind of metaphysics the category of relation has paramount importance. After all, the classical terminology of "unbegotten," "begotten," and "proceeds" clearly names relations. But what kind of relations? Here the thrust of the distinction and connection of the two "how" questions points in one direction. While there are in the triune God real relations—that is, relations that are constitutive for the particular being of the Father, the Son, and the Spirit—these relations must be clearly distinguished from the relations of the triune God to what is not God. The inner-trinitarian relations are in a sense mutually constitutive and reciprocal, though asymmetrical, relations. These inner-trinitarian relations constitute the respective trinitarian identities (Father, Son, Holy Spirit), and in this way constitute a real otherness; they also constitute, because they are constitutive relations, a real togetherness. This togetherness is further expressed by the fact that the relations which are constitutive for the hypostatic identities do not constitute a division in the divine essence. They are relations and distinctions in God, but do not involve any division or separation of the divine essence. The relations of the Trinity to the world are constitutive for the being of the world but not for the being of God. However, when this relational God relates to what is not God in creation, reconciliation, and eschatological consummation, God relates in such a way that God creates a relational world, a world of created particularities and created forms of togetherness.

What has been achieved by highlighting the importance of the "How?" question in both its forms, with regard to the being of the triune God, and with regard to the relation of the triune God to creation? The upshot can be summarized in five statements:

1. The category of relation as a real, reciprocal, constitutive, though asymmetrical, relation has been given a proper place in the understanding of the Trinity, both and at the same time for the understanding of the hypostatic identities of Father, Son, and Spirit and for the view of their togetherness.

2. If God is relational in this sense, there is eternally a place for personal particularity in God, the Father, the Son, and the Holy Spirit, which does not cancel out God's essential unity.

3. If God is relational in this sense, if this relationality is the "how" of the being of God, then this inner-trinitarian relationality must be sharply distinguished from God's relations *ad extra*. The relations of the trinitarian God to everything that is not God are constitutive for creation, but they are nonconstitutive for God.

4. However, if this relational God relates to what is not God, the divine relationality will shape that to which God relates so that when this God creates, there is a relational world with its own created relationality and its created patterns of particularity and togetherness. On the one hand, the network of created relationality of a contingent world is more diverse than the relationality of the triune

God, because it is not encompassed by the unity of the divine essence but characterized by the plurality of created substances. However, since it is created relationality, it is an open relationality that cannot sufficiently and completely be understood apart from its constitution in the relationship of God to creation.

5. Every attempt at expressing the correlation between the two "Hows?" must take their distinction and relationship into account. It is here that the relationship between kataphatic and apophatic modes of thought and speech must be worked through again and again.

It is precisely at this point that the third thesis must be considered:

The doctrine of the Trinity tries to answer the question "What is God?" in such a way that the answer neither cancels the relational plurality in God nor the unity of God's being but specifies the ways in which they can be spoken of.

It must be conceded that this question has to be in the background of reflections on the "Who?" and "How?" questions from the beginning. After all, we are considering the identity of God and the how of God's internal and external relations. The "monotheistic principle" that Christianity inherited from the Old Testament, and which Christian theology never questioned until quite recently, was presupposed and referred to in the development of discourse relating God, Jesus, and the Spirit from the beginning.[21] It acquired a specific significance in the development of trinitarian doctrine over against two positions that programmatically made appeal to it: Arianism and modalism.[22] What had to be shown was that the procession of the Son and the proceeding of the Spirit do not disrupt the unity of the one divine nature. The breakthrough for a clear conceptual formulation of the doctrine of the Trinity was certainly the distinction between what is common (*koinon*) to the three persons in the Trinity and what is characteristic for each one of them (*idion*).[23] The identification of the "what" with the shared *ousia* and the explication of Father, Son, and Spirit in the "how" of their relations with the particular *hypostaseis* that thus acquired a new meaning, generated a trinitarian ontology focused

---

21. See my article "Monotheismus V. Systematisch-theologisch," in *Theologische Realenzyklopädie* (Berlin-New York: W. de Gruyter, 1993), 23:256–62.

22. It is interesting to note that these two heresies were employed in medieval theology as paradigms for setting up the coordinates of the trinitarian question. See Thomas Aquinas, *Summa Theologiae* I, q. 27, a.1.

23. E.g., Basil, *Contra Eunom.* 2,28; Gregory of Nazianzus, *Or.* 25,16.

on the modes of origination (*tropos hyparxeos*),[24] the resulting relations (strictly interpreted as correlations, the "towardness" of the *hypostaseis* expressed by their identification with the *prosopa*), and the character of the resulting relation as *koinonia*, as communion relation or persons in communion.[25]

These differentiations, allowing for particularity, alterity, and relatedness, however, had to be bracketed by the one undivided, eternal *ousia*, excluding any ontological comparative and gradation. This formed the foundation of a rule of predication that could specify what had to be said of the one *ousia* and what could be predicated of the different persons. This rule of predication restricts all discourse of the "what" of God to the negation of specifying limitations. There is no positive content that can be predicated of the divine *ousia*; it remains beyond human grasp. "We have learned to honor in silence that which transcends speech and thought," insists Gregory of Nyssa.[26] However, this is not simply a case of "whereof one cannot speak, thereof one must be silent."[27] Rather, this is a silence that speaks, insofar as it directs our attention from the *ousia* to the *energeiai* of the triune God. The "unnameable" essence can be indirectly named by referring to the *energeia* of God, God's actions in the divine economy. Because they are rooted in the one *ousia*, the common *energeiai* are always the joint action of the three persons. Although what can be said directly about the divine *ousia* is that it remains incomprehensible and unnameable, indirectly it is needed to keep trinitarianism from falling into the ever-present pitfalls of Eunomianism or modalism. The apophatic restriction concerning the *ousia* regulates the kataphatic expression of language about the trinitarian God when it turns to the *energeia* of the Trinity.

We can thus summarize what needs to be said about the question "What is God?" in the Trinity:

1. Speaking of the divine essence as that which is common in the strong sense of the *homoousios* of the Father, the Son, and the Holy Spirit excludes both any form of ontological gradation between the three persons of the Trinity and any ontological difference between "what" the Father, the Son, and the Spirit are in relation to "what" God is. The denial of a difference of the ontological "what"-status of

---

24. Gregory of Nazianzus, *Or.* 31.9.
25. Gregory of Nyssa, *Pet.* 4 (= Basil, *Ep.* 38,4).
26. *Contra Eunom.* 3,5.
27. Ludwig Wittgenstein, *Tractatus logico-philosophicus* 7.

the three persons in the Trinity shows that their difference consists in the "how"-relationship.

2. The divine persons do not possess their common divine *ousia* in any other way than by virtue of their relations. Any other assumption would posit the divine essence as a fourth element in the Trinity, and necessitate speaking of relations that the persons have to the divine *ousia* in addition to the relations they have to one another. This implies, on the one hand—and this is one of the hallmarks of trinitarian orthodoxy—that the divine *ousia* is not understood as generative and that no form of fecundity is ascribed to the divine *ousia*. If, on the other hand, the originating relations between the three persons are the only way in which they possess the divine *ousia*, then *communication* is constitutive for the being and for the unity of the divine *ousia*. The three persons are "what" they are in virtue of their relations to one another, in virtue of "how" they are related in the communicative relations of origin.

3. Speaking of the one divine *ousia* of the Father, the Son, and the Spirit contrasts the divine essence to all forms of created substances. While created substances are always conditioned in some way in their "what"-ness by their relationship to something else, this is not the case for God. The conditionality of created substances implies necessity, whereas the unity of the divine essence is beyond all necessity. Only if the relations between the three persons are placed squarely within the unity of the divine essence can they be understood as relations of divine freedom. The relations of origin that apply to the three persons are therefore relations of absolute freedom-in-relation. The *homoousios to patri* which is predicated of the Son excludes any notion of the Father as "cause" (*aition*) that somehow restricts the freedom of the Son and, consequently, of the Spirit. The order between the three divine persons (*taxis*) is therefore the structure of coessential divine freedom, shared by all three in virtue of their common essence.

4. The divine essence can therefore only be spoken of in a sense that denies any form of restriction, limitation, or dependence that would restrict the freedom that God is in all three persons.

5. Speaking of the one divine essence therefore means speaking of the three divine persons and *vice versa*.

6. Being in relation with the trinitarian God means for God's human creatures to be in relation to the ground of freedom.

On the basis of the answers that are given to the questions "Who?," "How?," and "What?" is God, one can then proceed to speak of the attributes of God. This brings us to our fourth thesis:

The doctrine of the Trinity responds to the question "Which attributes can be predicated of God?" by regulating the way in which we can predicate attributes of God and points to the way in which these attributes are related.

When we develop the doctrine of the Trinity from the perspective of the "Who?" question, starting with the triune identity of God, then discourse about God's attributes must first of all be rooted in the personal self-communication and self-manifestation of God. God's self-communication is the foundation of Christian worship in which God is addressed by God's threefold divine name and the attributes of God are expressed in the form of the address to God in prayer. Thereby, the discourse about the divine attributes is placed within the relationship to the triune God as it is enabled by God's relationship to us and as it is enacted in worship. God and God's attributes are not spoken of as something external to who we are in relation to God. The situation of worship expresses explicitly that in predicating God we are implicitly predicating ourselves, and in predicating ourselves we are implicitly predicating God. For the Christian faith, the biblical Scriptures have paradigmatic function in exercising the predication of attributes to God in the relational context of worship. In this context, the personal attributes of God always come first, and they are connected to the original "scenes" of God's self-disclosure in God's word and actions as they are related in the biblical witnesses. The different personal attributes of God situate the worshiping community in relation to God so that predicating God is part of praising God, of petitioning God, of thanking God, of voicing our lament to God. Connecting the attributes of God to God's self-manifestation is intended to make sure that we are addressing and predicating God as God wishes to be addressed and allows us to predicate God.

It is important to note that this contextualization also includes the "names" of the Father, the Son, and the Spirit. When we address God as Father, we follow the invitation of Jesus: "Pray then in this way: Our Father in heaven . . ." (Matt. 6:9). When we talk about Jesus as the Son, we do so in the context of the application of Psalm 2:7 in the accounts of Jesus' baptism: "This is my Son, the beloved" (Matt. 3:17). When we call on the Spirit, we do so in the context of Jesus' announcement of the coming of the Spirit: "But the Advocate, the Holy Spirit, whom the Father will send in my name, will teach you everything" (John 14:26). The biblical accounts establish rigid designations, which are prior to descriptive naming, and establish the context in which descriptions are used. In other words: that Jesus called God "Father" and invites us to do so is prior to analogies between human fatherhood and the name "Father" for the one in the Trinity who is unbegotten, and defines the framework in which such analogous descriptions can secondarily be applied.[28]

Placing the question of the attributes of God in the context of worship establishes a strong link between the address of God and the predication of God. "Which attributes" can be predicated of God depends on who God is. In addressing God in this way, we are, in a sense, retracing in our relating to God the steps that the triune God has taken to relate to us in God's trinitarian self-disclosure. This is expressed clearly by Luther in his Large Catechism: "For we could never attain to the knowledge of the grace and favor of the Father except through the Lord Christ, who is a mirror of the paternal heart, outside of whom we see nothing but an angry and terrible Judge. But of Christ we could know nothing either, unless it had been revealed by the Holy Ghost."[29] Here we are already at the point where the "Who?" and the "How?" questions are interconnected. Predicating personal attributes of God necessarily involves us in the way God manifests Godself in the divine economy. This implies that the attributes predicated of God are based on God's self-manifestation in the divine economy.

At the same time, the attributes of God receive an important qualification here. In the context of the divine economy, the divine attributes are based on what God has done, does, and promises to do in the creation, reconciliation, and consummation of the world. In this connection, traditional attributes such as divine omnipotence are not defined primarily by what can be predicated of God—that is, that God can do anything that is logically possible—but by the creation of a world, the resurrection of Christ, or the justification of the sinner. What God's actions in the divine economy have in common is that they are truly creative in the sense that they are not restricted by any conditions

28. Cf. the causal theory of names that Saul Kripke suggests as an alternative to the descriptivist account of naming, in his *Naming and Necessity* (Cambridge: Harvard University Press, 1980). We have treated both accounts as complementary, while giving priority to the causal account.

29. "The Apostles' Creed," in Martin Luther, *The Large Catechism* (Radford: Wilder Publications, 2008), 62.

external to God's agency and they do not rely on presuppositions other than the being and will of God. This is most clearly seen in the understanding of the creation of the world *ex nihilo*, which does not presuppose anything apart from God's power to create. Christ's resurrection points in a similar direction. The end scenarios of created existence, finitude, and death have no determinative force that restricts the power of God. God is the Lord over life and death who transcends the polarities of created life. Similarly, the justification of the sinner does not presuppose merit on the part of the sinner, but makes the sinner righteous in virtue of Christ's righteousness. That God's agency does not have any presuppositions external to God does not mean that God cannot take the state of God's creation, death, and sin as the occasion for God's actions. God responds to the misery of creation, but God responds in the glory of God's own being. There is then a categorical difference between divine agency and any form of created agency, which in a material sense defines God's omnipotence.

One implication of divine omnipotence, as it is understood on the basis of God's self-manifestation in the divine economy, is that because of its creative character there is nothing that could frustrate or ultimately impede God's achieving the goal that God has set Godself. In this sense, God has foreknowledge of God's aim for God's relationship with creation, perfecting God's communion with God's reconciled creation, and is in this sense omniscient. God is omnipresent to every moment of the life of creation because God is the condition for its presence at every moment. And God's life brackets the time of creation from beginning to end.

If one takes the way the trinitarian God relates to that which is not God as the basis for defining the attributes of God, one can detect a trinitarian structure to how God acts in the divine economy which in turn shapes the view of God's attributes. If God's agency is understood as trinitarian agency, it has a trinitarian structure in the unity of the agency of the triune God. Basil has expressed this structure by talking about the Father as the unoriginate originating cause, the Son as the ordering cause, and the Spirit as the perfecting cause in everything that God does.[30] This leads to a trinitarian differentiation of all divine attributes which transcends the logic of negation that is based on the contrast between the Creator and the creation.

This can easily be shown with reference to divine eternity. As the unoriginate originating cause, God is the creative ground of all created time, and God as the creator is atemporally eternally present to every creature at every point in time of creation. If creation is to be understood as the actualization of

---

30. Basil, *De spir.* 15,38.

God's eternal will to be in communion with God's creation, then God must also be thought of as temporally eternally present for every creature and with every creature at every point in time of creation. God's temporality in this sense is God's free and eternal self-determination for communion with God's creatures.

The purpose of God's eternal creative will and temporal creative presence is disclosed in the incarnation of God the Son in Jesus Christ. As the eschatological event in time, it is both the fulfillment of the preceding history, and the anticipation of the perfection of God's communion with God's creation. In this way, Jesus Christ is the temporal self-disclosure of the eternal will of God to establish a communion of love and righteousness with God's creation. This illumines the purpose of creation by promising the perfection of creation in communion with God. God's temporal human creatures are thereby directed to the purpose of God's will and so to the ultimate destiny of their created life. The death and resurrection of Christ is therefore the paradigmatic reconciliation of time and eternity, of the time of mortal creatures and their eternal destiny. This has decisive implications for our view of the time of creation. In its exposition to death, in its bondage to decay, creation is destined to being transformed in participation in the communion with the eternal God.

The presence of God's Spirit in creation has a twofold significance. On the one hand, it is the presence of the eternal God in all forms of created life as the Spirit of life that makes creation responsive to the creative action of the Creator. On the other hand, the Spirit as the perfecting cause is the presence of the future perfection for creation. In God's Spirit, God is the future of every moment of creation. As such, the Spirit liberates from the bondage of creation to the past. As the presence of the absolute future, it counteracts the conditioning of created existence from the past, from its antecedent conditions. The Spirit is in this way the source of freedom for the creature, the way in which the eternal perfection in God's perfected communion with God's reconciled creation is already present here and now. Phenomena like emergence, which are not the predicted result of their antecedent conditions according to deterministic laws, appear in this way as the correlate of the presence of the Spirit in the natural world. The Spirit's time is the actualization of novelty already before the end of history. However, the liberating Spirit may establish discontinuity with antecedent courses of events, but as the perfecting cause of God's action it is not discontinuous with God's action as the originating cause and the ordering cause. What may appear as discontinuous novelty on the plane of worldly events must nevertheless be continuous with God's overarching will and action and the patterns of the eternal and the temporal in which it is actualized.

Talking about the eternity of God on this trinitarian basis has a rich content, which is not expressed by interpreting eternity simply as timelessness. Talk about God's eternity must comprise the forms in which God is present to creation as its eternal ground, eternally and temporally, in the *chronos* of physical time, in the *kairos* of the reconciliation of time and eternity, and in the *eschaton* where time is taken up into the eternal presence of God. God's eternity is the unity of the eternal relation of God the eternal Father, as the unoriginate origin, to a temporal creation, of the ordering of times through the presence of the eternal Son for time and in time, and of the life-giving and life-perfecting temporal presence of the eternal Spirit. And in this rich sense God's eternity is, as Boethius defined, "the complete, simultaneous and perfect possession of everlasting life."[31]

Boethius's definition gives a good indication of how divine simplicity—the doctrine that there is no real distinction between God and God's attributes, so that God is what God has—should be understood: God is God's nature and God's existence. Divine simplicity denies God that is a composite being characterized by such kinds of composition as form and matter, individual and nature, essence and being, and substance and accident. None of these distinctions may be applied to God and God's attributes. In philosophical discussion, it is questioned whether this doctrine does make any sense at all. Alvin Plantinga has famously argued that if God is identical to God's properties, then God is a property. However, properties are abstract entities, and abstract entities are causally inert, so that God cannot be conceived as a personal creator of every contingent being.[32] This objection is based on a distinction between concrete individuals as active, and abstract properties as inert. One can see, from this objection alone, that divine simplicity requires to be supplemented in order to exclude this kind of straightforward objection. That God is simple is simply not enough, because particular things might be simple, too, in the sense of indivisibility. On the other hand, if God is *simplicitas* "*simpliciter*," it becomes difficult to distinguish God from the formal being of things as that which appears when a composed reality is reduced to its most elementary principle. Simplicity either claims not enough by making God a being among other beings, or it claims too much by identifying God with being as such, with all its pantheistic consequences.

---

31. Boethius, *De consolatione philosophiae* V,6,4: "interminabilis vitae tota simul et perfecta possessio." For a slightly more detailed account, see Christoph Schwöbel, "Time," in *Religion Past and Present* (Leiden: Brill, 2012), 12:720–24.

32. Alvin Plantinga, *Does God Have a Nature?* (Milwaukee: Marquette University Press, 1980), 47.

Thomas Aquinas, who structures the *Summa Theologiae* (hereafter *ST*) in such a way that the doctrine of the Trinity (*ST* I, qq. 27-43) is the core from which the procession of creatures from God (*ST* I, qq. 44-119) is to be explained, therefore prefaces this account with a reflection on the divine essence (*ST* I, qq. 2-26), including their modes of operation (*agere sequitur esse*), in order to clarify the distinctions of the persons by means of active processions (cf. *ST* 2 prol.). In this account of the attributes that make up the divine essence, divine simplicity comes first in order to clarify that God's essence is indivisible, so that we cannot know God through God's parts, which is, of course, the way in which we know created entities. If we cannot know God from God's parts, it is not only clear from the start that the three persons cannot be conceived of as parts of God, but also that we cannot know God from the rational investigation of things as they are caused by God. In the end, we arrive at positive knowledge of God only by means of revelation. The reflections of the first section of the threefold division of the *prima pars* lead into the doctrine of the Trinity as it is revealed to faith. Simplicity provides the starting point, but nothing more. Simplicity (q. 3) must be supplemented by perfection (q. 4)—after all, a particular being could be simple and God could simply be being. *Perfectio* therefore presents God as the *ipsum esse*, as the cause of all things, clearly distinguished from its effects, but in a fully determinate and concrete form (*ipsum esse per se subsistens*). Only God, as the perfect being, can be perfectly simple, so that now God's goodness (qq. 5 and 6) and infinity (q. 7) can be considered, leading to omnipresence (q. 8), immutability (q. 9), and eternity (q. 10), culminating in divine unity (q.11).[33] This is the point where all the arguments lead, so that divine unity is, so to speak, the telos of the argument, starting from simplicity. One could say: divine simplicity is *indivisibilis essentiae tota simul et perfecta possessio in tribus personis Trinitatis*. In other words, Thomas designs the exposition of the understanding of the divine essence and its attributes in such a way that he arrives at the first foundational concept of his doctrine of the Trinity, the *mia ousia*. In this connection, divine simplicity makes perfect sense because of the conjunction with divine perfection. However, from being a knock-out argument against

---

33. See the excellent account offered by Rudi te Velde, whose particular strength is that he considers in each step Thomas takes in his argument the structure of the whole *prima pars: Aquinas on God: The "Divine Science" of the* Summa Theologiae (Aldershot, UK: Ashgate, 2006). Te Velde's contribution to *The Oxford Handbook of the Trinity*, ed. Gilles Emery, O.P., and Matthew Levering, on "The Divine Person(s): Trinity, Person, and Analogous Naming" (New York: Oxford University Press, 2012), 359–70, can be read as following *Aquinas on God*.

trinitarian relatedness, it has become an element in defining divine unity in the sense of the *mia ousia*. Whatever can be said about the three persons, it must not break this divine unity, because otherwise we would no longer be talking about divine persons. We would—at least on Thomas's account—no longer be doing trinitarian theology.

DOING TRINITARIAN THEOLOGY

If one surveys the developments in the field of trinitarian theology in the last twenty years, one has the impression of a lively flourishing of approaches and investigations focused on the doctrine of the Trinity, its foundations, developments, and constructive expositions in all theological disciplines. Two weighty handbooks on the Trinity have been published in recent years, attempting to give a comprehensive picture of the sources and debates that have characterized the development of trinitarian thought in the history of Christianity.[34] Peter C. Phan, the editor of *The Cambridge Companion to the Trinity*, lists in his introduction around twenty new collaborative volumes in recent years that attempt to assess trinitarian teaching and its implications.[35] One of the most recent of these collections offers a comprehensive overview under the title *Rethinking Trinitarian Theology*, combining historical studies and constructive approaches and their critique.[36] It would be difficult to point to any other theological topic that has attracted so much scholarly attention in recent decades. Interest in trinitarian theology is truly ecumenical, in that it unites the different churches, denominations, and theological traditions, and it is truly interdisciplinary, bringing the different theological fields together in theological and, increasingly, philosophical conversations. The rapidly intensifying encounter between the religions in a globalizing world has also led to a new interest in the doctrine of the Trinity as that which is perceived by other religions as distinctively and problematically Christian. When in the 1970s a series of theological books was launched for a wider readership with the series title *Themen der Theologie* ("Topics of Theology"), the volume *Gott* (1971), written by Heinrich Ott, Karl Barth's successor as the chair of dogmatics in Basel, only mentioned the Trinity in passing. When a different publisher launched a new series with the same title in 2011, the volume had the title

---

34. Peter C. Phan, ed., *The Cambridge Companion to the Trinity* (Cambridge: Cambridge University Press, 2011); Emery and Levering, eds., *Oxford Handbook of the Trinity*.

35. Peter C. Phan, "Systematic Issues in Trinitarian Theology," *Cambridge Companion*, 25–26n.1.

36. Robert J. Woźniak and Giulio Maspero, eds., *Rethinking Trinitarian Theology: Disputed Questions and Contemporary Issues in Trinitarian Theology* (Edinburgh: T&T Clark, 2012).

Trinität.[37] Looking back on the beginnings, one has to say that the Trinity is no longer forgotten. It is much thought about and talked about—so much so that this very discussion has now also come under criticism.

It is possible to discern several stages in the recent development of trinitarian thought. The first phase is a *programmatic phase*, trying to establish trinitarian theology as a field of theological reflection in the churches and in academic theology. On the British scene, *The Forgotten Trinity* is typical for this stage of the discussion. There followed an *explorative phase*, when the impetus of a programmatic reorientation was taken up in order to explore the new theological possibilities that had been opened up by the trinitarian reorientation. Colin Gunton's Bampton Lectures, titled *The One, the Three and the Many*, are typical of this phase, focusing not so much on the exposition of the doctrine of the Trinity, but on the view of the "culture of modernity" that was opened up by viewing it from a trinitarian perspective.[38] Elizabeth A. Johnson's *She Who Is: The Mystery of God in Feminist Theological Discourse* is also characteristic for this phase.[39] One could also count Miroslav Volf's *After Our Likeness*, the comprehensive exploration of trinitarian thought for ecumenical theology in conversation with the ecclesiologies of Joseph Ratzinger and John Zizioulas, as an example of this phase.[40]

During the next phase, which one could call *critical ressourcement*, the impetus spread to exegetical studies and especially to historical investigations, many of the initial intuitions of the programmatic phase were put to the test of historical scholarship. Is the contrast between Western and Eastern theologies, which had influenced most of the earliest sketches of trinitarian theology, historically and theologically correct?[41] Can the negative view of Augustine's

---

37. Volker Henning Drecoll, ed., *Trinität. Themen der Theologie* 2 (Tübingen: Mohr Siebeck, 2011).

38. Colin E. Gunton, *The One, the Three and the Many: God, Creation and the Culture of Modernity*, The 1992 Bampton Lectures (Cambridge: Cambridge University Press, 1993).

39. Elizabeth A. Johnson, C.S.J., *She Who Is: The Mystery of God in Feminist Theological Discourse* (New York: Crossroad, 1992).

40. Miroslav Volf, *After Our Likeness: The Church as an Image of the Triune God* (Grand Rapids: Eerdmans, 1998). German original: *Trinität und Gemeinschaft. Eine ökumenische Ekklesiologie* (Mainz-Neukirchen: Grünewald Verlag-Neukirchener Verlag, 1996).

41. This contrast was established as a paradigm by Théodore de Régnon, S.J., *Études de théologie positive sur la sainte Trinité*, vol. 2 (Paris: Victor Retoux, 1892–1898), who introduced the Greek/Latin scheme to account for the differences between the Greek tradition (Pseudo-Dionysius, Richard of St. Victor, Alexander of Hales, Bonaventure), which approaches the Trinity from the diversity of the three persons, and the Latin tradition (Augustine, Anselm, Peter Lombard, Albertus Magnus, Thomas Aquinas), which begins with the unity of nature. The paradigm has then been popularized by Michael Schmaus, *Der* Liber Propugnatorius *des Thomas Angelicus und die Lehrunterschiede zwischen Thomas von*

doctrine of the Trinity, which for Zizioulas has an almost constitutive function for his own exposition of the doctrine, a view that Colin Gunton and Robert Jenson echo in their own ways, be substantiated in a detailed analysis of Augustine's writings on the Trinity? To what extent is "the Cappadocian view" of the Trinity a faithful historical reconstruction or a neopatristic modern adaptation of the writings of the Cappadocian Fathers? Can the rich medieval resources of the theoretical explication of the Trinity be made fruitful for its contemporary reconstruction? How are the contributions of the Reformers and the later conscious returns to trinitarian thinking, for instance in Reformed scholasticism or in German idealism, be assessed? The historical *ressourcement* has led to many revisions of earlier assessments and reappraisals of the sources. If one understands the term *ressourcement* not only as a retrieval of the historical resources for trinitarian theology, but also as a way of developing new conceptual resources for the explication of trinitarian doctrine, one would also have to see the new interest in the doctrine of the Trinity by philosophical theologians, mostly from the analytic traditions, as an important development in discovering new resources for the reflection of trinitarian doctrine.

Where do we stand now? Has the critical *ressourcement* led to a less programmatic but more differentiated way of doing trinitarian theology, or should it simply be abandoned in the name of divine simplicity, as one recent author has suggested, because it proved to be not a renaissance at all but the projection of modern and postmodern ideas on the sources of Christian doctrine, which has led not to a revival of orthodox trinitarian faith but only to the resurrection of old heresies?[42] Confronted with this, no doubt rather simplistic, choice, it seems advisable that we seek orientation from the criteria that constitute and regulate the activity of doing systematic theology.[43] Systematic theology can be understood as the self-explication of Christian faith,

---

Aquin und Duns Scotus, vol. 2: *Die Trinitarischen Lehrdifferenzen* (Münster: Aschendorff, 1930), 574–66, and was then adopted also for the contrast between the patristic doctrines by Yves Congar, Eberhard Jüngel, Walter Kasper, Jürgen Moltmann, and many others who normally combined it with Rahner's insistence on the importance of the economic Trinity. De Régnon had employed the distinction primarily as a paradigm for analyzing the contrasts between the different medieval schools. See Michel René Barnes, "De Régnon Reconsidered," *Augustinian Studies* 26 (1995): 51–79, and Kristin Hennessy, "An Answer to de Régnon's Accusers: Why We Should Not Speak of 'His' Paradigm," *Harvard Theological Review* 100 (2007): 179–97.

42. See Stephen R. Holmes, *The Quest for the Trinity: The Doctrine of God in Scripture, History, and Modernity* (Downers Grove, IL: InterVarsity Academic, 2012). The points Holmes presents can already be found in his contribution to the celebratory volume of the *Neue Zeitschrift für systematische Theologie* presented to Colin Gunton on his sixtieth birthday: "'Something Much Too Plain to Say': Towards a Defence of the Doctrine of Divine Simplicity," *NZSTh* 43 (2001): 137–54.

on the basis of its sources and traditions, with regard to its truth-claims and its ethical orientations for the Christian life. Christian faith has from the beginning been a reflective faith. This is rooted in the conviction that the very subject matter of Christian faith is such that the reflective explication of Christian faith is required. There is no Christian faith without theology, although theology has many forms and institutional settings.[44]

The critical context of doing systematic theology is a situation of disagreement concerning the teaching or the practices of the church in which a new understanding is sought by means of theological reflection. The criteria for doing systematic theology can be generated from the structure of the Christian faith:

> 1. Because the Christian faith is based on the self-disclosure of God as it is witnessed in the biblical sources, the doctrines of the Christian faith must be developed in accordance with Scripture.
>
> 2. Since the Christian faith is handed on in the traditions of the church, which together with Scripture make up the external word that requires vindication by the internal testimony of the Spirit, Christian teaching must be in critical continuity with the normative traditions of the church.
>
> 3. Because of its subject matter, the Christian faith claims to be true for all situations, therefore it must also be true and relevant for our contemporary situation.

These historical-hermeneutical criteria need to be extended by three systematic-analytical criteria.

> 4. Because the Christian faith relies on intelligible comm-unication—after all, faith comes from what is heard (Rom. 10:17) and claims that its subject matter is the supreme ground of all truth and reason—its propositions must be internally consistent, both logically and semantically.

---

43. Christoph Schwöbel, "Doing Systematic Theology," *King's Theological Review* 10 (1987): 51–57. A slightly elaborated German version can be found in idem, *Gott in Beziehung* (Tübingen: Mohr Siebeck, 2002), 1–24.

44. I have tried to develop these rather sweeping statements in my article "Theology," in *Religion Past and Present* (Leiden: Brill, 2012), 12:621–51.

5. Because the Christian faith claims to be based on the self-disclosure of God, who is the source and standard of all truth and the unity of all truth (*Deus est veritas*), the propositions of the Christian faith must be externally defensible, for instance in conversation with other sciences.

6. Since the Christian faith claims to offer orientation for Christian *praxis* in all spheres of life, its capacity of orientation has to be shown.

It is clear that working with these criteria necessarily involves systematic theology in close cooperation with the other theological and nontheological academic disciplines. Each of the six criteria displays in specific ways the interrelationship between the different theological disciplines. For assessing where we stand in trinitarian theology, it therefore seems possible to apply these criteria in order to get a glimpse of what the problems and the state of discussion in trinitarian theology are.

1. IN ACCORDANCE WITH SCRIPTURE

There used to be a consensus in New Testament scholarship that in the New Testament "there is no doctrine of the Trinity but there is material for the development of a doctrine,"[45] and that a critical historical interpretation shows there is a wide gap between the texts of the New Testament and later doctrinal formulations. Frances Young has approached the topic from the opposite perspective by asserting: "Trinitarian theology is the product of exegesis of the biblical texts, refined by debate and argument, and rhetorically celebrated in liturgy."[46] Approaching trinitarian theology in this way directs the attention not only to the way in which the biblical texts were employed in order to try settling doctrinal questions in the early church, but also invites us to focus on what it is about the biblical texts that made them amenable to such an interpretation. While earlier research primarily looked at the presence of triadic formulae that somehow appeared as approximation to later doctrinal formulae, more recent attempts have focused on the underlying patterns of talking about God, the God of Israel, in connection with Jesus and the Spirit in the different theological conceptions of the New Testament. There is, it seems, agreement that in the different theologies of the New Testament there is

---

45. Arthur W. Wainwright, *The Trinity in the New Testament* (London: SPCK, 1962), 242.

46. Frances Young, "The Trinity and the New Testament," in Christopher Rowland and Christopher Tuckett, eds., *The Nature of New Testament Theology: Essays in Honour of Robert Morgan* (Oxford: Blackwell, 2006), 288.

no evolutionary development from a "low" Christology in earlier layers of the tradition to a "high Christology" in later strata, to which a pneumatology was later added. Rather, it seems a "fact that . . . early Jewish Christians (apparently) felt thoroughly justified in giving Jesus reverence in terms of divinity *and* at the same time thought of themselves as worshipping *one God.*"[47] The significance of Jesus in worship was not expressed by turning him into a second God, but by expressing his relationship to the one God as "image of the invisible God" (Col. 1:15), or as the "Son" (for instance Gal. 4:4). In several texts, especially in Paul, Luke, and John, there is a close and already carefully structured relationship between God, Jesus, and the Spirit.[48]

With the Farewell Speeches of John's Gospel (chs. 14–17) we have reached a stage where one can see a fully developed prototrinitarian discourse. There seems to be specific prototrinitarian grammar undergirding this discourse where the Father is always the "ultimate point of origin" and the "ultimate terminus" in the relationship between the Father, Jesus, and the Spirit, and the three identities that are named from one ordered relational unity of God over against everything that is created and therefore not God.[49] It would be a mistake to contrast these grammatical rules to the experiential side of early Christian beliefs and practices, which are reflected in the writings of the New Testament, and oppose them to the "ontological" view of the reality of God. Rather, it seems to be the other way around: because the reality of God is experienced in ways that enable and provoke early Christians to speak of the Father, the Son, and the Spirit, their discourse about God displays a depth structure that supports the prototrinitarian grammar of talking about God.

Is this a radical departure from the "monotheism" of the Hebrew Scriptures? The opposite seems to be the case.[50] If one looks at the understanding of God in the Hebrew Scriptures from the perspective of the history of religions, one can see it as a process of integration, where elements that were external to the reality of YHWH are included in the sphere of YHWH's being and activity. The integrative monotheism, which appears in

---

47. Larry W. Hurtado, *One God, One Lord: Early Christian Devotion and Ancient Jewish Monotheism* (London: T&T Clark, 1998), 2. Cf. also Hans-Joachim Eckstein, "So haben wir doch nur einen Herrn. Die Anfänge trinitarischer Rede von Gott im Neuen Testament," in idem, *Kyrios Jesus. Perspektiven einer christologischen Theologie* (Neukirchen: Neukirchener Verlag), 2–22.

48. For an overview, see Ferdinand Hahn, *Theologie des Neuen Testaments, Bd. II: Die Einheit des Neuen Testaments. Thematische Darstellung* (Tübingen: Mohr Siebeck, 2002), 301–306.

49. See my article (above, n. 17) "The Trinity between Athens and Jerusalem," 28.

50. See Christopher Seitz, "The Trinity in the Old Testament," in Emery and Levering, eds., *Oxford Handbook of the Trinity*, 28–40.

writings such as Second Isaiah, insisting on "YHWH alone," can claim this exclusivity, because the reality of YHWH includes everything that in earlier stages had been associated with other deities. Integrative monotheism, however, is differentiated monotheism, which allows for the possibility of talking about aspects of YHWH's reality as somehow independent hypostatic beings, as God's agents, without breaking the all-encompassing and therefore exclusive unity of YHWH.[51] It is here that discourse about "wisdom," the "word," the "angel of the Lord," "Torah," and the like can serve as a matrix for early Christian discourse about God by being adapted to the Christian experience of Jesus, God the Father, and the Spirit. Jesus' story is read as the continuation of God's story with Israel, and the prototrinitarian discourse of the New Testament takes its clues from the differentiated forms of talking about the one integrative reality of God in the Hebrew Scriptures.

If we approach the biblical writings with the questions that structure the doctrine of the Trinity, we find that the question "Who is God?" is answered by referring to God, Jesus, and the Spirit interdependently and, on the basis of their interdependence, also independently. With regard to the question "How is God?," we find the first steps of rooting the way in which God relates to the world, in Jesus and the Spirit, in the relationship God has to Christ and the Spirit "in the beginning." The eschatological finality of the speaking of God in the Son as the culmination of a history of God addressing God's people points to God's protological primordiality (if such a word may be allowed) at the beginning (Heb. 1:1-4), and so distinguishes the Son from the angels. The "What is God?" question is answered by discourse about God which integrates the different aspects of God's activity that are named by talking about the Father, the Son, and the Spirit: God is the sovereign creator, the sole source of salvation, and the ultimate end of everything.

Doing trinitarian theology in accordance with Scripture offers not only rich material for seeing how trinitarian theology developed from the exegesis of Scripture, but also shows why that could be the case. Bringing the questions of trinitarian theology into the realm of biblical interpretation has produced a rich harvest of fresh investigations into the biblical ways of speaking to

51. An alternative way is the integration of the different stages of history in one final stage, associated with a single place of worship, which we have in the Priestly source. God appears in primeval history as *Elohim*, establishes as covenant with Abraham as *El Shaddai*, and finally makes Godself known as YHWH, whose worship is to be exclusively focused in one place. The question "Who is God?" can therefore be answered in different ways, referring to God in different relationships, and yet it is one God who now has humankind as God's image and partner. See Christoph Levin, "Integrativer Monotheismus im Alten Testament," *Zeitschrift für Theologie und Kirche* 109 (2012): 153–75.

God and speaking of God. Recent research has underlined one particular point that seems significant: trinitarian language appears specifically in contexts of worship. While the Bible has been used throughout history in different ways as a doctrinal manual, as a law book, or as a historical textbook, it is the dimension where the Bible is employed as "Scripture" in contexts of worship that we see as the strongest link to the formulation of trinitarian doctrine.[52] The use of the Bible in worship is the basis for employing the Bible for the clarification of doctrinal issues. Employed as Scripture in worship, the Bible is a liturgical book. We have here the transition where the Bible is not used as a collection of historical sources, but as the matrix for addressing God and proclaiming God. Doing trinitarian theology in accordance with Scripture therefore also means doing trinitarian theology in accordance with the use of the Bible in worship.

2. IN CRITICAL CONTINUITY WITH THE TRADITION

It is probably with regard to this second criterion that the renaissance of trinitarian theology has generated the most lively debates. Part of the programmatic stage of trinitarian theology were a number of rather radical judgments about the contrast between East and West in approaching the doctrine of the Trinity, or about the role representatives of the Western tradition, such as Augustine or Thomas Aquinas, in the subsequent marginalization of the doctrine of the Trinity. The debate between systematic and historical theologians has led to remarkable revisions in the views of the history of the doctrine of the Trinity, and in the way contemporary theology refers to the conceptions of trinitarian theology in the early church, in medieval times, or in the early modern period. Schematic views have been discarded in favor of a close *relecture* of the tradition. Théodore de Régnon's scheme of contrasting East and West, the one starting from the plurality of the persons, the other from the unity of the divine substance, first developed with regard to medieval theologies of the Trinity, and then applied to patristic times, had to be discarded as historically inaccurate and systematically misleading. This is just one example where the renaissance of trinitarian theology has led a renewed engagement with the tradition that ultimately leads to a radical questioning of the usefulness of the contrast of East and West, Latin and Greek theologies of the Trinity, the psychological and the social model for doing trinitarian theology. In the course of these debates, points that were originally made *against* parts of the tradition now have to be made *with* the tradition.

---

52. See Christoph Schwöbel, "Bible, IV. Dogmatics," in *Religion Past and Present* (Leiden: Brill, 2007), 2:13–17.

There is for systematic theology, so it seems, no other way to come to a clear view of the doctrinal debates than to work its way through the discussions, as they are documented in the texts, to the decisions of the ecumenical councils.[53] Appealing to conciliar orthodoxy without such a careful reassessment of the debates behind it will create more confusion than normative canons of truth.

A particularly interesting example is Augustine's *De trinitate*, which in the early phases of trinitarian theology was blamed by some for the relegation of the doctrine of the Trinity to a place of irrelevance in Christian teaching and living.[54] The opposite seems to be the case. Reconstructing the argument in books 5 to 7 of *De trinitate*, and relating it to the argument of books 8 to 15, it seems inevitable to conclude that, for Augustine, the unity of the divine essence and the distinctness of the persons in their relations are inextricably interwoven. Rowan Williams concludes: "Augustine, so far from separating the divine substance from the life of the divine persons, defines that substance in such a way that God cannot be other than relational, Trinitarian. Because the divine life in its coming forth to creation can only be grasped as self-imparting, *sapientia* and *caritas* are inseparable; and *caritas* is inconceivable without relatedness."[55] Summing up the argument of book 7, Lewis Ayres writes: "We do not identify the unity [of the Trinity] by focusing on something other than the persons: it is focusing on the persons' possession of wisdom and 'being in themselves' that draws us to recognise their unity. The triune communion *is* a consubstantial and eternal unity; but there is nothing but the persons."[56]

These findings require extensive revisions of the critical assessment of Augustine's trinitarian theology in the first phase of the renaissance. However, at some points a re-reading of *De trinitate* also seems to call into question constructive points that were close to the heart of some proponents of trinitarian

---

53. See Lewis Ayres, *Nicaea and Its Legacy: An Approach to Fourth Century Trinitarian Theology* (Oxford: Oxford University Press, 2004).

54. See, among others, Michel René Barnes, "Re-reading Augustine's Theology of the Trinity," in Steven Davis and Daniel Kendall, eds., *The Trinity* (New York: Oxford University Press, 1999), 145–76; Lewis Ayres (in addition to the reference in the previous note), *Augustine and the Trinity* (Cambridge: Cambridge University Press, 2010).

55. Rowan Williams, "*Sapientia* and the Trinity: Reflections on the *De Trinitate*," in Bernard Bruning, Mathijs Lamberigts, and Jozef van Houtem, eds., *Collectanea Augustiniana. Mélanges T.J. van Bavel* (Leuven: Peeters, 1990), 325.

56. Lewis Ayres, "The Fundamental Grammar of Augustine's Trinitarian Theology," in Robert Dodaro and George Lawless, eds., *Augustine and His Critics: Essays in Honour of Gerald Bonner* (London: Routledge, 2000), 67.

theology. Maarten Wisse's close reading of the whole work suggests that the focal point of Augustine's conception is a careful distancing from ideas of participation in the divine life, which at least some of the proponents of trinitarian theology see as the soteriological and eschatological core of the doctrine.[57]

A similar case can be made for Thomas Aquinas's doctrine of God in the *Summa theologiae*. Karl Rahner had argued that the marginalization of the doctrine of the Trinity in Christian doctrine and in the devotional life of Christians was closely connected to the separation of the treatise *De Deo uno* from the development of the doctrine of the Trinity in *De Deo trino*. This, he suggests, goes back to Thomas Aquinas's structuring of the material in the *Summa theologiae*, which became normative for Catholic teaching when the *Summa* replaced Peter Lombard's *Book of Sentences*. This, Rahner argues, leads the doctrine of the Trinity into a situation of "splendid isolation," which prevents Christian theology from being practiced as trinitarian theology.[58] Is Thomas and his *Summa*, then, one of the factors for the marginalization of the doctrine of the Trinity?

Recent studies on Thomas Aquinas's doctrine of the Trinity present the whole conception of the *Summa* as a trinitarian theology. The divine essence that is discussed in qq. 2–26 is not to be understood as the divine essence apart from the persons, later discussed in qq. 27–43, but as the "total divine reality" that is one according to essence. There is therefore no derivation of the persons from essence in q. 27, and the relations are not accidental with regard to the absolute essence. As Gilles Emery interprets the distinction in his magisterial *The Trinitarian Theology of Thomas Aquinas*:

> It is not, as some have said, about dividing the treatise into *De Deo Uno* and *De Deo Trino* in the style of certain neo-scholastic theology manuals. Still less is it a matter of a division between a philosophical approach to God and a theological one, as if the first part of the treatise had a philosophical nature and the second was

---

57. Maarten Wisse, *Trinitarian Theology Beyond Participation. Augustine's* De Trinitate *and Contemporary Theology* (London: T&T Clark, 2011).

58. Rahner writes: "Thus, the treatise on the Trinity occupies a rather isolated point in the dogmatic system. To put it crassly, when the treatise is concluded, its subject is never brought up again. Its function in the whole dogmatic construction is not clearly perceived. It is as though this mystery has been revealed to us for its own sake, and that even after it has been made known to us, it remains, *as a reality*, locked up within itself. We make statements about it, but as a reality it has nothing to do with us at all." Karl Rahner, *The Trinity*, trans. Joseph Donceel (New York: Crossroad, 1970), 14.

properly theological. In effect, the whole treatise on God is about the Triune God seen in the light of revelation.[59]

Thomas Aquinas's approach to the doctrine of the Trinity, with a consideration first of the unity of the triune God, does not diminish the significance of the persons (qq. 29–43), as they are distinguished by their relations of origin (q. 28). Rather, it helps to build a bridge via the "missions" of the persons (q. 43), which make the whole Trinity relevant for the divine economy, since already the first part presupposes the light of revelation, the economy, for the speculative grasp of the unity of the triune God. The soteriological dimension is in this way present from the start, since Thomas's doctrine of the one God is an integral part of his trinitarian theology.[60] This is systematically developed by the exposition of "the immanent processions as the grammar of God's action in the world."[61] The trinitarian character of the immanent Trinity is retained in God's relations to what is not God. God's action in the world is therefore not the action of God's undifferentiated essence. With regard to creation, one therefore has to say that the divine persons "according to the logic of their processions, have causality with regard to the creation of things": "God the Father made the creature through his Word, which is the Son, and through his love, which is the Holy Spirit. And accordingly, processions of the persons are the reasons [*rationes*] for the production of creatures, insofar as they include the essential attributes, knowledge and will."[62]

The interrelationship between the exposition of the immanent Trinity and the trinitarian economy that is in this way conceptually clarified would become even clearer, one can safely assume, if one looked more closely at the way in which Thomas applies the trinitarian grammar of being and act in his biblical commentaries. Here is another revision of the view of the history of trinitarian thought that informed the first programmatic stage of the renaissance of trinitarian theology. What some felt they had to say against Thomas Aquinas,

59. Gilles Emery, *The Trinitarian Theology of St Thomas Aquinas* (Oxford: Oxford University Press, 2007), 44.

60. The implications of such an integrated view for Thomas's theological method are carefully analyzed by Timothy L. Smith, *Thomas Aquinas' Trinitarian Theology: A Study in Theological Method* (Washington, DC: Catholic University of America Press, 2003). Anselm K. Min has shown how productive it can be to bring the insights of Thomas's doctrine of the Trinity in conversation with the contemporary debate: *Paths to the Triune God: An Encounter between Aquinas and Recent Theologies* (Notre Dame, IN: University of Notre Dame Press, 2003).

61. Anselm K. Min, "Thomas Aquinas on the Trinity," in Phan, ed., *Cambridge Companion to the Trinity*, 100.

62. *Summa theologiae* I, q. 45, a. 6.

one can now say with Thomas Aquinas. From being perceived as a foe, Thomas Aquinas has become a friend for the trinitarian theologian. One might still disagree with one's friends, but in the context of a shared endeavor and a continuing conversation.

Another example is the theology of the Reformers, and specifically of Martin Luther. Classical studies from the first half of the twentieth century had stated that the doctrine of the Trinity stood isolated as something like an "erratic block"[63] in Luther's theology.[64] In more recent research, the doctrine of the Trinity appears as an "integral problem" of Luther's theology.[65] If one looks a little closer, one can see that in many of his works, especially in his sermons,[66] but also in his lectures, Luther practices an applied trinitarian theology, based on the teachings of the ecumenical councils, which he then employs as a hermeneutic tool for interpreting Scripture. From the interpretation of Scripture he then gains a much fuller, lively description of the unity of the one God in the difference of the persons, which, in turn, supports the teaching of the ecumenical councils. This does not imply that Luther regarded the dogma of the church as an independent authority beside the authority of Scripture. Rather, this hermeneutical procedure is based on the assumption that the creeds of the church are, in any case, summaries of scriptural truth. For Luther, this trinitarian hermeneutic is to be applied in all areas of Christian preaching and teaching, because it is that which distinguishes the Christian understanding of God from that of Jews and Muslims. In his catechetical writings, this applied trinitarian theology is given a particular emphasis. The trinitarian faith is rooted in the self-presentation of the triune God through the Son in the Holy Spirit who creates certainty of faith concerning the truth of the Gospel of Christ. The mode of knowing the triune God is therefore anchored in the way the triune God relates to believers in the threefold structure of God's trinitarian action, and this discloses the very being of God in its unity and personal difference-

63. See Werner Elert, *Morphologie des Luthertums, Bd. 1: Theologie und Weltanschauung des Luthertums* (Munich: Beck, 1965), 191.

64. See Christoph Schwöbel, "The Triune God of Grace: The Doctrine of the Trinity in the Theology of the Reformers," in James M. Byrne, ed., *The Christian Understanding of God Today* (Dublin: Columba Press, 1993), 49–64.

65. Ulrich Asendorf, "Die Trinitätslehre als integrales Problem der Theologie Martin Luthers," in Joachim Heubach, ed., *Luther und die trinitarische Tradition. Ökumenische und philosophische Perspektiven* (Erlangen: Martin-Luther-Verlag, 1994), 113–30. See also Christine Helmer, *The Trinity and Martin Luther: A Study on the Relationship between Genre, Language, and the Trinity in Luther's Works (1523–1546)* (Mainz: Philipp von Zabern, 1999.)

66. Ulrich Asendorf, *Die Theologie Martin Luthers nach seinen Predigten* (Göttingen: Vandenhoeck & Ruprecht, 1988), 25–46.

in-relation.[67] In the Large Catechism this is summarized in the formula of the threefold divine self-giving:

> . . . for here in all three articles He has Himself revealed and opened the deepest abyss of his paternal heart and of His pure unutterable love. For He has created us for this very object, that He might redeem and sanctify us; and in addition to giving and imparting to us everything in heaven and upon earth, He has given to us even His Son and the Holy Ghost, by whom to bring us to Himself. For (as explained above) we could never attain to the knowledge of the grace and favour of the Father except through the Lord Christ, who is a mirror of the paternal heart, outside of whom we see nothing but an angry and terrible Judge. But of Christ we could know nothing either, unless it had been revealed by the Holy Ghost.[68]

The constitution of faith illuminates the structure of the whole divine economy, and this mirrors the immanent relationships in the divine Trinity. If the understanding of the Trinity is in this way grounded in the self-giving of God, it is clear that reason apart from faith cannot gain access to the triune majesty. However, that does not exclude that the strategies of reason can be employed, not in a foundational but in an explicatory function, in order to state as clearly as possible in philosophical terms what Scripture tells us in the language of narrative and promise. This is especially apparent in the doctoral disputations of Erasmus Alberus (1543), Georg Major and Johannes Faber (1544), and Petrus Hegemon (1545), which show Luther on the one hand fully conversant with the medieval debates, but at the same time quite reckless in combining otherwise incompatible positions.[69]

With regard to the doctrine of the Trinity in the Reformers, it seems that the renaissance of trinitarian theology has led to a new engagement with the doctrine of the Trinity in the Reformation and the way it shapes the whole practice of theology. For Luther, it appears that the self-presentation of the triune God in the constitution of faith is understood as the self-presentation of the *res* of faith through the *signa* of communication. This is the core of

---

67. Christoph Schwöbel, "Offenbarung, Glaube und Gewißheit in der reformatorischen Theologie," in Eilert Herms and Lubomir Zak, eds., *Grund und Gegenstand des Glaubens nach römisch-katholischer und evangelisch-lutherischer Lehre* (Tübingen: Mohr Siebeck 2008), 214–34.

68. "The Apostles' Creed," in Luther, *Large Catechism*, sections 64–65.

69. See Simo Knuuttila and Risto Saarinen, "Luther's Trinitarian Theology and Its Medieval Background," *Studia Theologica* 53 (1999): 3–12; Helmer, *The Trinity and Martin Luther*, 41–120.

his trinitarian theology, which binds the immanent Trinity and the economic Trinity in its different forms of discourse together. This relationship between being and communication is already inscribed into God's trinitarian being, and this is communicated in God's address to humans through Christ in the Spirit. "Just like the Father is an eternal Speaker, so the Son is spoken in eternity, and so the Spirit is from eternity the Listener."[70]

The criterion of developing the self-explication of Christian faith "in critical continuity with the tradition" in recent research illustrates a retrieval of the history of trinitarian theology which casts a critical light on the thesis of the "forgotten Trinity." The fact that the church and theology are from time to time overcome by forgetfulness does not mean that what is forgotten is not there. It needs to be rediscovered. When it is rediscovered, revisions and reassessments are required. These reappraisals have involved historical theologians and systematic theologians in passionate debates, but through these debates the questions of trinitarian theology have inspired significant historical research and systematic reconstruction. The recent debates on, for instance, Augustine's or Thomas Aquinas's theology of the Trinity are good examples for the mutually corrective effects historical and systematic theology can have on one another, which curb their respective relativist tendencies. And this seems quite appropriate for a doctrine like the Trinity.

3. APPROPRIATE TO OUR CONTEMPORARY SITUATION

It is in this area, where the appropriateness of theological reflection to its ecclesial, social, and cultural contexts is at stake, that the renaissance of trinitarian theology has produced its most immediate effects. Theology always has social effects, because it concerns the fundamental orientations of human beings for their being-in-the-world. These effects are often, but not exclusively, mediated through the church, because the church as a community of faith is also the social embodiment of faith. The understanding of God that informs the beliefs and practices of the church is therefore one of the decisive factors of the social shape of faith, in the church and through the church in society at large. This can be seen by the effects the trinitarian reorientation has had in correcting the theological self-understanding of the church, in giving a new direction to ecumenical efforts, and in trying to find a new orientation in a religiously pluralistic world. Zizioulas's criticism,

---

70. See, in more detail, Christoph Schwöbel, "God as Conversation: Reflections on a Theological Ontology of Communicative Relations," in Jacques Haers, S.J., and Peter de Mey, eds., *Theology and Conversation: Towards a Relational Theology* (Leuven: Leuven University Press/Peeters, 2003), 43–67, esp. 62–67.

echoed by many others, that the theological self-understanding of the church lacked a trinitarian foundation and tended to a one-sided Christomonism, was quickly taken up in all major denominations. Beginning in the 1980s, attempts flourished in official statements by representative bodies of different churches to employ the trinitarian language of communion and *koinonia* to establish a revised understanding of the being and life of the church that gives the church a place in economy of the triune God.[71] Not only different churches and church families sought to describe the foundation of the church in trinitarian terms, but it was also attempted to reflect on questions of church order and the mission of the church in the world from the perspective of a trinitarian vision. In retrospect, it seems fair to say that these efforts proved to be more successful if the trinitarian description of the foundation and structures of the church could connect with the churches' historical self-understanding and their authoritative traditions.

In ecumenism, the trinitarian reorientation was taken up enthusiastically as, for instance, the documents and papers from the Fifth World Conference of Faith and Order at Santiago de Compostela 1993 show.[72] A more skeptical note is already sounded by the statement *The Nature and Purpose of the Church: A Stage on the Way to a Common Statement*.[73] The statement begins, under the heading "The Church of the Triune God," like this: "The Church belongs to God. It is the creation of God's Word and Holy Spirit."[74] A little later, the document states: "The notion of *koinonia* is being used today by many churches

---

71. In the Roman Catholic Church, the interpretation of *Lumen gentium*, the Vatican II dogmatic constitution on the church, in the sense of a communion ecclesiology was characteristic for this period. See Walter Kasper, "Kirche als *communio*," in idem, *Theologie und Kirche* (Mainz: Grünewald Verlag, 1987), 272–89; Paul Josef Cordes, *Communio. Utopie oder Programm?* (Freiburg: Herder, 1993); and Joseph Ratzinger, "Die Ekklesiologie der Konstitution *Lumen gentium*," in *Weggemeinschaft des Glaubens. Kirche als Communio. Festgabe zum 75. Geburtstag*, ed. Stephan Otto Horn and Vinzenz Pfnür (Augsburg: St. Ulrich Verlag, 2002), 107–31.

72. Thomas F. Best and Günther Gassmann, eds., *On the Way to Fuller Koinonia* (Geneva: World Council of Churches, 1996). For an analysis of the role of the trinitarian notion of communion in ecumenical dialogues, see Risto Saarinen, "The Concept of Communion in Ecumenical Dialogues," and "East-West Dialogues and the Theology of Communion," both in Heinrich Holze, ed., *The Church as Communion: Lutheran Contributions to Ecclesiology*, Lutheran World Federation Documentation no. 42 (Geneva: Lutheran World Federation, 1997), 287–316; 317–38. See, in the same volume, my own attempt at interpreting the notion of communion from a Lutheran perspective: "The Quest for Communion: Reasons, Reflections and Recommendations," 227–86.

73. *The Nature and Purpose of the Church: A Stage on the Way to a Common Statement*, Faith and Order Paper no. 181 (Geneva: World Council of Churches, 1998).

74. Ibid., 9.

and in ecumenical texts as a major idea towards a common understanding of the nature and purpose of the Church. The question is being asked whether this notion is being called to bear more weight than it is able to carry."[75]

This self-critical question on the part of the Faith and Order study document can also be phrased in the following way: Are we divided precisely in our understanding of what constitutes communion on the ecclesial level? If one looks critically at the *koinonia* models of ecumenism, it seems that they suffered from an overconfident application of the categories of some versions of trinitarian theology to the understanding of the church and the view of communion between the churches. *Prima facie* the categories of person, communion, otherness, and relationship seemed to be eminently well suited for a stage of ecumenism where the quest for a doctrinal consensus had become problematical. However, the vision of an ecumenical *koinonia* quickly lost its appeal when the otherness of the other asserted itself in the desire for a preservation of one's own ecclesial identity and communion over against communion with other churches. One may also ask whether the attempt at "short-circuiting" the *koinonia* of the Trinity (itself not an easy concept for some versions of trinitarianism in the West) with the *koinonia* of the church is not a contradiction to one of the most important insights of trinitarian theology concerning the relationship between the immanent and the economic Trinity. The view of the trinitarian economy as the self-manifestation of the immanent Trinity implies that no direct analogies are possible between the being of the church and the being of the triune God, since the way the Trinity and the church are connected is mediated through the divine economy, as the gospel is proclaimed and celebrated in word and sacraments. Put in the language of communion: How is the communion that the triune God *is* related to the communion of saints that the triune God *creates*? To answer this question, a comprehensive account of the divine economy is needed, culminating in a trinitarian theology of the word and the sacraments. Viewed from this perspective, one could say that the apparent failure of *koinonia* ecumenism points to the task of developing a fully trinitarian vision of ecumenism. In this way, the project of trinitarian theology might still prove to be appropriate to the situation of the church and the communion of the churches today.

One area in the ecumenical community where the inspiration of trinitarian theology seems to have had wide-ranging effects for our contemporary situation is the liturgy of the church. It seems not an exaggeration to say that

75. Ibid., 28.

the trinitarian renaissance has led to an enhanced trinitarian sensibility in all Christian churches when they celebrate the liturgy. This is noticeable in the liturgical reforms since the 1990s.[76] Could it be that the built-in conservatism of liturgies offered more opportunities for a retrieval of trinitarian language because it had never been completely lost? Or is the reason for the new trinitarian sensibility of the language of worship to be seen in the fact that the primary form of trinitarian discourse is the invocation of the triune name, whatever its theological explication?

Our view of the contemporary situation can, of course, not be restricted to the situation of the churches apart from the wider cultural contexts. The fact that the churches exist today in a situation of religious pluralism in its global and local contexts is therefore a significant factor for assessing the appropriateness of the explication of Christian doctrine. The situation of religious pluralism makes the question of the identities of religions and their relations central. The religions are distinguished by the deities they worship and which they regard as the source of salvation or (to include nontheistic religions) what they see as the goal of the fulfillment of the human destiny. At least for the theistic religions, the "Who?" question acquires in this situation primary importance. The particular trinitarian identity of the Christian God as Trinity receives a new significance for the encounter of the religions.[77] This opens the view also for the particularities of the religions in their respective self-interpretations.

One requirement of the situation of religious pluralism is that one starts conversation and reflection from the standpoint of one's own perspective. Claiming a position beyond all concrete standpoints in the religions amounts to an imperialist claim for one's own position. Starting from a Christian standpoint, defined by the identity of the God of the Christian faith, one has to start from a trinitarian perspective. This has pushed a number of questions specifically connected to a trinitarian understanding of the divine economy into the foreground. If the divine economy is understood consistently as a trinitarian economy, is it possible to distinguish between the activity of the *logos asarkos* and the economy of the *logos ensarkos*, and if so, how should they be related?[78]

76. See the brief but magisterial account of Geoffrey Wainwright, "The Trinity in Liturgy and Preaching," in Emery and Levering, eds., *Oxford Handbook of the Trinity*, 457–71, and the contributions to Bert Groen and Benedikt Kranemann, eds., *Liturgie und Trinität* (Freiburg: Herder, 2008).

77. See Veli-Matti Kärkkäinen's overview, *Trinity and Religious Pluralism: The Doctrine of the Trinity in Christian Theology of Religions* (Aldershot, UK: Ashgate, 2004).

78. See the discussion triggered by the work of Jacques Dupuis, S.J., and the response from the Congregation of the Doctrine of Faith: *Towards a Christian Theology of Religious Pluralism* (New York, NY: Maryknoll, 1997).

It has been part of a major strand of the theological tradition to speak of the activity of the *logos asarkos* in creation and in the history of salvation before the incarnation. Could this be extended in such a view that God's presence in other religions is also understood as part of the activity of the *logos asarkos*, not only before Christ but also after Christ? And is the work of God the Spirit to be understood in a sense that transcends the understanding of the Spirit as the Spirit of Christ, so that one should speak of the Spirit's presence in other religions before and after the incarnation?[79]

In one sense, these proposals can maintain that there is no salvation in the religions apart from the saving activity of the Logos and that the presence of the divine must be encompassed by the activity of the Spirit who, according to the traditional understanding, is the universal Spirit of eschatological fulfillment. In another sense, the identity of the *logos asarkos* can become problematical if we distinguish the *logos asarkos* sharply from the incarnation, and it becomes unclear who the Spirit is that blows everywhere if the identity of the Spirit is not defined by reference to Christ. Trinitarian proposals for a theology of religions working with these distinctions have to confront one difficulty: we can speak of the divine Trinity only on the basis of revelation, that is, when God's self-disclosure through the Son in the Spirit has created the certainty of faith in God the Father, the Son, and the Spirit. For this faith, the identification of the Logos with Jesus Christ and the identification of the Spirit as the Spirit of Christ is constitutive. It is this identification that creates the possibility of talking about the saving activity of this Logos before the incarnation, and of this Spirit before the Christ event, as the tradition did when they talked about the "Fathers of the old covenant" or about the Spirit "who spoke through the prophets." The distinction between the *logos ensarkos* and the *logos asarkos*, and the Spirit of Christ and the Spirit of eschatological fulfilment, therefore cannot be interpreted as a disjunction, so that the incarnation becomes just one of the instantiations of the Logos and the Spirit of Christ just an example of how the Spirit works. The criteria of identification are bound to God's trinitarian self-disclosure though Christ in the Spirit. The trinitarian relationality does not lead to a general relativism. The tension between the revelation of God in Christ through the Spirit and the hiddenness of God in the world, including the world of religions, must be maintained, as long as we are bound to see everything in

---

79. This emphasis plays a major role in writings of the Pentecostal theologian Amos Yong. See his works: *Discerning the Spirit(s): A Pentecostal-Charismatic Contribution to Christian Theology of Religions*, Journal of Pentecostal Theology Supplement, 2000; and *Pneumatology in Christian-Buddhist Dialogue: Does the Spirit Blow Through the Middle Way?* (Leiden: Brill, 2012).

the light of grace (*lumen gratiae*), interpreting the light of nature (*lumen naturae*) before the full illumination of everything in the light of glory (*lumen gloriae*).

What does that mean for an encounter of religions that is inspired by the trinitarian faith? First of all, confessing the triune God, the Father, the Son, and the Spirit, as the one who creates, reconciles, and perfects God's creation, and understanding this God as omnipresent, omnipotent, and eternal, implies that God is somehow present in the religions. To claim God as the omnipresent creator contradicts any view that treats the religions somehow as "enemy territory" or as a "Godless zone." However, from their own experience of faith, Christians know that the presence of God in the world, and so also in the religions, including their own Christian religion, is distorted by sin, the alienation from God, and by the bondage to idolatry that characterizes alienation from God in all its aspects. Therefore, Christians encounter the religions with the expectation of finding the presence of God in them as well as distortions of the presence of God that are caused by sin. This they know from their experience of their own Christian religion. Second, Christians believe that God the triune Creator makes Godself known through God's revelation through Christ in the Spirit, which brings liberation from bondage to sin and so reveals God the Creator and consummator of everything. The only criteria they have for discerning the presence of God are those given by the trinitarian self-disclosure of God. It would therefore seem problematical to contrast a christocentric with a theocentric, a salvation-centered, or a kingdom-centered perspective on the theology of religions. Third, in applying these criteria, Christian theologians have to listen to the believers of other religions explaining their beliefs from their particular perspective. Christian theology of religions and the dialogue of religions belong inextricably together. Fourth, such conversations will be most fruitful if they engage in comparative theology from the respective perspectives that will engage the partners in dialogue also in new conversations in their own faith communities. A trinitarian theology of religions that is shaped by faith in the three divine persons in relations cannot be surprised that such an enterprise leads to conversations between human persons in relation, even when it denies all direct analogies between the divine and the human.

These historical-hermeneutical criteria of doing systematic theology, which we have applied to trinitarian theology, are closely connect to the systematic-analytic criteria that focus on questions of meaning, truth, and orientation in the self-explication of Christian faith. Only because the Christian faith claims to assert or imply meaningful propositions with genuine truth-claims can it be part of a tradition of interpretation that is the focus of the historical–hermeneutical criteria.

4. INTERNALLY COHERENT

The fourth of the criteria and the first of the systematic criteria states that the exposition of Christian faith must be internally coherent, in the sense that it does not violate the syntactic rules of logic and the semantic rules of meaning, so that it can be used to state a real truth-claim. The doctrinal formula that the Christian God is three persons in one essence has from the beginning attracted reflection and critique that have focused on the logical consistency of the formula. Can it make sense to claim that God is three in one? Dealing with this question with a focus on its internal coherence necessarily involves Christian theologians in conversations with philosophers.

During the first phase of the renaissance of trinitarian theology, philosophy, and philosophy of religion in particular, discussed questions of the meaning and truth of religious statements in abstraction from their specific religious content and from their "embeddedness" in doctrinal schemes and religious practices. Problems like the nature of religious experience, the cognitive status of religious language, the theistic proofs, and so forth dominated the discussion, and from time to time an interlocutor called "the theist" would enter the discussion, arguing for modest claims referring to any gods and none. There has been a momentous change in recent years, which has placed questions of specific Christian doctrines on the agenda.[80] While theologians were worrying about the "Myth of God Incarnate,"[81] philosophers attempted to expound the "Logic of God Incarnate"[82] with the help of the whole sophisticated toolkit at the disposal of philosophy in the analytic tradition. This has brought the doctrine of the Trinity back onto the philosophical agenda. Prominent philosophers who used to defend the coherence of theism with a unipersonalist conception of God found themselves persuaded to offer a philosophical exposition of the understanding of the Christian God as Trinity.[83] This has led to curious role reversal. It is still quite common to find theologians presenting a radically revisionary view of God, or arguing for a radically apophatic attitude, before engaging with the intricacies

---

80. The story is told in Thomas V. Morris, *God and the Philosophers: The Reconciliation of Faith and Reason* (Oxford: Oxford University Press, 1994).

81. John Hick, ed., *The Myth of God Incarnate* (London: SCM, 1977).

82. Thomas V. Morris, *The Logic of God Incarnate* (Ithaca: Cornell University Press, 1986).

83. See Richard Swinburne, *The Coherence of Theism* (Oxford: Clarendon, 1977), as well as idem, *The Christian God* (Oxford: Oxford University Press, 1994).

of traditional doctrine, while philosophers take the logical and metaphysical questions of orthodox trinitarian teaching head-on. Only in recent years have the two groups begun to engage in serious conversations.[84]

The "renaissance of philosophical theology"[85] has within a short time brought forward four main directions of justifying orthodox trinitarian faith by philosophical reasoning.[86] For all of them, the commitment to the traditional formulae of trinitarian dogma and the attempt at doing justice to the biblical witnesses has a normative function. They differ not in the doctrine of the Trinity they try to defend, but with regard to its precise interpretation as well as to the philosophical criteria that the conceptual exposition of trinitarian doctrine has to satisfy. Philosophical "social trinitarians" (Cornelius Plantinga, Richard Swinburne, James P. Moreland, William L. Craig, et al.) maintain that Father, Son, and Holy Spirit should be seen as three divine individuals fully in possession of the divine kind essence, so that God has certain properties because the persons do (Swinburne[87]), or that the three persons are seen as three parts of the whole Godhead, so that the Godhead can be understood as one divine soul (Moreland/Craig[88]). The main issue that is raised with regard to the so-called social trinitarian approaches is always whether their notion of the consubstantiality of the three persons is strong enough to reflect the *homoousios* of the classical creedal tradition. Is it enough to speak of the consubstantiality of the persons of the Trinity, or is a notion of identity required to fend off the dangers of tritheism? Is a stronger sense of identity required?

A further central issue that has been raised with regard to such proposals is whether they do not tend to posit a fourth entity, that is, the Trinity, in addition to the three persons, so that we end up with a quaternity of divine beings. The countermodel of "Latin trinitarianism" (Brian Leftow) tries to avoid this danger

---

84. A fascinating contribution to this conversation, treating the voices of systematic theologians and philosophical theologians with equal seriousness and engaging them in a lively exchange, is Thomas H. McCall, *Which Trinity? Whose Monotheism? Philosophical and Systematic Theologians on the Metaphysics of Trinitarian Theology* (Grand Rapids: Eerdmans, 2010).

85. Ibid., 1.

86. For an excellent overview, see Michael C. Rea, "The Trinity," in Thomas P. Flint and Michael C. Rea, eds., *The Oxford Handbook of Philosophical Theology* (Oxford: Oxford University Press, 2009), 403–29; and Ronald J. Feenstra, "Trinity," in Charles Taliaferro and Chad Meister, eds., *The Cambridge Companion to Christian Philosophical Theology* (Cambridge: Cambridge University Press, 2010), 3–14.

87. Swinburne, *The Christian God*, esp. 179–90.

88. James P. Moreland and William L. Craig, *Philosophical Foundations for a Christian Worldview* (Downers Grove, IL: InterVarsity, 2003), 575–95, now also in Michael C. Rea, ed., *Oxford Readings in Philosophical Theology*, vol. 1: *Trinity, Incarnation, Atonement* (Oxford: Oxford University Press, 2009), 21–43.

by starting, much like the criticized paradigm of the contrast between East and West, with the oneness of God.[89] Leftow accounts for the threeness in God by claiming that their distinctness can be understood as event-based, so that at some points in God's eternal life God is the Son, at others the Father, while this identity is held together so that the distinctness is part of our lives but not a part of God's eternal life. The identity of consciousness (in the Lockean sense of the continuity of one eternal consciousness) is never broken, because God lives God's life in all three strands of the trinitarian persons at once. Father, Son, and Spirit are "phased sortals" (like "infant" and "man"), picking out one substance under particular event-based circumstances. There is just one divine substance, and "the Persons are somehow God three times over," but there is only one trope of God and not three individualized cases of deity. Leftow even thinks that his theory can account for the communicative encounter between Father and Son, because on his presuppositions they never coincide: "God eternally has three parts of His life going on at once, without succession between them. One is the Father's life, one the Son's, one the Spirit's."[90] The eternity of God's life, free of all temporal relations, guarantees that this unity is not "disturbed" by the events that constitute the persons who have no temporal sequence. While Leftow can guarantee the oneness of God—"the triune Persons are event-based persons founded on a generating substance, God"[91]—the status of the persons remains rather weak. They are not substances in any sense of term, and the question of their consubstantiality does not arise. If there are relations, their mode of subsistence seems curiously weak, since in its distinctness it depends on us.

The alternative explications of the doctrine are, like Leftow's, impressive in their technical elegance while they leave the theologian sometimes wondering what has been gained. This also seems to be the case, at least *prima facie*, of the application, which has been elegantly argued by Peter van Inwagen, of Peter Geach's theory of relative identity to the Trinity.[92] For Geach, Leibniz's

---

89. Brian Leftow, "A Latin Trinitarianism" (2004), now in Rea, ed., *Oxford Readings in Philosophical Theology*, 76–106.

90. Brian Leftow, "Modes without Modalism," in Peter van Inwagen and Dean Zimmerman, eds., *Persons: Human and Divine* (Oxford: Oxford University Press, 2006), 374.

91. Ibid., 373–74.

92. Peter Geach, *Logic Matters* (Berkeley: University of California Press, 1980), 238–49; Peter van Inwagen, *God, Knowledge, and Mystery: Essays in Philosophical Theology* (Ithaca: Cornell University Press, 1995). See also Van Inwagen's essay "Three Persons in One Being: On Attempts to Show that the Doctrine of the Trinity is Self-Contradictory," in Melville Y. Stewart, ed., *The Holy Trinity* (Dordrecht: Kluwer, 2003), 83–97.

Law of the Indiscernibility of Identicals is ill-formed because no language can express indistinguishability *simpliciter*. All identity statements and any form of equivalence are always relative. The pay-off of this notion for defending the traditional doctrine of the Trinity against the charge of incoherence is, as van Inwagen shows, considerable, because relative identity abolishes the notion of absolute counting. We always count with respect to something. If we are counting "Divine Beings by beings, there is one; counting divine Persons by beings, there is one; counting divine Beings by Persons, there are three; counting divine Persons by persons, there are three."[93] Given that the logic of identity we apply is that of relative identity, then all the propositions that make up the traditional doctrine of the Trinity can be shown to be coherent. However, does this not make the distinctness of the persons of Father, Son, and Spirit dependent on a philosophical theory? And, since van Inwagen does not underwrite Geach's claim that there simply is no absolute identity, the possibility is left open that the Father, Son, and the Spirit are absolutely distinct. The important point is that, in addition to demonstrating how the logic of relative identity works, there needs to be an account of the metaphysics of relative identity to make the claim stick that it solves the coherence problems of the doctrine of the Trinity.[94]

Such a metaphysical account is offered in developing the parallels between the problem of material constitution, as considered by Aristotle, and the doctrine of the Trinity, as Michael Rea and Jeffrey Brower have suggested. On the analogy of hylomorphic compounds (such as, in their example, a statue and a lump of bronze), the divine essence can be understood as having the role of matter, whereas the being of the Father, the Son, and the Spirit are the distinct forms that are instantiated by the divine essence:

> Each Person will then be a compound structure whose matter is the divine essence and whose form is one of the three distinctive Trinitarian properties. . . . According to the Aristotelian solution to the problem of material constitution, . . . the three Persons are *three* distinct Persons but numerically one God . . . , there will be three distinct Persons, each Person will be God (and will be the same God as the other Persons); and there will be exactly one God.[95]

93. Ibid., 250.

94. Michael C. Rea, "Relative Identity and the Doctrine of the Trinity," *Philosophia Christi* 5 (2003): 431–46.

95. Jeffrey E. Brower and Michael C. Rea, "Material Constitution and the Trinity," *Faith and Philosophy* 22 (2005): 68–69, also in Rea, ed., *Oxford Readings in Philosophical Theology*, 127–47.

If we survey these different attempts to render the doctrine of the Trinity logically coherent, while remaining true to the biblical witnesses and to the doctrinal tradition, one cannot but applaud the intellectual rigor apparent in the work of the philosophers. The different schools of thought seem to approach the explication of the doctrine from different ends of the main questions that were briefly sketched in the second section. The social trinitarians are happy to start with the "Who?" question, affirming the particular identity of God the Father, the Son, and the Spirit as something required by the biblical witness and by the tradition. They are much more audacious than the majority of systematic theologians to talk about three individuals or even three parts in the Godhead. Their problem seems to be what they can say in answer to the "What?" question. Do they really succeed in doing justice to the unity of the divine essence? The "Latin trinitarian" approach takes this as the starting point. However, there seems to be a difficulty in expressing the eternal hypostatic identity of the Father, the Son, and the Spirit if they are "event-based" in their identities. The crucial question is in each account: What kind of metaphysics can support the respective demonstration of the logical coherence of the doctrine of the Trinity? The real advantage of the constitution theory is that it addresses this question squarely and that it can show how much can be gained from the analogy with the Aristotelian theory of material constitution. However, there is also a theologically required correction of Aristotle's account. While Aristotle arrives at "accidental sameness" with regard to the lump of bronze and statue, the trinitarian constitution theorists arrive at essential sameness, as it is clearly required by trinitarian teaching. Essential sameness is clearly more than the consubstantiality, which seems to be all the social trinitarians can say. Is this a transition from a standard Aristotelian metaphysics to a revisionary Aristotelian metaphysics? And indeed, that seems to be required if we wish to maintain that the triune God is not like any other being.

This seems to be particularly relevant when one understands the one divine *ousia* as constituted in the relations between the three trinitarian persons. If the divine *ousia* is understood as being instantiated by the three persons, one is in danger of ending up with a fourth entity in the Trinity, a divine quaternity. If the three persons are constituted by the divine *ousia*, the problem arises whether one has to ascribe some sort of fecundity to the *ousia*, which the tradition in important parts (for instance Thomas Aquinas) was very keen to avoid. If the divine *ousia*, however, is nothing else but what the three persons hold in common in virtue of their originating relations, one is confronted with the question whether it can be understood in the sense of divine simplicity, or whether the divine essence has to be understood as complex in a certain sense.

The one thing the tradition tries to avoid is speaking of the divine essence as somehow a composite nature, because that would imply that it can be known by way of its parts—which is exactly the way in which we know finite beings. If the divine essence is simple in the sense of having no parts, it can only be known by way of the trinitarian self-disclosure of God. Any account of divine simplicity must therefore retain the fact that we know the trinitarian God only as the Father, the Son, and the Spirit. If the Father, the Son, and the Spirit are related in such a way that the Father cannot exist without the Son and the Spirit, the Son not without the Father and the Spirit, and so on, we come to a view of the divine *ousia* as an inseparable communion. There are therefore no parts in God in the sense that one person could be divided from the others. On such an account, the trinitarian relationality of God is complex because of the constitutive internal relations between the three persons, but this complexity is exactly what constitutes God's simplicity in that it cannot be divided into parts. Such an argument itself is by no means unusual in trinitarian theology, since it is a structurally similar argument which defines the hypostatic identities through the relations, and the relations as that which pertains between the hypostatic identities. The point of trinitarian theology—and the main point from a metaphysical point of view—seems to be that the One and many seem to be co-constitutive in the Trinity.

From the perspective of philosophical theology, some of the main difficulties in the theological proposals arise from the account systematic theologians give of the two "How?" questions and their relationship: How are the three persons related in the one divine essence? How is the triune God related to creation in the divine economy? And how are the two "Hows?" related? In his critical discussion of Robert W. Jenson's trinitarian theology, Thomas H. McCall, while fully acknowledging the serious challenge of Jenson's revisionary metaphysics, wonders whether it is right to proceed from the identification of God by God's revelatory speech and action to claiming that God is identical with God's speech and action. Does that mean that God's identity is thus dependent on the events in which God is identified? If God is "whoever raised Jesus from the dead," and if this is in a strong sense constitutive for the being of God, then God would seem to be dependent on the world and would fail the test of Anselm's formula that God is *id quo maius cogitari nequit*.[96] McCall criticizes Moltmann's notion of perichoresis in a similar way by diagnosing that it states "not enough for divine triunity" but "too much for the

---

96. This is the punchline of David Bentley Hart's criticism of Jenson, in Hart's book *The Beauty of the Infinite: The Aesthetics of Christian Truth* (Grand Rapids: Eerdmans, 2003), 160. This echoes Colin Gunton's question whether some aspects of Jenson's thought take us "dangerously near a Hegelian

God–world relation."[97] Does Moltmann's rejection of monotheism lead him to a monism where God and the world become co-constitutive? Both criticisms, which McCall supports with strong philosophical arguments while remaining sympathetic to the overall endeavor of Jenson's and Moltmann's trinitarian theologies, concern the way both theologians relate the two "hows" of the God–world-relation and of God's immanent trinitarian relations, and point to the effects their account of the relationship has on what can be said about the divine essence ("What?") and the divine attributes. What makes McCall's analysis so helpful is that he proceeds from diagnosis to therapy, offering ways to repair what he sees as the risks of both conceptions for the understanding of the Trinity.

If we consider the criterion of internal consistency in the light of these discussions, one can say that the philosophical theologians are able to offer interpretations of the doctrine of the Trinity which show the internal coherence of trinitarian doctrine. However, this also involves a transition from logical to metaphysical reflection and to considerations whether there is need for a revisionary metaphysics to account for what the doctrine says. In general, one has the impression that while the philosophical theologians are at points too cautious to consider possible metaphysical revisions, systematic theologians seem to be a little too audacious in introducing revisions so that philosophical theologians have to remind them of the conceptual price they have to pay for these revisions. One aspect of the discussion is truly illuminating. While philosophy of religion in the analytic tradition remained in the twentieth century for the longest time largely forgetful of the philosophical and theological traditions, understanding their own approach as a new beginning that was not in need for extended conversations with the tradition, the new engagement of philosophical theology with substantive doctrinal issues, with all the philosophical rigor that is required, unlocks the gates to the tradition in a new way. Taking the doctrine of the Trinity philosophically seriously opens up the conversation with the tradition in such a way that theologians such as Gregory of Nyssa and Thomas Aquinas appear as the conversation partners from whom philosophical theology—and systematic theology that takes philosophical issues seriously—still has much to learn.

---

conception of self-realisation through the other." Colin E. Gunton, *The Promise of Trinitarian Theology* (Edinburgh: T&T Clark, 1993), 135.

97. McCall, *Which Trinity*, 164–67.

5. EXTERNALLY DEFENSIBLE

The fifth criterion for doing systematic theology claims that the self-explication of Christian faith must be externally defensible in relation to other fields of knowledge outside theology. It might seem that even a stronger criterion of external coherence is required. However, while it is certainly true that if God is the ground and unity of all truth, as it is claimed with the classical statement "*Deus est veritas*," then true propositions in theology must be externally coherent with all other true propositions. Indeed, in this strong version, it seems hardly justified to speak of "external" coherence. Although it is not difficult to grasp what the criterion says, it is by no means easy to handle. "All other true propositions" is not identical with "all other propositions that are believed to be true." Applying the criterion in a rigid way might involve us into arguing for the compatibility of a theological theory with, for instance, scientific theories that we believe to be true but which later prove to be false. I therefore prefer to understand this criterion in a way that is less strict but also less risky, when I claim that the theological self-explication of the Christian faith must be externally defensible. "Externally defensible" should not mean "can be defended" in an independent court of reason but, rather, "can be argued for in conversation with other fields of knowledge." This means that the implications of the doctrine of the Trinity for understanding the world and ourselves must be capable of being defended in a way that is compatible with our engagement with the world in other fields of knowledge.

With regard to its relationship to other fields of knowledge, the status of the doctrine of the Trinity as the framework for what is being said in Christian dogmatics must be observed. Because of this status as the integrative frame for all doctrines, the relationship to many fields of knowledge is mediated and indirect, and not immediate. It normally has the form of asking, for instance: "How does the doctrine of creation relate to what we know in other fields if we consider creation as a work of the triune God?" Schleiermacher's rule that every statement of Christian dogmatics can be stated in related propositions about God, the world, and humanity (*Glaubenslehre* §30) does not apply to the doctrine of the Trinity. This is the reason why Schleiermacher discussed the doctrine as the "coping stone" of the whole system in the last paragraphs of the *Glaubenslehre*, the *epilegomena* (§§170-72), which have relevance for the whole enterprise. There is then no way of circumventing the way in which the Trinity is mediated in the divine economy, if we wish to grasp its significance for the Christian understanding of reality.

We can briefly refer to the conversations between Christian theology and the natural sciences as an example of how the criterion of external defensibility works, and how it can be applied to trinitarian theology. Given that there is no way of arguing around the trinitarian mediation of our understanding of the triune God, it would be problematical to expect direct analogies between God and the structure of reality as it is investigated by the various other sciences. Rather, we should expect to see a mediated consonance between a view of the world and of humanity as it is investigated in the sciences and in the humanities, and the contours of the Christian understanding of reality as it is shaped by faith in the triune God who creates, reconciles, and perfects God's creation. The so-called science and religion dialogue tends to be focused on questions of scientific and religious epistemology, very much like the early stages of analytic philosophy of religion, and therefore has not much to say about the doctrine of the Trinity and the relevance of a trinitarian metaphysics for our understanding of the universe in the natural sciences. An exception is John Polkinghorne's *Science and the Trinity*, and the symposium *The Trinity and an Entangled World*.[98] Here the sensitivity for consonances between a trinitarian metaphysics and the present state of our knowledge of the universe leads to a trinitarian vision of reality where the Christian faith and scientific theories are brought into a mutually enlightening critical contact.

If we understand, with Basil, Calvin, and many others, every form of divine action as unified structured action where the Father is the unoriginate cause, the Son the ordering cause, and the Spirit the perfecting cause,[99] and if we maintain with the doctrine of *creatio ex nihilo* that there are no presuppositions for creation apart from the triune God's being, we would expect the universe to be a contingent creation with ordered intelligibility in the sense of a contingent rationality where meaning, truth, and value are disclosed in contingent events, a universe that is an open process in which relative novelty and freedom are possible, because its consummation is not the effect of immanent necessary forces. If we believe that the creator Logos, the word that was God from the beginning, became incarnate, we would expect that in the reality of experience the truth about the universe is in some sense disclosed. If we believe that the Father is revealed through the Son in the Spirit in such a sense that the certainty

---

98. John Polkinghorne, *Science and the Trinity: The Christian Encounter with Reality* (New Haven: Yale University Press, 2006); and idem, ed., *The Trinity and an Entangled World: Relationality in Physical Science and Theology* (Grand Rapids: Eerdmans, 2010).

99. Basil, *De spiritu* 15,38,2 and Calvin's rule (*Inst* I,13,18): ". . . Patri principium agendi, rerumque omnium fons et scaturigo attribuitur: Filio sapientia, consilium, ipsaque in rebus agendis dispensatio: at Spiritui virtus et efficacia assignatur actionis." *Opera selecta*, vol. 3, ed. Peter Barth and Wilhelm Niesel (Munich: Chr. Kaiser, 1928), 132. Cf. Philip W. Butin, *Revelation, Redemption, and Response: Calvin's Trinitarian Understanding of the Divine Human Relationship* (New York: Oxford University Press, 1995).

of faith is created, which enables God's human images to cooperate with the Creator, we would understand the cosmos not as a process that is moved quasi-mechanistically by meaningless dumb forces and their interaction. Instead, we can understand it as a process in which information is communicated that is meant to be received. Rather than like a clockwork, the universe would in our view be more like a book that can be deciphered. If the universe is created, redeemed, and perfected by the triune God in whose being particular identity (Father, Son, and Spirit) has a place defined by essential relatedness, we would expect a creation where created particularity and created relatedness matter.

Even such a loose list of expectations, which can be grounded in faith in the triune God as creator, redeemer, and consummator of the world, already provokes many resonances from the developments of modern science that can illustrate the consonance between trinitarian theology and the sciences. It is to be expected that once the science and religion dialogue turns from the entanglement in methodological issues to an engagement with substantive questions of Christian belief, and also discovers the historical dimension of the interaction of science and theology, the significance of the doctrine of the Trinity will become clearer. The examples also show that external defensibility does not mean that the truth of doctrines of faith should be justified on the basis of the findings of science. Rather, theology and science can engage in a fruitful conversation the more theology is willing to spell out the view of reality that faith in the trinitarian God opens up. The better trinitarian theology can clarify its internal rationality, the better it can be talked about in a reasonable conversation with the sciences. The role of theology in such conversations is not to look for alleged parallels between the knowledge of faith and the findings of science but, rather, to point to the significance of meta-scientific beliefs, basic orientations, and plausibilities of a metaphysical character, which are always present in science but often implicitly assumed. The role of theology is to make such meta-scientific beliefs and attitudes explicit, and to show by its own example that it is willing to put them under rigorous scrutiny. Starting the conversations with the science from the Christian faith in the triune God would very quickly take us beyond the alternative of a fundamentalist creationist account and an equally fundamentalist evolutionist ideology.

6. PROVIDING ORIENTATION FOR CHRISTIAN PRAXIS IN SOCIETY

The sixth criterion for explicating the truth-claims of Christian faith is to show that the Christian faith has a capacity for providing orientation for Christian praxis in society. The debates in recent years whether the trinitarian faith does have such a capacity for orientation, and what it consists in, have centered around the title of a paper by Miroslav Volf: "The Trinity Is Our Social Program."[100] The most outspoken criticism of attempts at grounding views of the church and human society based on the analogy of the Trinity comes from Kathryn Tanner, Volf's colleague at Yale Divinity School. In order to avoid the strange mix of an ontology based on Orthodox eschatology—where through the resurrection of Christ humanity finds its ontological place in the communion of the triune God—futurism, and transhumanism, as it is found in the thought of Nicolai F. Fyodorov (from whom Volf borrows his title), Volf begins with two qualifications. First, he asserts that instead of Fyodorov's futuristic vision, we can state the relationship between the Trinity and the shape of human society only in an analogous way and by means of the "historically appropriate ways" in which the eschatological destiny can be grasped while we are still *in via*. From this, he claims to build on "the narrative of the triune God's arrangements with the world"[101] against the "ultimate horizon" of the immanent Trinity.

In the discussion of Volf's program, these two steps that were designed to qualify Fyodorov's futuristic vision turn out to be the crucial problem. Most of the criticism centers on the use of analogy here, and on the possibility of transferring the metaphysical concepts of the Trinity, albeit mediated through the narrative of the divine economy, analogically to human action in history.[102] Tanner's penetrating critique spells out the dissimilarities between the trinitarian persons and relations, and the relations between human persons,

100. Miroslav Volf, "'The Trinity Is Our Social Program': The Doctrine of the Trinity and the Shape of Social Engagement," *Modern Theology* 14 (1998): 403–23. Also in Michael Banner and Alan J. Torrance, eds., *The Doctrine of God and Theological Ethics* (London: T&T Clark, 2006), 105–24.

101. Ibid., 108.

102. Volf (ibid., 122n.40) agrees with Stephen Williams's criticism of Colin Gunton's approach in *The One, The Three and the Many* to the question of the One and the many and to the issues of relatedness and otherness, insofar as it is seen as "excessively abstract," focused on "getting . . . concepts . . . right." Stephen N. Williams, *Revelation and Reconciliation: A Window on Modernity* (Cambridge: Cambridge University Press, 1995), 171. Gunton's reticence, however, is motivated by the desire to respect the world's otherness as created, and to resist all attempts at a direct analogical transfer from the relationships of the trinitarian divine life to created life. The concepts of the doctrine of the Trinity can serve as "open transcendentals" for exploring the conceptual possibilities for giving an account of created life. However, the way in which these transcendentals are realized is bound up with the full structure of the divine economy from creation to eschatological fulfilment. See Christoph Schwöbel, "The Shape of Colin Gunton's Theology: On the Way Towards a Fully Trinitarian Theology," in Lincoln Harvey, ed., *The Theology of Colin Gunton* (London: T&T Clark, 2010), 182–208. For a spirited reply to Volf, see Mark Husbands, "The Trinity Is Not Our Social Program: Volf, Gregory of Nyssa, and Barth," in Daniel J. Treier and David Lauber, eds., *Trinitarian Theology for the Church: Scripture, Community, Worship* (Downers Grove, IL: InterVarsity, 2009).

of which the Cappadocian Fathers were acutely aware, and then offers a reconstruction of the vision of community that can be developed on the basis of Jesus' message and praxis. But she also ends up by positing an analogy, "but not a very specific one": "The Trinity is coming to us to give us the sort of life-giving relations of mutual flourishing which the Trinity itself enjoys."[103] This "giving," however, follows a logic of participation and not of modeling ourselves on the imitation of the trinitarian relation. This logic, Tanner argues, can be better grasped in the incarnation: "In some ways, indeed, the incarnation is a better model for the sort of human community or kingdom to be set up: when every human being becomes one in Christ this overrides in a significant sense forms of already established kinship that would otherwise keep people apart; this is an unnatural community one might say, made up of what is naturally disparate and dissimilar."[104]

In trying to assess the significance of trinitarian theology for our social engagement and so for its political relevance, Erik Peterson's thesis that the doctrine of the Trinity had a predominantly critical function in debunking the political theologies of the Constantinian court theologians serves as a salutary reminder of the limits of analogy.[105] In 1935, Peterson's treatise was an attempt to challenge the notion of "political theology" that had been introduced into public debate by Carl Schmitt, a scholar of law and political theorist whose theory of sovereignty (the sovereign is "he who decides on the state of exception") was gratefully lapped up by the Nazi regime. Peterson argues that the philosophical notion of monarchy, for instance in Aristotle, and the single rule of the emperor, a political reality since Augustus, had been developed theologically by Eusebius in such a way that one ruler on earth corresponds with one ruler in heaven. This offered a theological legitimation for Constantine's rule: "political theology," in Schmitt's sense. Peterson wanted to show that the theology of the Cappadocian Fathers, claiming the concept of monarchy for all three persons of the Trinity, destroyed the theological foundations by denying the analogy between monarchy in heaven and monarchy on earth.[106] The theological legitimacy of the rule "on earth as it is in

---

103. Kathryn Tanner, "Social Trinitarianism and Its Critics," in Maspero and Woźniak, eds., *Rethinking Trinitarian Theology*, 368–86. See also Tanner's Warfield Lectures, *Christ the Key* (Cambridge: Cambridge University Press, 2009), esp. chs. 4 and 5: "Trinitarian Life," 140–206, and "Politics," 207–46.

104. Tanner, "Social Trinitarianism," 386.

105. Erik Peterson, *Der Monotheismus als politisches Problem* (Leipzig: Hegner, 1935), now in idem, *Ausgewählte Schriften*, vol. 1, ed. Barbara Nichtweiß (Würzburg: Echter, 1994), 23–83. An English translation has now been published: *Theological Tractates*, ed. Michael Hollerich (Stanford: Stanford University Press, 2011).

heaven" is demolished by the fact that there is no analogy between the Trinity and rule on earth. In Peterson's words: "We have attempted to demonstrate with the help of a concrete example the theological impossibility of a 'political theology.'"[107]

We are back to the question of the relationship to the two "Hows?," God's immanent trinitarian relations and the relations of the triune God to creation. Peterson's example clearly shows that there is no direct analogy, at least not in the sense of *analogia entis*, between the Trinity and created communities. The *epinoiai*, which the Cappadocians employed to clarify the meaning of the Trinity, are a conceptual tool that falls short of analogous predication. The Trinity therefore cannot function as a "model" for the shape of social relationships. It has a powerful critical role in unmasking all attempts at claiming a theological foundation for a particular form of organization of political life as implicitly idolatrous.

If there is no direct analogy, how is the criterion of "providing orientation for Christian *praxis* in society" then to be met? Volf and Tanner both point to the trinitarian structure of the divine economy, Volf primarily to self-donating love, Tanner to our unity in Christ, based on the union of humanity and divinity in Christ. Even Peterson states: "For the Christian there can only be political action under the presupposition of faith in the triune God."[108] "Faith in the triune God" seems to be the decisive pointer here. If we want to establish the link between the Trinity and the shape of human relationships, then we have to start from faith in the triune God as it is rooted in the self-disclosure of God the Father through the Son in the Spirit, as it is communicated in the word of preaching and the celebration of the sacraments. Faith does not only have epistemic significance. It must also be understood in an ontological sense, as the mode of being in the relationship that the triune God establishes with God's human creatures. The life of faith is thus characterized by God's overcoming the human contradiction of sin in God's justifying grace and by relocating humans in the relationship of createdness against the dislocation of sin. The destiny of humans to live as creatures created in the image of God is realized

106. Peterson's main "proof-text" is from the second chapter of Gregory Nazianzen's *Third Theological Oration*: ". . . monarchy is that which we hold in honor. It is, however, a monarchy that is not limited to one person, for it is possible for unity if it is at variance with itself to come into a condition of plurality; but one that is made up of an equality of nature, and a union of minds, and an identity of motion, and a convergence of its elements to unity—a thing which is impossible for created nature." E. R. Handy, *Christology of the Later Fathers* (Philadelphia: Westminster, 1954), 161 (PG 36, 76A-C).

107. Ibid., 81n.168. See my paper "Radical Monotheism and the Trinity," *NZSTh* 43 (2001): 54–74.

108. Ibid., 24.

as life in the image of Christ. This, however, is not primarily characterized by actively imitating Christ, but by being conformed to Christ and by being made one in Christ through God's justifying grace. The church is thus the personal and communal expression of the restoration of humanity's created sociality as redeemed sociality. The life of faith in the church is in this way the participation of humans in the realization of God's purpose for God's reconciled creation as God's co-operators. In this way, the church is the witness and the anticipation of the perfect fulfillment of God's communion with God's reconciled creation in the kingdom of God.[109]

This brief sketch indicates that if we want to spell out the way in which Christian praxis relates to the triune God, we have no other option than to tell the full story, the trinitarian drama in its three acts of creation, reconciliation, and the eschatological perfection of the world, in order to understand the relationship between the triune God, human created and redeemed relationality, and social praxis. We cannot isolate two or three elements to establish an analogical imaging relation, because the different acts of the drama are inherently connected and are modified by their connection. Any talk of "models" that somehow relate God's being and our being contains pitfalls, if such "models" are not placed in the whole trinitarian economy. After all, imitating God is also the very character of sin in giving in to the temptation of the serpent: "*eritis sicut Deus.*"

Furthermore, the God who is love in the immanent relations of the Trinity relates to the world in the divine economy in creative, reconciling or redeeming, and perfecting love. The capacity of God's eternal and unchanging love to adapt to the state of creation introduces a differentiation that is crucial for God's human creatures. God's reconciling love restores the original destiny of God's human creatures and places them again on the way to being perfected in the realized communion with the triune God in the kingdom of God. God's being as eternal love is differently "tuned" in relation to his human creatures and their relationship to God than it is in the immanent relations of the divine Trinity. God's self-giving love has a different form when it is appropriated to the Father, the Son, and the Spirit, and this form does not coincide with the immanent relations of the Trinity. It seems that in the Christian faith, the love of the believers follows that pattern. It is not a love that is exclusively reciprocated to the triune God. The conjunction of loving God and loving one's neighbor (Matt. 22:34-40) implies that loving God means participating in the movement of God's love to God's creatures. Being perfect (*teleioi*) like

---

109. This is a brief summary of a more detailed account in my paper "Human Being as Relational Being," in Schwöbel and Gunton, eds., *Persons, Divine and Human*, 141–65.

the heavenly Father is perfect (Matt. 5:48) is not so much an analogy of perfection but, rather, the call for God's human creatures to cooperate in the asymmetrical fashion that is fitting for creatures in directing their action toward the *telos* that God intends for God's creatures. The social program of faith in the Trinity informing the shape of social engagement of the community of faith therefore differs from the being of the Trinity and follows the logic of the divine economy rather than reflecting the trinitarian being of the immanent Trinity.

In a similar manner, one would have to spell out what participating in Christ means following the narrative ordering of the trinitarian economy, in order to distinguish it from a form of participation that has emanationist overtones. In faith we are one in Christ (Gal. 3:28), in being the *koinonia* of the Holy Spirit (2 Cor. 13:13), and in this way we share in Jesus' relationship to the Father as God's daughters and sons. The trinitarian structuring of the relationship cannot be ignored in focusing on the incarnation alone, as Tanner suggests. It provides the framework for understanding the incarnation.

One may well ask: If the relationship of the Christian community of faith to the triune God is mediated in this way by the divine economy, are there any points of contact to the immanent being of God in a metaphysical sense? In baptism, the personal identity of the human person is anchored in the relationship to the triune God so that it is not ontologically rooted in the relationships human persons have with one another. That is significant for the understanding of human personal being, because if created persons could constitute one another, they could also deconstruct one another. Baptism tells a different story. Again, in celebrating the Eucharist, it is indeed celebrated that the community of believers is to be "a community of mutual fulfillment in which the good of one becomes the good of all."[110] However, this can only be said because the "life-giving relations" are not constituted by the members of that community but by the death and resurrection of the incarnate Son, and in this way the "life-giving relations of mutual flourishing that the Trinity itself enjoys"[111] are graciously communicated to the believers, truly a foretaste of the fulfillment of the communion of the triune God with God's reconciled creation. The orientation that the doctrine of the Trinity provides for the praxis in society needs to be spelled out in a trinitarian theology of mediation, in order to avoid the short–circuiting of divine and human personhood and of the uncreated and eternal life of the Trinity with the life of created communities on the way to find their fulfillment in communion with the triune God.

110. Tanner, "Social Trinitarianism," 385.
111. Ibid., 386.

* * *

Where do we stand in trinitarian theology? The picture I have tried to sketch following the six criteria for the self-explication of Christian faith in systematic theology appears quite complex. During the last twenty years, trinitarian theology has lost much of its original programmatic drive and has made room for a critical and reflective differentiation, involving all theological disciplines and philosophy as the main conversation partners. Reflection on the doctrine of the Trinity involves the collaboration of biblical studies, the historical disciplines, philosophy, and systematic theology together with practical theology, in order to avoid stereotypes and claims that in the end cannot be supported by the findings and reflections of the other disciplines. The way in which the different theological disciplines draw upon one another reflects crucial characteristics of the doctrine of the Trinity and of the ways it has been argued for throughout Christian history. Since the doctrine of the Trinity responds to the question "Who is God?" with the triune name, it is inevitable that the modes of God's self-identification by proper name and identifying description according to the biblical writings are discussed with the exegetical disciplines. Since these modes of address continue to be used in Christian worship today, supported by the use of the Bible as a liturgical book, this engages practical theologians and liturgists in the conversation. When we understand the doctrine of the Trinity as pointing to an answer to the question "How is God in the immanent Trinity?" the metaphysical concepts employed in this answer necessarily draw the historians of doctrine and the philosophers into the discussion, not just for a historical inquiry but also for testing the metaphysical implications of the concepts employed in such an answer.

However, the question "How is God in the immanent Trinity?" cannot be answered without raising the question: "How is God in relation to creation?" It is in the relations of God to creation that God reveals Godself as the Father through the Son in the Spirit, and this is the foundation on which the whole doctrine rests. Nevertheless, it seems crucial to distinguish sharply between God's relation to creation and the immanent relations in the divine Trinity, since it is one of the central convictions of the Christian faith, expressed in the doctrine of *creatio ex nihilo*, that the world does not constitute God in any sense. While the move to the divine economy again points to the work of biblical studies, the distinction between God's immanent relatedness and God's relationship to everything that is not God makes us careful not simply to read back the accounts of the triune God's dealings with creation into the immanent Trinity. However, we also cannot proceed the other way around and presuppose a fully formed understanding of God in God's tri-personal relatedness and essential unity in order to read it into the divine economy. Without the divine economy, the doctrine of the Trinity does not have any material content. Without the immanent Trinity, the freedom of God in relating to the world God creates, reconciles, and has promised to bring to fulfillment, is lost.

It is here, in the relation of the two "Hows?," that the most perplexing problems arise, making a full-scale cooperation of all the theological disciplines necessary. If the question "What is God?" is also answered by the doctrine of the Trinity, it restricts and specifies the claims that can be made for the proposals of trinitarian theology in a significant way. Remembering that the divine essence cannot be comprehended, as the Cappadocians claimed against Eunomianism, points us to the limits of our conceptual grasps and to the boundaries of language. It is important to note that the warning implied in asserting the incomprehensibility of the divine essence does not arise because we do not know enough about God, or dare not speak of God the Trinity. Rather, it is because we know God in God's trinitarian self-revelation, and so feel compelled to invoke God by no other name, that the incomprehensibility of God must be emphasized. All we know and all we can say about God does not give us a comprehending take on God, but points us back to the divine self-communication, which we cannot but receive as a gift that constitutes the Christian faith.

In theology one can make mistakes by saying either too much about God, or by saying not enough, thereby denying the way in which God has given Godself for us to know in such a way that we dare to address God by the triune name. It is not because they claimed to know less about God than the Eunomians that the Cappadocians and all following their lead insisted on the incomprehensibility of the divine essence, but because they felt that they knew more and knew better than their opponents, which made them exercise reserve at this point. This problem, of course, returns when we ask "Which attributes?" can be predicated of the triune God. Positive statements based on the rich predications of God in the biblical sources must thus be accompanied and qualified by indicators of negation and expressions of excess in order to maintain the logic of perfection. The very practical issues behind these conceptual questions concern the ever-present danger of relapsing into mythology or falling prey to idolatry.

When trinitarian theology is done in this way, it no longer appears as a name for a theological program that can be compared to other theological orientations, or as a theological school, keen on distinguishing itself from other schools. In this way, doing trinitarian theology appears—at least to one participant observer—as just another name for doing Christian theology.

2

Trinity, Tradition, and Politics

Karen Kilby

A great deal has been written about the Trinity in recent decades. Much of the language used to describe this mass of publication—a flourishing, a flowering, a revival, or a "renaissance"—has distinctly positive connotations, for most of those writing about the phenomenon, or writing from within it, see the outpouring of trinitarian theology as fundamentally a good thing, a moment in which Christian thought is simultaneously returning to its roots to rediscover a distinctive richness, and exhibiting fresh creative power—both going back and moving forward.

There is also, however, a more skeptical minority. The doubts are directed, not toward the doctrine of the Trinity itself, but toward the so-called trinitarian revival, or at least a significant portion of it.[1] Is this *really* a revival, a retrieval and development of a key dimension of the tradition, or is it something else—something more like a foreign growth, the flowering of a slightly different plant?

The essay that follows will fall into three parts. I will first indicate some of the reasons for this skepticism, giving a brief overview of what we might term the minority position in contemporary trinitarian theology. In the remainder of the essay I will seek to explore and develop the position in two ways. In the second section, I will consider what I take to be a key issue between the minority and majority positions—divine ineffability—in the light of some recent and interesting work by Kendall Soulen. In the third section, I will turn to

---

1. That there is no lively debate in English-speaking theology about the status of the doctrine is itself a point worth noting. The John Hick and Maurice Wiles who stimulated *The Myth of God Incarnate* (London: SCM, 1977) debate seem to have no obvious successors in the current generation of theologians. It may be that those with a similar sensibility now tend more toward an engagement with Jacques Derrida and continental philosophy.

the relation between Trinity and politics. Although, as we shall see, the way much contemporary trinitarian theology moves from something like a map of the Trinity to the commendation of an overarching ecclesial or sociopolitical program can be very problematic, at the same time this sense of political relevance gives it much of its attraction. In this third section, then, I will try, if not to match this relevance, at least to suggest the possibility of a different way of thinking about the relation of Trinity and politics.

1. Critiques of Social Trinitarianism

What criticisms have emerged against the mainstream of recent trinitarian theology? One set of concerns, as already indicated, revolve around the way recent trinitarian theologians, especially social trinitarians, seek to make the Trinity relevant by deriving a politics from it, contrasting, typically, the tendencies of "mere monotheism" to support empire, authoritarian regimes, and patriarchy with the tendency of the doctrine of the Trinity to support equality, mutuality, and the appreciation of diversity. The criticism usually focuses not on *what* the social trinitarians actually recommend about society or church—that we should be more egalitarian, more loving, that we should positively value difference, that communion or community is important—but on the legitimacy of deriving these conclusions from the doctrine in this *way*.

Kathryn Tanner has recently set out a fairly comprehensive critique of this position. She points out, first of all, the simplistic thinking involved in aligning monotheism with monarchy, and Trinity with more progressive forms of social arrangement: such an alignment is not particularly borne out by history—where the rise of the doctrine of the Trinity and rising Christian support for centralized empire coincide—nor does it take into account that a whole variety of political programs can in fact be correlated with any one kind of belief in God.[2] Second, there is the fundamental perversity of trying to get a grip on, as Tanner puts it, "what is difficult to understand—the proper character of human society" on the basis of "what is surely only more obscure—the character of divine community."[3]

---

2. This is a point Tanner has also made at length in her volume *The Politics of God: Christian Theologies and Social Justice* (Minneapolis: Fortress Press, 1992).

3. Kathryn Tanner, "Social Trinitarianism and its Critics," in *Rethinking Trinitarian Theology: Disputed Questions and Contemporary Issues in Trinitarian Theology*, ed. Giulio Maspero and Robert J. Wozniak (London: T&T Clark, 2012), 378.

I think this point could be taken a little further. I have argued elsewhere[4] that it is not only a matter of trying to learn about the obscure from the still-more-obscure, but that there is a particularly distinctive pattern of projection built into such arguments. Because the Trinity is obscure—because we do not know how to understand how the three can be one—the social trinitarian perfectly reasonably draws on those things that to some degree bind people together in our experience—love, empathy, mutual giving—and proposes that perhaps it is like this in the Trinity, only unimaginably more so. We must add this last proviso, this "unimaginably more so," since three human persons, however much in accord and empathy they may be, remain three, while the three divine persons are one. But then, in a second movement, what was first put forward to overcome a difficulty—some concept of love, relatedness, empathy, self-gift—is itself offered as the basis for a social and political program: we can learn from the wonders of trinitarian community how best to structure human communities. So we first project our best ideas about human community onto the Trinity, and then claim to have discovered in the Trinity a new map for structuring human communities.

A further point Tanner makes is that if one *were* going to try to draw the most obvious political conclusions from the doctrine of the Trinity, they might not necessarily be the progressive ones that social trinitarians tend to find: there is a kind of fixity in the classical doctrine of the Trinity (Father cannot be Son and Son cannot be Father), an ordering that would seem to underwrite hierarchy, a dominance of the male gender, and an insistence on the sameness of the persons that would seem to leave little space for difference. To get a progressive social program from a social doctrine of the Trinity, you have to work quite hard: "What these theologians are trying to do," Tanner writes, "is systematically modify as many of the politically problematic aspects of classical Trinitarianism as they can."[5] And, finally, of course, there are a series of severe *disanalogies* between the Trinity and human society: "unlike the peaceful and perfectly loving mutuality of the Trinity," Tanner writes, "human society is full of suffering, conflict and sin. Turned into a recommendation for social relations, the Trinity seems unrealistic, hopelessly naïve, and for that reason perhaps even politically dangerous."[6]

One element in some of the criticisms just outlined is a tension between the program of social trinitarians and "classical trinitarianism"—that is, between the

4. Karen Kilby, "Perichoresis and Projection: Problems with Social Doctrines of the Trinity," *New Blackfriars* 81 (2000): 432–45.

5. Tanner, "Social Trinitarianism," 375.

6. Ibid., 381.

recent social trinitarians and the tradition that they see themselves as retrieving and developing. The question of the relation of recent trinitarianism to the tradition has also been raised directly by a range of scholars, including Michel René Barnes, Lewis Ayres, and Sarah Coakley. The most recent and comprehensive treatment of this issue is given by Steve Holmes in *The Holy Trinity: Understanding God's Life*.[7] Interestingly, Holmes had been a student of Colin Gunton, one of the foremost social trinitarians in the English-speaking world, and early in his career Holmes himself wrote as a social trinitarian. Subsequently, however, he repented: in his recent book he calls into question quite comprehensively the very notion of a renaissance or retrieval of the Trinity. In patristic trinitarianism, divine simplicity is always central, as is divine ineffability. And in patristic trinitrianism, there is much less to say about the three. The three *hypostases*, according to the Fathers, are distinguished by their relations of origin—the Father begets the Son, the Spirit proceeds from Father or Father and Son—but not in any other way. One can speak of these relations of origin, and one can speak of a distinction between the persons that is tied to this, but that is all, according to the Fathers.[8]

There is a kind of discipline and austerity to earlier trinitarian thought—a discipline and austerity that continued to be felt in the early and mid-twentieth century in the work of theologians like Rahner and Barth—which has been lost in the sudden increase in trinitarian volubility of our time. One might say that the whole enthusiasm for imagining the Trinity as ideal persons in community stems from a concept of "person" which has nothing to do with the traditional technical trinitarian term. Recent thinkers, then, have been lulled into thinking they have discovered some great new key by the coincidence of a long-standing technical term with one of the favored ideas of our period. According to Holmes, "The practice of speaking of three 'persons' in this [contemporary] sense in the divine life, of asserting a 'social doctrine of the Trinity', a 'divine community' or an 'ontology of persons in relationship' can only ever be, as far as I can see, a simple departure from (what I have attempted to show is) the unified witness of the entire theological tradition."[9]

---

7. Stephen R. Holmes, *The Holy Trinity: Understanding God's Life* (Milton Keynes: Paternoster, 2012). A new version of this book is available under the title *The Quest for the Trinity: The Doctrine of God in Scripture, History, and Modernity* (Downers Grove, IL: IVP Academic, 2012).

8. See also my article "Is an Apophatic Trinitarianism Possible?," *International Journal of Systematic Theology* 12 (2010): 65–77, which touches on the very limited nature of what the Cappadocians thought could be said of the Trinity.

9. Holmes, *The Holy Trinity*, 195.

2. DIVINE INEFFABILITY

Weaving its way through all these criticisms, I believe, is a fundamental problem that recent trinitarianism has become, quite simply, too *knowing*. Contemporary theologians often seem to "have a concept" of the Trinity, and to be able to talk with confidence about the inner life of the Trinity, in a way that sets them at odds with the tradition. And what is most needed, then, is to learn again how to be trinitarian without pretending to know more than in fact we do.

An obvious objection to this perspective is that if the tradition insisted heavily on God's unknowability, and contemporary thinkers tend to venture to say more about the Trinity, it could be the tradition, rather than the dominant contemporary view, that is at fault. The problem, it might be suggested, needs to be found not in modern over-volubility but, rather, with the excessively heavy influence of neo-Platonism on so many of our predecessors. Freed as we now are from captivity to this philosophy, the objection might run, we have realized that there is no reason to be so apophatic. God has given Godself to be known in revelation, after all, and in the incarnation. Is it not therefore right that we have something robust, something powerful, exciting, and particular, to say about the God who reveals Godself as Trinity?

In many cases, of course, modern volubility about the inner life of the Trinity and its social and political relevance seems rooted not so much in re-immersion into Scripture as in speculative possibilities of the language bequeathed by the tradition—the terminology of "person," for instance, or of "perichoresis." There is arguably something a little odd in settling on a very specific language precisely because of the authority invested in it by its usage in the tradition, and then deploying the language in a way unimagined by and at odds with this same tradition. It can seem not so much a development of the tradition as a misunderstanding of it.

Still, even if the legitimacy of this point is granted, it does not fully address the objection: Is the restraint and austerity, the apophaticism, of the tradition when it comes to understanding the Trinity, something to be regretted rather than admired? Is it the unfortunate result of too much neo-Platonism obscuring the Fathers' capacity to see what is just there in the Bible?

This is, of course, an issue, or a version of an issue, that has been with us for some time—since the work of Harnack at least. A somewhat fresh approach to the question may be possible, however, by way of a consideration of some recent work by Kendall Soulen. His book *The Divine Name(s) and the Holy Trinity*[10] is, in my view, the most significant intervention to be made in recent years in trinitarian theology, and although the question of how "knowing" trinitarian theology ought to be is not its explicit theme, there are important ways in which it touches on this question.

The focus of Soulen's work is, as its title indicates, on issues of naming God. The Christian tradition, he proposes, in fact has three distinct, noninterchangeable ways of naming the Trinity. One, as might be expected, is "as Father, Son, and Holy Spirit." A second, nearly as familiar, way is to name the Trinity by a proliferation of names: the Trinity is root, tree, and fruit, fountain, river, and stream; it is lover, beloved, and love; it is memory, will, and understanding; and so on.

In the third way of naming (which actually comes first, in Soulen's scheme) we move into what can seem less familiar territory. Soulen, whose most important earlier work has involved grappling with problems of Christian supersessionism, argues that there is a pattern of naming the Trinity that centers on the Tetragrammaton, the unspoken name of God which is given in Exodus 3:15 and occurs approximately six thousand times in the Hebrew Bible. In Jewish tradition, reverence for the divine name is marked among other ways by its nonpronounciation: it is alluded to in various kinds of indirect ways, including the use of a surrogate. Both Jesus and the authors of the New Testament continued to observe the traditional forms of reverence for the divine name, but quite early in the church's history these patterns of indirect allusion to God's proper name had been forgotten, so that later readers, including those in the fourth century, could read the New Testament without actually hearing the frequent allusions to the name given on Mount Horeb.

When we hear, for instance, of Jesus being given the "name above every name" (Phil. 2:9), though Christians in the fourth or the twenty-first century might not immediately understand the significance, no Jew in New Testament times could fail to catch the allusion to the Tetragrammaton. Similarly, Soulen suggests that when we read of baptizing in the *name* (not *names*) of Father, Son, and Holy Spirit, we should consider that this may well be a reference to precisely the name revealed to Moses in Exodus. Or again, in Paul's proto-creed of "One God, the Father . . . and one Lord, Jesus Christ" (1 Cor. 8:6), we must hear in "Lord" *kyrios*, a Greek translation of *Adonai*, itself substituted for the Tetragrammaton.

One consequence of Soulen's proposal is that God's having a proper name, given in Exodus, is not something which should, for Christians, be seen as a strange archaism, or a name which has been surpassed or displaced now that

10. Kendall R. Soulen, *The Divine Name(s) and the Holy Trinity: Distinguishing the Voices* (Louisville: Westminster John Knox, 2011). A second volume, *The Divine Name(s) and the Holy Trinity: Voices in Counterpoint*, is projected.

we "have" Jesus, or now that we instead know God as Trinity. Rather, both the significance of "Jesus" and the trinitarian naming of God are fundamentally rooted in the one proper name of God. Something fundamentally shifts here, then, in Christian trinitarianism's relation to Judaism.

On Soulen's view, there is an irreducible pluralism to the ways in which the Trinity is named. All three patterns of naming—which he terms the "theological" (by way of the Tetragrammaton), the christological (as Father, Son, and Holy Spirit), and the "pneumatological" (through an endlessly open multiplication of names)—are necessary, and none can be collapsed into the others.[11] One of the things his proposal does is to provide a framework through which to look again at certain contemporary stand-offs. Soulen considers, for instance, the so-called inclusive-language debate, where on one side feminist theologians such as Elizabeth Johnson insist on the importance of coining fresh ways of naming God in new contexts, and on the other side those like Robert Jenson are anxious to reaffirm the centrality and inescapability of the language of Father, Son, and Spirit.[12] On Soulen's reading, such conflicts are not so much about gender as they seem to be but, rather, are the outcome of a conflict between parties, each of whom is championing *one* of the legitimate patterns of trinitarian naming.

So how is this relevant to the question of whether the reserve, the restraint, and austerity surrounding the Trinity in much of the tradition should be seen as the unfortunate effect of excessive neo-Platonism? In one respect, the story Soulen tells clearly supports the objection I have been entertaining. Large portions of the Christian theological tradition have been unable to see the

---

11. There is a sense in which the way of naming that makes reference to the Tetragrammaton is most primordial—the other patterns are in a certain way rooted in this, because this pattern alone is to do with a proper name. There is a delicate tension in Soulen's thought here, one that parallels the tension in classical trinitarianism between the equality of the three persons and the primacy of the Father as unoriginate origin. In general, in fact, Soulen establishes quite an elaborate parallelism between the three patterns of naming and the three persons of the Trinity. The patterns, which he names "theological," "christological," and "pneumatological," are distinct but related; they are envisaged as three strands in a single cord, or three voices in a single harmony; certain theological strategies are seen as in danger of falling into a kind of subordinationism, where one pattern is insisted upon as orthodox to the detriment of others, or modalism, where the real difference between the various patterns is denied; and so on. In my view, the elaborate tidiness of this parallelism between the Trinity itself and the three ways of naming the Trinity is the most worrisome aspect of his project. One wonders whether the pull of intellectual elegance is sometimes a little too strong.

12. Robert W. Jenson, in fact, at least in the work that Soulen focuses on, *The Triune Identity: God According to the Gospel* (Philadelphia: Fortress Press, 1982), 1–20, quite implausibly takes "Father, Son, and Holy Spirit" as the *proper* name of God.

significance of the Tetragrammaton in the Hebrew Bible, and part of the explanation for this is precisely the grip of neo-Platonism.[13] From Hellenistic philosophy the Fathers imbibed the notion that divine transcendence requires that God is beyond all names, and with the Cappadocians the motif of namelessness is no longer just presumed but actually put center stage in the articulation of orthodoxy. The Fathers are so thoroughly in the grip of this presumption of divine namelessness, indeed, that each time in Scripture they come across a reference to the divine name they simply take it as another occasion to discuss the unnameability of the divine essence.[14]

Together with an understanding of God's namelessness comes the divine "polyonomy"—one must use many names of God because no one is adequate. The classic articulation of this "anonymous polyonomy" is of course in Dionysius, but it is presumed by a large part of the theological tradition. It is characteristic of Soulen's recasting of the tradition, however, that his presentation of the doctrine of anonymous polyonomy is not simply negative. While it is regrettable that it blocked recognition of the importance of the Tetragrammaton, it led the Fathers and their medieval successors to explore "the deep logic of God's many names." So, writes Soulen, "the same preconception that ruled out the search for the *divine name* spurred on the search for the *divine names*."[15] In other words, while one pattern of trinitarian naming, the one here termed the theological, was occluded, another pattern—the pneumatological—was vigorously developed.[16]

So Soulen's attitude toward neo-Platonism is complex, but it does at least lend some support to the notion that neo-Platonically derived apophaticism is to blame for a certain inability to see what is just *there* in the Bible. If we consider the broader implications of his view, however, I think it can be argued that as a whole it cuts *against* recent theology's trinitarian confident volubility.

First, there is the fact that, while Soulen brings us back to attentiveness to the fact that God has a proper name, it is a name that is not spoken, that is indicated, circled around, indirectly alluded to rather than simply pronounced. One could say, I think, that we relate to God, but neither God, nor God's name, nor an understanding of God, are at our disposal.

13. Another reason, and in the context of Soulen's thought perhaps a more important one, that the Fathers became unable to notice the role of the Tetragrammaton was their loss of contact with, and their disinclination for any sympathetic interest in, Jewish practice.

14. Soulen draws this point from Jaroslav Pelikan.

15. Soulen, *The Divine Name(s)*, 55 (his emphasis).

16. It is also worth noting that, on Soulen's account, the Reformation tradition comes off no better than what he calls the "Dionysian" tradition.

Second, there is the emphasis on the *irreducibility* of the threefold pattern of naming. If we cannot settle on a single way of approaching the Trinity, might it not follow that we cannot have something like a map, a description of God as Trinity in our grasp, a concept at our disposal which we could then put to use in other areas, as social trinitarians seem to think that they have?

And linked to this, third, is Soulen's very focus on *naming* the Trinity. Naming and describing are quite close, particularly if "naming" is used in the extended sense that it has had in the tradition, but there is perhaps still a significant difference. If we are focused on naming, God as Trinity never becomes akin to an object on which we reflect and theorize in a disengaged way, because naming is always an action within a relationship.

So while it may be right to say that the particular shape of the Fathers' trinitarian apophaticism need not be normative for subsequent trinitarian development, I think it can be argued that Soulen's work lends support in a broader sense to a trinitarian apophaticism, a restraint, a resistance to a too-knowing approach to the doctrine. Indeed, perhaps one should view the tradition's deployment of notions of ineffability and simplicity as simply a way, drawing on the best available intellectual resources, of responding to the biblical pressures of the mysteriousness, absolute uniqueness, and transcendence of God. They may not be the only way of doing so; they may not be a necessary way of doing so; but they are *a* way. And what is therefore disturbing about contemporary trinitarian volubility is not quite that it has abandoned the particular mode of restraint derived from neo-Platonism, but that no new mode of restraint has been found: contemporary thinkers, from Moltmann to Gunton to the analytic theologians, seem disturbingly unfettered.[17]

What is fundamentally troubling about much contemporary trinitarian theology, then, is that many seem to *have* a concept of God in a way that it seems to me we have no business having a concept of God. The worry is that such a theology can become a form of idolatry, out of step with the mystery and transcendence of God, out of tune with the Bible's portrayal of God whose ways are beyond our ways and whose thoughts beyond our thoughts, with the fact that while the God whose self-description is "I am who I am" has a name, it is a name which is to be revered but not pronounced; and also oddly untouched by the baffling and ungraspable quality of the Jesus of the Gospels and the elusiveness of the Spirit.

---

17. Hans Urs von Balthasar should also perhaps be included on this list. Although he is not a typical social trinitarian, his theology of the Trinity is distinctly unrestrained. Cf. my *Balthasar: A (Very) Critical Introduction* for a consideration of the unfettered quality of his thought in general, and his trinitarianism in particular.

3. Trinity and Politics

But what is the *point* of the doctrine of the Trinity, one might ask, if we can have no concept, no map, no understanding, no grasp of it? The answer I would propose is that the Trinity must be considered, not as something we stand outside of and gaze at, but as something with which we are involved. When we pray, it is to the Father, in the Son, through the Spirit. The Spirit works in us, catching us up into a movement, a life, which is trinitarian. Whatever the pattern of the Trinity is, whatever the life of the Trinity is, it is something we find ourselves in the midst of, and what I have suggested is that it may be an ill-advised courting of the dangers of idolatry to suppose that we can, in doing theology, extract ourselves sufficiently from this in-the-midst-ness to form for ourselves a representation, an image, a picture, a map, of what the Trinity is.

To follow this view is, of course, to block off the path that moves from Trinity to politics by way of the application of key concepts: if we lack a concept of the Trinity to begin with, we clearly cannot put it to use in recommending how to organize society. It need not, however, rule out a trinitarian political theology altogether. What follows, then, will be an outline of what an apophatic trinitarian political theology might look like.

In addition to the proposal that we should not think of ourselves as in possession of a comprehensive grasp of God, I will begin from the assumption that we are not in possession of a comprehensive grasp of society, either how it is or how it ought to be. I want to explore, in other words, the possibility of a political theology that does not rely on commitment to an overarching narrative and an all-inclusive analysis of economic, social, and political life as it is or as it needs to become.[18]

The first point to establish is that if an overview of how everything is and how everything ought to be eludes us, this need not in itself lead to a stance of political indifference and irresponsibilty. People who have at their disposal no overarching narrative may nevertheless be able to see with reasonable clarity that a variety of things are not as they ought to be, that there are features of the world which cry out for change. And it is possible to work for such changes without a comprehensive map of how society is and ought to be. A sense of justice and compassion, and the willingness to see the realities one encounters as best one can, with whatever partial vision and provisionally useful analytical tools one can find, is enough.

18. My assumption that we do not have a comprehensive grasp on social reality is parallel to the assumption that we have no grasp on the Trinity. It is not, however, I should add, a necessary correlate—it would be perfectly possible to be apophatic in one's trinitarianism while at the same time confident in one's overarching narrative of socioeconomic reality.

In fact, I think it can be argued that what most inhibits sociopolitical engagement is not the lack of an overarching account of society and politics, but something Jon Sobrino calls "fidelity to the real"—something like the willingness to look around and take what one sees into account. Many of the non-poor in the rich world live with a knowledge that we mostly want to suppress, I think, a knowledge that the circles of comfort and stability in which we move do not really reflect to us the real story of the world.[19] To look at the suffering of those in absolute poverty, unable to feed and educate their children properly, or at the suffering of those who are mentally ill, or of those who are trafficked, or those caught in the asylum system, is something that those who live in comfort, on the whole, simply do not want to do. This brokenness and monumental injustice and suffering are part of the reality of the world, but it is hard to be faithful to them. They are a little too disturbing. We sense that they will unsettle us, call us into question, that to look and to keep looking and act in a way that is in keeping with what we see might destabilize our own existence.

My suggestion here is not that proper sociopolitical engagement requires no theoretical moment, no attempt at analysis of social or economic or political forces. I *am* suggesting, however, on the one hand, that this engagement does not necessarily require the utterly generalized sorts of vision that one might hope to deduce from just the right concept of the Trinity. And, on the other hand, the greatest difficulty, the key sticking point, I am suggesting, lies not with the more limited and provisional sorts of analysis that we do need, but with our capacity for fidelity to reality, our willingness to look at and really take seriously the world around us. I am assuming, in other words, that the most significant truth is not that we fail to engage because we lack the right analysis but, rather, that we lack the analysis because we are not willing to engage.

This last point may be worth illustrating. Let's suppose, for instance, that I hear on the radio of a serious problem of trafficked women in Britain. I am, we can imagine, troubled to think of such slavery and oppression going on nearby. What should I do? I don't know. I don't entirely understand what global forces of capitalism and crime are conducive to such trafficking, and I do not know what exactly might be at fault in border control or policing, or what regulatory reform might be necessary, or where if anywhere pressure could be applied, or what organizations are working on this problem that are worthy of support. So I go about my daily tasks, and I listen to other items on the radio. But whatever I tell myself in this situation, the ignorance is not the true block from engagement, but is, rather (in the longer term anyways), the outcome

19. This article takes a distinct turn toward "contextual" theology at this point: I will explicitly be speaking from precisely this perspective of the non-poor of the rich world.

of disengagement. I do not look away and do nothing because of my lack of understanding of what to do—even if that is how it can seem to me—but I lack an understanding of what to do because I have opted to look away and do nothing.

We most urgently need the resources of faith and theology, then, I am proposing, not in constructing an absolutely general idea of politics, or society, or the way economies should be structured, or the shape of a perfectly constructed community—we do not fundamentally need theology either for the definitive vision of utopia or for the definitive analysis of globalization. We most urgently need them, rather, in grappling with this problem of being faithful to the real, being willing actually to allow ourselves to be moved, disturbed, decentered, destabilized, even, by the tragedy and suffering and injustice that we routinely both see and refuse to see.

Does this have anything to do with the Trinity? It is not too hard to see that it might have something to do with Jesus. Any temptation we might have to think that the way to relate to God is by rising directly above the sufferings and injustices and particularities of this world—any such temptation is thwarted by the pattern of Jesus' life, incarnate and entangled as it is in a particular political moment, responsive to the concrete injustices and sufferings of a distinct time and place. I do not propose that we should abstract from the life and teaching of Jesus a tidy political program and then apply it at will in any other time and place, but if we understand Jesus as the Word of God spoken into creation, then we have to see this speaking as taking place in the midst of things, in the midst of the messy, suffering, conflicted reality that is the world—this is how and where we have to listen for God. And if we understand Jesus as the fundamental pattern of human response to God, then again we have to see the response as taking place in the midst of things, through and not apart from the engagement with the messy, suffering, conflicted reality that is the world.

But, one might respond, if there is no concrete program to be transferred from his time to ours, how do we know in *particular* what to do? And there is the deeper problem on which I have already touched, the danger that we do not necessarily *want* to know, do not want to be disturbed and destabilized from a comfortable, secure existence. Where can we find the strength, the resolve, to genuinely confront the demands justice and love require, wrapped up as most of us are in our own secure cocoons?

Both these questions, it seems to me, lead to reflection on the role of the Holy Spirit. A classic Christian affirmation is that the Spirit incorporates us, in our variety and difference, into Christ, and this has bearing on the first question.

Trinitarian faith legitimates a certain trust, as Christians seek to engage with the social and political demands of their time, that the Spirit may be at work aligning them with and incorporating them into Christ's own relation to the world. While there may be no algorithm for making the transition from Christ's engagement to the one required of the contemporary church and contemporary Christians, there can legitimately be a kind of confidence that this is a gap the Spirit can bridge.

And what of the reluctance, the disinclination, to really see what is before us? Here again, we can be led to reflection on the Spirit, although by way first of a reflection on *sin*. For surely this evasion of the real is, and must be acknowledged as, a dimension of the sin of the rich world. Indeed, I have been suggesting that it is a sphere in which sin has a particularly strong grip, so strong that it can be hard to see how to escape, how as individuals or communities we could be really willing to look at the real when to do so would so discomfort and destabilize us. But it is part of the fundamental grammar of the Christian faith that where we know there is sin, we must also trust in and look for the reality of grace, the movement of the Holy Spirit. It is a basic Christian conviction that the Holy Spirit is at work in the world, the church, and in individuals, freeing and making new things possible, and so it is a fundamental Christian requirement to attend to, to listen for, the promptings of the Spirit. In the realm of the political, then, faith in the Holy Spirit means not needing to remain simply trapped and frozen, caught between an awareness of the injustices and oppression of the world on the one hand, and one's own fear of confronting them, on the other: the individual or community is, rather, in a position, first, to acknowledge the sin of their own situation, and, second, to seek out and attend to the movements of the Holy Spirit which, on one level or another, allow a new fidelity to the real.

Both Son and Spirit have something to do, then, with what I take to be the most urgent question for a political theology, but what of the Father? Here we may find a way in by considering the almost inevitable frustration of political engagement. NGOs often like to encourage by telling supporters that they *can* end hunger, make poverty history, eradicate debt, and so on, but Christians who engage with any of these things must do so in the knowledge that in all likelihood we will not end hunger or make poverty history or usher in a new age of justice. At best, political efforts may contribute to some partial success, and they may utterly fail. What is it that can make ongoing engagement, ongoing "fidelity to the real," possible under these conditions? One strategy might be to ignore the complexity and ambiguity of the world and attend only to a limited problem where there is hope of seeing full success—but this would not quite count as being faithful to the real. It would once again be a kind of escapism. But what if the whole of our engagement in the world is itself—and is lived as and understood as—part of an orientation and a movement toward a horizon that transcends the world, toward the Father who is the source and goal of all?

In brief, then, one can conceive of political engagement as the Spirit at work in us, seeking to overcome our selfish blindness, seeking to unite us with Jesus, whose own involvement with the world and "fidelity to the real" is at the same time always his pointing beyond the world to the Father.

The aim of this essay has been to find a path toward quite a *different* way of relating trinitarian theology to politics than is most often found in the recent literature. What I am suggesting is that it is not advisable to imagine, *either* with respect to God *or* with respect to politics, that we are in a position to have an integrated grasp of the whole, a vision which we can ponder and play with and then decide to do something about. In both cases, we are already in the midst, always already related, always already implicated, but with no overview. Both our politics and our relation to God must be lived in the lack of an integrating grasp. It may be true that we *want* an overview, a single, integrating vision—this attracts us, because there would be a kind of security to it, a satisfaction, a closure. There is a strong pull to the kind of theologies Jürgen Moltmann and Leonardo Boff and the others offer, for this reason. But perhaps if trinitarian theology can help us come to terms with living in the midst of a relationship with a God who is not grasped, it can also be of some use in helping us think about what is needed to be faithful to a reality whose demands unsettle and destabilize us.

3

The Necessity for *Theologia*

Thinking the Immanent Trinity in Orthodox Theology

Aristotle Papanikolaou

In this essay, I will discuss the three most dominant trajectories of trinitarian theology in contemporary Orthodox theology: the apophaticism of Vladimir Lossky, the communion models of John Zizioulas and Dumitru Stăniloae, and the sophiology of Sergius Bulgakov. While none of these thinkers are anglophone theologians, and none of them wrote in English, with the exception of Zizioulas, the English translations of works by these particular theologians have dictated the influence of Orthodox trinitarian theology in the anglophone world. Indeed, there really is no anglophone Orthodox theology to speak of other than the influence of the translated works of these theologians. I will end by bringing Bulgakov in conversation with Rahner in order to offer suggestions for what is needed not simply in current Orthodox discussions of the Trinity, but in the wider discourse of Christian theology on the Trinity. Let me give a hint by simply saying that a Christian theology of the Trinity is deficient if it does not recognize the doctrine of the Trinity as the rationally defensible Christian response to understanding the God–world relation in terms of communion, and against both nominalism or pantheism.

THE APOPHATIC TRINITY

Vladimir Lossky is one of the best-known Orthodox theologians of the latter half of the twentieth century, and the one who exercised the most influence on the construction of a particular metanarrative of the history of Orthodox Christian thought. According to this narrative, the core of Eastern Christian thought has been an understanding of theology as mystical union with God.

In defining theology in this way, Lossky was contrasting this core of Eastern Christian thought with what he perceived to be the rationalism and propositionalism characteristic of the neo-Scholasticism of his time. Throughout his writings, Lossky is a bit harsh on Thomas Aquinas, but in later writings he hints that Aquinas is not so much the problem but, rather, his interpreters.[1] The danger with the neo-Scholastic approach to the Trinity, according to Lossky, is that its emphasis on a rationalism in theology, whose end result is propositions to which one must assent in faith, simply diverts attention from the Christian struggle to be united with the living God. The most obvious manifestation of this danger for Lossky is the *filioque*. As Lossky himself states, "[t]he positive approach employed by Filioquist Triadology brings about a certain rationalization of the dogma of the Trinity. . . . One has the impression that the heights of theology have been deserted in order to descend to the level of religious philosophy."[2] More than simply diverting attention, the neo-Scholastic approach appears to deny the very realism of divine-human communion, which is the very heart of the incarnation. Such is the danger of any rationalistic approach to theology, according to Lossky, which is also evident for him in the Russian sophiologists, including Bulgakov. (As an aside, it strikes me as worthy of discussion for trinitarian theology how many of the greatest theologians of the twentieth century, their differences notwithstanding, had as a common enemy the neo-Scholastic manual style of theology).

The doctrine of the Trinity, for Lossky, is a "primordial fact" of revelation, the expression of which defies the rules of formal logic.[3] The goal in theology is not so much understanding as it is an articulation to that which is faithful to the paradoxical realism of a God who is transcendent to all human knowing but radically immanent in the person of Christ; and to the paradoxical realism of the created being united with the uncreated. The realization of this divine-human communion was revealed by God as Trinity, that is, in the kenosis of the Son and Spirit, both sent by the Father. Since God revealed Godself as Trinity in order to unite the created with the uncreated, the goal of theology is to provide language to the *datum* of revelation in such a way that is faithful to the unity-in-distinction of God as Trinity, and in such a way that the dogma serves the

---

1. Vladimir Lossky, review of E. L. Mascall, *Existence and Analogy*, in *Sobornost* 3 (1950): 295–97.

2. Vladimir Lossky, "The Procession of the Holy Spirit," in *In the Image and Likeness of God,* ed. John H. Erickson and Thomas E. Bird (Crestwood, NY: St. Vladimir's Seminary Press, 1974), 81.

3. Vladimir Lossky, *The Mystical Theology of the Eastern Church* (Crestwood, NY: St. Vladimir's Seminary Press, 1976), 64.

function of guiding the Christian struggle to the union that the trinitarian God effected and, hence, made possible.

The theological approach must then be antinomic, which Lossky defines as the nonopposition of opposites.[4] Only an antinomic approach to the Christian doctrine of the Trinity can prevent the dogma from degenerating into a mere rational proposition, and keep the Christian focus on the realism of divine-human communion, which the dogma attempts to express. This antinomic approach, according to Lossky, is what explains the early Christian use of the categories of *ousia* and *hypostasis*. It was no accident for Lossky that these concepts are synonymous, as the goal was to employ categories that referred to each other while expressing a reality irreducible to the other.[5] *Ousia* is not *hypostasis* and vice versa, but the *ousia* would give rise in thought to the trinitarian distinction, while the *hypostasis* would give rise in thought to the common *ousia*.

Crucial to this antinomic approach to the Trinity, according to Lossky, is the affirmation of the monarchy of the Father, in which the Father is the cause of the Son and the Spirit. The Father as the principle of unity in the Trinity gives rise to both person and nature simultaneously. As Lossky states, "[t]hus the monarchy of the Father maintains the perfect equilibrium between the nature and the persons, without coming down too heavily on either side. . . . The one nature and the three hypostases are presented simultaneously to our understanding, with neither prior to the other."[6] The monarchy of the Father also grounds Lossky's understanding of the theological notion of person as irreducibly unique and *ekstatic*, by which Lossky means freedom from the necessity of nature. It is in this theological notion of person, however, especially its grounding in the monarchy of the Father, that Lossky seems to violate his own apophatic approach to the Trinity. For Lossky, apophaticism is not simply a negation of a more positive statement about God in order to arrive at an analogical naming of God; it is an attitude to the revelation of God that involves antinomic expression in theology, but whose end goal is a union with God that goes beyond the capacities of human knowing. In grounding his theological notion of person, however, in the monarchy of the Father, who as cause is irreducibly unique in relation to the Son and the Spirit, and *ekstatic* in relation to the divine *ousia*, Lossky is going beyond simply an antinomic expression of

---

4. Ibid., 50.

5. Vladimir Lossky, "The Theological Notion of the Human Person," in *In the Image and Likeness*, 113.

6. Lossky, "Procession of the Holy Spirit," 81.

the Trinity; he is engaging in trinitarian speculation, which is not allowed by his rules of apophaticism.

There are a few other tensions in Lossky's thought. The first entails his emphasis on the essence/energies distinction as antinomic categories of expression of the realism of divine-human communion.[7] If divine-human communion is through the energies of God, then what is the point of the Trinity? Lossky would say there is no point, as it is simply a revealed fact, but there is a disconnect between the revelation of God as Trinity as effected divine-human communion in the person of Christ and the Christian participation of God through the energies. Ironically, this disconnect may be the result of Lossky's own propositionalism. Like the neo-Scholastics, Lossky affirms that the revelation of the Trinity is a *datum* of revelation. The difference is that Lossky subjects this *datum* to the logic of apophaticism rather than Aristotelian logic.

The emphasis on the essence/energies distinction, which Lossky single-handedly succeeded in popularizing in contemporary Orthodox theology and which has come to dominate Orthodox Christian theology, betrays a deeper problem in Lossky's apophatic approach to the Trinity. It forgets the history that the development of the doctrine of the Trinity was and is simultaneously the development of the Christian response to a God–world relation in which God is radically immanent in creation while simultaneously transcendent to creation. Contrary to Lossky's protestations, trinitarian theology is not simply about *oikonomia*, but about *theologia*, that is, about the being of God.

LOVE AND COMMUNION

Within the generation of Greek theologians of the 1960s stands John Zizioulas as the most ecumenically influential, and who has self-consciously characterized his own theology as continuing the neo-patristic synthesis of Georges Florovsky, his professor at Harvard. Zizioulas cannot be accused of anti-Westernism in the sense of seeing the entire cultural heritage of the "West" since Augustine as culminating in the nihilism of Nietzsche, and as diametrically opposed to the Hellenistic-Byzantine ethos. He does, however, set up a diametrical opposition between an Augustinian-inspired trinitarian theology that is grounded in the one essence of God and the Cappadocian trinitarian theology that prioritizes the person.[8] According to Zizioulas, the Cappadocian fathers accomplished nothing less than an ontological revolution

7. Lossky, *Mystical Theology*, 67–90.

8. John D. Zizioulas, *Communion and Otherness* (London: T&T Clark, 2006), 162.

in articulating a trinitarian theology that simultaneously affirms an ontology in which being-as-communion prioritizes the particular over that which is the same. This trinitarian theology is itself rooted in the Christian experience of the Eucharist, which is the event of the eschatological body of Christ, and, as such, *is* church. The eucharistic event is such an event of communion because the presence of the Holy Spirit constitutes the assembly as the resurrected body of Christ.[9] As such, the work of the Holy Spirit is both eschatological, as it makes present in the present the future unity of all in Christ, and communal, insofar as this unity is one of a communion of persons in the person of Christ, in whom humans are constituted by the Holy Spirit as *hypostatic* (unique) and *ekstatic* (free from the necessity of created nature) beings in and through relations to God the Father and to all of creation.[10]

Such an experience of the divine requires two ontological leavenings: (1) the radical distinction between the uncreated and the created as the basis for a communion that is free and loving, and not of necessity. The creation *ex nihilo* also indicates that creation itself is surrounded by nothing and the only hope for creation's longing to be free from the necessity of death and finitude is through an eternal relation with the divine. (2) The second leveling is the grounding of the trinitarian being of God in the person of the Father. Regarding the latter, Zizioulas famously asserts: "the Father out of love—that is, freely—begets the Son and brings forth the Spirit. If God exists, He exists because the Father exists, that is, He who out of love freely begets the Son and brings forth the Spirit. Thus God as person—as the hypostasis of the Father—makes the one divine substance to be that which it is: the one God."[11] In Zizioulas's early work, his claims about the monarchy of the Father are informed by existential concerns: he identifies as basic to human existence a longing for uniqueness, but one that is only realizable in relations of love and in a freedom from nature, that is, as *ekstasis*. This hope can only be fulfilled in relation to the eternal God, but only if God's being is itself free from the ontological necessity of nature, since God can only give what God *is*. As Zizioulas himself states in a passage worth quoting in full:

> the ground of God's ontological freedom lies not in His nature but in His personal existence, that is, in the "mode of existence" by which

9. See John D. Zizioulas, *The Eucharistic Communion and the World*, ed. Luke Ben Tallon (London: T&T Clark, 2011).

10. John D. Zizioulas, *Being as Communion* (Crestwood, NY: St. Vladimir's Seminary Press, 1985), 123–42.

11. Ibid., 41.

He subsists as divine nature. And it is precisely this that gives man, in spite of his different nature, his hope of becoming an authentic person. The manner in which God exercises His ontological freedom, that which makes him ontologically free, is the way in which He transcends and abolishes the ontological necessity of the substance by being God as *Father*, that is, as He who "begets" the Son and "brings forth" the Spirit. This ecstatic character of God, the fact that His being is identical with an act of communion, ensures the transcendence of the ontological necessity which His substance would have demanded—if the substance were the primary ontological predicate of God—and replaces this necessity with the free self-affirmation of divine existence.[12]

Zizioulas has since nuanced both this position of the importance of asserting the monarchy of the Father as the principle "cause" of the trinitarian being of God—that is, of the Son and the Spirit—and his understanding of human personhood as freedom from the necessity of nature. Regarding the latter, freedom from the necessity of nature cannot be understood as a transcending or abolishing of created nature, but as a freedom from the necessity created by the effects of sin on created nature. Human personhood, then, is not a transcendence of created nature per se, but a personal realization of all that created nature was created to be.[13] Similarly, on the question of the monarchy of the Father, he argues that this freedom within the divine being cannot be understood as a freedom *from* the necessity of nature, in the same way that human personhood is understood as freedom from the necessity of sinful created nature. In the divine being, there is no "given" as there is in created existence, and, thus, nature and person are not antinomical but coincide. Zizioulas writes that "[f]reedom, therefore, in its Trinitarian sense is not a freedom *from* but a freedom *for* the other to the point of raising the other to the status of absolute uniqueness irreducible to the sameness of nature."[14] This freedom for the other is not primarily for creation, the not-God, but within the very being of God:

---

12. Zizioulas, *Being as Communion*, 44. See also idem, *Communion and Otherness*, 101–108.

13. For this nuancing, see Zizioulas's important essay, "Person and Nature in the Theology of St. Maximus the Confessor," in Bishop Maxim Vasiljević, ed., *Knowing the Purpose of Creation Through the Resurrection: Proceedings of the Symposium on St. Maximus the Confessor* (Alhambra, CA: Sebastian Press/ The Faculty of Orthodox Theology–University of Belgrade, 2013), 85–113.

14. John D. Zizioulas, "Trinitarian Freedom: Is God Free in Trinitarian Life?," in *Rethinking Trinitarian Theology: Disputed Questions and Contemporary Issues in Trinitarian Theology*, ed. Giulio Maspero and Robert Wozniak (London: T&T Clark, 2012), 197.

"The essence of Trinitarian freedom, therefore, lies in God's capacity to be *ek-static* not in relation to something other than God, but *in himself*."[15] This freedom is personal and grounded in the person of the Father, and not in the essence of God, and it is this freedom within the being of God that is the condition for the possibility of God's freedom for creation and, thus, creation's freedom for God. As Zizioulas argues, "[i]t is the Trinity that makes God free from the necessity of his essence; had it not been for the Trinity God would require an eternal creation in order to be free to reach beyond his essence, and then he would bind himself necessarily and eternally to creation."[16] Zizioulas is, thus, asserting that thinking the immanent Trinity as the freedom of God's being grounded in the monarchy of the Father is the only way we can think of God's freedom for creation and creation's freedom for God.

The ontological revolution to which Zizioulas attributes patristic trinitarian theology is one that is implied in the Christian experience of Christ in the Eucharist. Even if Zizioulas moves away from Lossky's apophaticism (to which Lossky himself had difficulty remaining faithful) by offering speculations about the being of God—*theologia*—with his particular understanding of the necessity of the monarchy of the Father,[17] it is a mistake to characterize Zizioulas as a social trinitarian thinker, as Zizioulas nowhere begins with an idea of the trinitarian persons in reciprocal relations from which he then deduces patterns of human relations in either the church or the political community. In fact, one of the biggest theological problems in Zizioulas is his emphasis on the monarchy of Father, which raises the question of reciprocation between Son and the Holy Spirit to the Father.[18] Zizioulas's theology of personhood, for which he has become famous, is actually radically christocentric, in the sense that the two constitutive aspects of personhood—irreducible uniqueness and *ekstatic* freedom from necessity—are given in the human experience of immanent Trinity in Christ in the Eucharist.[19] To be constituted as hypostatic, that is, irreducibly unique, and *ekstatic*, that is, free from necessity, is possible only relationally, specifically in the relation that Christ shares with the Father.

15. Ibid.

16. Ibid.

17. For an account on speculation within contemporary Orthodox theology, see David Tracy, "Contemplation, Speculation, Action: Reflections on Orthodox Theology," Orthodoxy in America Lecture Series, Orthodox Christian Studies Center, Fordham University, http://www.fordham.edu/orthodoxy.

18. Even with his nuancing of what he means by freedom within the existence of God grounded in the monarchy of the Father, Zizioulas does not really address this issue. He does say that "there is no such an entity as a person prior—and therefore given—to the Son and the Spirit, since the Father himself emerges in and through his relationship (communion) with them" ("Trinitarian Freedom," 202).

The logic of Zizioulas's argument flows from below, insofar as what he affirms about God's trinitarian being is grounded in the experience of God in Christ. The space of the fullness of this union is, for Zizioulas, the Eucharist.

As is well known, Zizioulas has been criticized by patristic scholars for reading too much into the patristic texts. Although there is some merit to this claim, I also think that Zizioulas should be credited for drawing out implications that were not previously noticed. First, it should be noted that Zizioulas's theology of personhood is not original to him; he gets the initial building blocks from Lossky.[20] The understanding of personhood as irreducibly unique and *ekstatic* is a legacy of Lossky's that Zizioulas develops. Second, I think what Zizioulas noticed quite correctly is that the category of *hypostasis* in trinitarian theology cannot simply be that which expresses the distinctive properties of the trinitarian persons. It is the category that emerges in order to render coherent the union between two ontological others, the uncreated and the created, something not possible within the framework of an ontology of essence. Despite all his protestations, Lossky's essence/energies distinction traps him into the same logic of essence for which he accuses the neo-Scholastics. *Hypostasis* emerges as the category necessary to express the divine-human communion in Christ, which is the basis for the claim that God is Trinity, and Zizioulas is quite right to see that an ontological revolution is implied in this move insofar as Christian thought is attempting to think the being of God as free to be in communion with the not-God; or, in other words, to think a God–world relation that is one of free loving communion in which the distinctive otherness of the created is not absorbed but the basis for such a loving communion. I must admit that although no thinker is ever above criticism, especially when writing about God, I simply cannot understand the attack by patristic and systematic theologians alike against what I cannot otherwise but see as very retrievable insights in Zizioulas's trinitarian theology.

The Romanian theologian Dumitru Stăniloae (1903–1993) is similar to Zizioulas in that he searches for that aspect in human experience which would allow for clarification and understanding of the dogmatic tradition. The dogmas are not sterile propositions, but must speak to the realism of divine-human communion and, thus, must resonate with life experiences. Stăniloae, Zizioulas, and Bulgakov all attempt to interpret the dogmatic tradition in light of some aspect of human experience, though Stăniloae and Zizioulas do so in a more

19. For more on Zizioulas's understanding of the Eucharist as an experience of the immanent Trinity, see Aristotle Papanikolaou, *Being with God: Trinity, Apophaticism, and Divine-Human Communion* (Notre Dame, IN: University of Notre Dame Press, 2006), 94–106.

20. A fact that Zisioulas recognizes for the first time, to my knowledge, in "Trinitarian Freedom," 197.

exploratory fashion, rather than, as we will see with Bulgakov, locating a foundationalist grounding within the human experience of self. Whereas for Zizioulas the aspect of human experience by which he clarifies his trinitarian theology is the human experience of longing for irreducible uniqueness and freedom from necessity colliding tragically with death and finitude, the point of focus for Stăniloae is the movement of dialogue in relationships of love. In unison with all contemporary Orthodox theologians, Stăniloae affirms that humans were created for union with God. Human beings, like no other living beings, realized this union through a dialogue of love that God initiated from the moment of creation. Stăniloae affirms a notion of creation as God's gift that initiates the possibility of an exchange of gifts between God and human beings, who function as priests of creation. This exchange of gifts is simultaneously a dialogue of love enabling a personal communion between God and creation. The fact that the world was created for the purpose of communion between the personal God and human persons is a truth of revelation confirmed by the human experience of freedom and relationality. As Stăniloae states, "[i]t is only with other persons that man can achieve the kind of communion in which neither he nor they descend to the status of being objects of exterior knowledge used always in an identical way. Instead, they grow as sources for an inexhaustible warmth of love and of thoughts that are ever new, brought forth and sustained by the reciprocal love of these persons, a love that remains always creative, always in search of new ways of manifesting itself."[21] That the human experience of love shapes Stăniloae's trinitarian theology is especially clear when he wrestles with the question of why a third in God; it is also in addressing this question that Stăniloae's speculative tendencies become evident. He argues that "[i]t is only through the third that the love between the two proves itself generous and capable of extending itself to subjects outside themselves. Exclusiveness between the two makes the act of a generous overflow beyond the prison walls of the couple impossible."[22] Although Stăniloae was an independent thinker in his own right, this particular quote reveals his indebtedness to Bulgakov, to whom I will now turn my attention.

---

21. Dumitru Stăniloae, *Orthodox Dogmatic Theology: Revelation and Knowledge of the Triune God*, vol. 1, *Orthodox Dogmatic Theology*, trans. and ed. Ioan Ionita and Robert Barraniger (Brookline, Mass.: Holy Cross Orthodox Press, 2005), 10.

22. Ibid., 267.

SOPHIA

It may seem a bit out of order to discuss Bulgakov after Lossky, Zizioulas, and Stăniloae since he is, of course, their senior and wrote his most mature theological synthesis before any of these three were barely writing theology. Bulgakov, however, was forgotten soon after his death and only now is he experiencing a revival. So, in terms of theological ideas, it makes perfect sense to deal with Bulgakov at this point in this paper.

Sergius Bulgakov is the most profound and yet the most neglected Orthodox theologian of the twentieth century. The neglect is puzzling in light of the fact that he was the first dean of St. Serge Orthodox Theological Academy in Paris, after his exile from Russia in 1922. He is known for the most sophisticated theological development of sophiology, which makes this silence even more puzzling, given that sophiology is a form of Russian religious and philosophical thought that dominated Russia's intellectual scene in the late nineteenth century and early twentieth century, and whose roots can be traced back to Vladimir Solov'ev. What makes it even more puzzling is that Bulgakov's three-volume *On Divine-Humanity* is the first comprehensive systematic theology in the East since John of Damascus.

This neglect of Bulgakov, I think, is attributable to several factors, not least of which is the complexity of his theological sophiology, which resulted in the lack of any disciples who could explicate, clarify, and carry his thought forward. One sees aspects of Bulgakov's sophiology in his student Paul Evdokimov, but with little systematic development. The most important cause for this neglect, I think, can be traced to the attacks on Bulgakov's theology by two of the most prominent Orthodox voices in the twentieth century: Vladimir Lossky and George Florovsky. Bulgakov's sophiology was accused of heresy in the 1930s, and both Lossky and Florovsky were directly involved in providing negative assessments of it, in spite of the fact that both felt a deep, personal respect for Bulgakov.[23] One cannot really understand Lossky's apophaticism and Florovsky's "neo-patristic" synthesis without understanding that in the background lurks Bulgakov; in other words, their theologies were constructed in part in opposition to Bulgakov's thought. Ironically, Bulgakov can be interpreted as offering the first "neo-patristic synthesis," a fact that Florovsky himself later recognized, their deep differences notwithstanding.[24] Also ironic

---

23. See Bryn Geffert, "The Charges of Heresy Against Sergeii Bulgakov"; and Alexis Klimoff, "Georges Florovsky and the Sophiological Controversy," *St. Vladimir's Theological Quarterly* 49, no. 1-2 (2005): 47–66; 67–100.

24. I owe this point to Matthew Baker.

is that all of Lossky's major categories—antinomy, the distinction between person-as-freedom and nature-as-necessity, the kenosis of the Son and the kenosis of the Holy Spirit, the distinction between individual and person—are all found in Bulgakov, though Lossky presents them as emerging from the patristic tradition. It appears as if Lossky co-opted these central categories of Bulgakov and apophaticized them so as self-consciously to present an anti-sophiological theology.

Both Lossky and Florovsky became the voices for Orthodox theology to the non-Orthodox world, especially since it was their work that was being made available in French and English. It was also their thought that would exercise the most influence on the next generation of Orthodox theologians, such as John Zizioulas, which was basically convinced that Russian sophiology was an aberration of Orthodox theology. This sentiment is even conveyed by the editors of the recently published *Cambridge Companion to Orthodox Christian Theology*, to which I am a contributor. In an otherwise remarkable production, the editors claim that "'Orthodox theology' is not synonymous with 'Eastern Christian thought'. The fascinating area of Russian religious philosophy therefore falls outside the proper scope of this volume."[25] I don't agree with this distinction: anyone who reads Bulgakov carefully will soon realize that he is doing Orthodox theology, especially if one sees Orthodox theology as being the ongoing interpretation of the heart of Orthodox thought: the principle of divine-human communion. In fact, I would argue that the debate between Lossky's and Florovsky's neo-patristic synthesis and Bulgakov's sophiology, which is also patristic, is one over the interpretation of this principle of divine-human communion for trinitarian theology. Insofar as the principle of divine-human communion was at the heart of his thought, as I will soon argue, Bulgakov's position within the narrative of twentieth-century Orthodox theology needs to be seen more positively.

Before I dive into Bulgakov and the Trinity, I should note that Bulgakov anticipates so many of the classic insights of twentieth-century theology. His understanding of the relations of the persons of the Trinity in terms of *kenosis* anticipates Hans Urs von Balthasar, who credits Bulgakov for this insight in *Mysterium Paschale*, even if he adds that Bulgakov's theology should be divested of its sophiological presuppositions. Bulgakov's identification of the Father as the revealing *hypostasis*, the Son as the revealed *hypostasis*, and the Holy Spirit as the revelation, bears a striking resemblance to the formulation of Karl Barth

25. Mary B. Cunningham and Elizabeth Theokritoff, "Preface," in idem, eds., *The Cambridge Companion to Orthodox Christian Theology* (Cambridge: Cambridge University Press, 2008), xvii–xviii.

in *Church Dogmatics* I/1. Bulgakov's claim that the Father suffers the crucifixion of the Son anticipates Jürgen Moltmann's *The Crucified God*. Bulgakov was a trained, quasi-Marxist economist who, prior to his conversion to Orthodoxy, debated Lenin in prerevolutionary journals. He disavowed his quasi-Marxism, but his attempt to link dogmatic speculation to economic and political realities anticipates Gustavo Gutiérrez and Latin American liberation theology.[26] His reappropriation of the Christian symbol of *sophia* for understanding God as Trinity, and his declaration that the Father is *Sophia*, the Son is *Sophia*, and the Spirit is *Sophia*, anticipates my colleague Elizabeth Johnson, though when one reads Bulgakov, one will immediately realize his thought is in need of the feminist corrective she provides in her now-classic work, *She Who Is*.[27] There are also clear affinities between Bulgakov's explication of God as Spirit in terms of *sophia* and Pannenberg's linking of God as Spirit with field theories in physics, especially in their attempts to tackle the problem of God's relation to time and eternity. A theologian who anticipates so many classic and enduring theological insights of the twentieth century is certainly one who should not be neglected.

What separates Bulgakov from this sophiological predecessors, such as Solov'ev, is the way he embeds his own thought within the broader, linear tradition of thinking on divine-human communion that is evident in the Greek patristic tradition. What separates Bulgakov from his better-known contemporaries, Vladimir Lossky and Georges Florovsky, is that Bulgakov was more willing to engage critically the patristic tradition, demonstrating how each of the major patristic authors contributed to making sense of the God–world relation in terms of divine-human communion, and where he thinks they failed. It would be misleading to accuse him simplistically of saying that the Fathers were wrong, or that the Fathers need to be corrected by German Idealist philosophy. Bulgakov sees the Orthodox tradition as attempting to construct a theology of the God–world relation that is grounded in the revelation of the divine in Christ, and sees his own work as continuing that effort. It is important also to remember Bulgakov's context—his mature theology developed during a time in Russia where there were competing worldviews. Bulgakov very much thought that trinitarian theology provided an account of the whole that had to compete with a Marxist worldview, and,

---

26. For the affinities, see Aristotle Papanikolaou, *The Mystical as Political: Democracy and Non-Radical Orthodoxy* (Notre Dame, IN: University of Notre Dame Press, 2012), esp. 37–42.

27. Elizabeth D. Johnson, *She Who Is: The Mystery of God in Feminist Theological Discourse* (New York: Crossroad, 2002).

thus, had to be rationally defensible. If trinitarian theology is about God's transcendence-as-radical-immanence-in-creation, then theology must give an account of how God's being exists so as to be in a free communion with the not-God. The Trinity is given in revelation, but Bulgakov argues that "thought is called to fathom this revealed fact to the extent this is possible in human knowledge."[28]

Thought attempts to understand this revealed fact by turning to human experience. But which aspect in particular? Bulgakov follows the logic of revelation, and specifically the logic of self-revelation in human experience, since it is self-consciousness as self-revelation that is the condition for the possibility of relationality with the other. Bulgakov begins with created spirit.[29] Created spirit is the consciousness of self to the self-as-I. Existing as I is a consciousness of self; this consciousness of self is also a knowledge of self; a revelation of self to the self. The I, however, is not an empty, formless, contentless I; it is some thing; it has content; it is an object; it has a nature. Spirit is the realization for itself of this nature, of this content, of this givenness, for itself and through itself. The I as self-consciousness as self-revelation is the actualization of the I in relation to an other than the I, than spirit, which is nature, which the I as spirit realizes in itself for itself. This other, formally, is the nature of spirit, which is the predicate of the I-as-subject; nature is the object of the I-as-subject. This nature is not something that the I freely chooses, but is given to the I to be realized as spirit, to exist as spirit. Nature in and by itself does not exist, but exists only as spirit. Spirit is the actualization of the I as it confronts itself in its own nature, which is given to spirit. Thus, spirit is the unity of subject and object, of subject and predicate, as the I is the movement to realize all that it is as given to it in nature, and this realization is nature becoming more transparent to the I; it is also the movement to overcoming the antithesis between freedom and necessity, and toward the existence of the I as free necessity. Self-consciousness is the relation of the self to the self, but in the self's relating to the self it confronts the givenness of its own nature.

God is Absolute Spirit. As Spirit, God is self-consciousness of God's self. As self-consciousness, God knows God's self, which means that God reveals God to God's self. Self-consciousness-as-self-revelation of self is a relation to self through an other than the self. In God, there can be no givenness, so this relation of God to God's self cannot exist "outside" of God. The self-consciousness as self-revelation of God is through the positing of God to God's

28. Sergius Bulgakov, *The Comforter*, trans. Boris Jakim (Grand Rapids: Eerdmans, 2004 [1936]), 56.

29. For what follows on the phenomenology of created spirit and Absolute Spirit, see ibid., 53–73; and idem, *The Lamb of God*, trans. Boris Jakim (Grand Rapids: Eerdmans, 2008 [1933]), 89–101.

self; that is, the other in and through which God knows God's self is not given to God, but is God, though God as other to God's self. This other is God's Word, Logos, and Son. The Logos/Word/Son is God's predicate, object, content of all that God is, reflected back to the self-positing Absolute Spirit, that is, the Father. In self-positing the Word/Logos/Predicate/Object/ Content of God to God's self, Absolute Spirit is positing love of this content, which is distinct from the content itself. The Son as spirit/person returns all that the Father is to the Father through a reciprocating love for the Father; without this reciprocating love, then Absolute Spirit is narcissistically loving itself in its reflection of itself. Also, the self-consciousness-as-self-revelation is the actualization of the Word/Content/Object/Predicate that is posited, which is a reciprocal return of this Word to the self-positing Absolute Spirit/Father. This actualization is the Glory and Beauty as Life of this Word/Content/Object/ Predicate. This phenomenology of Absolute Spirit is what Bulgakov means by trinitarian "deduction."

Sophia, a central concept in Bulgakov's thought, is *ousia* hypostatized. *Ousia* is not simply that to which one assigns attributes; it is the being of God as God's self-revelation. It is the unity of spirit and nature in God, without the absorption of each to the other. As *ousia* hypostatized, and identified with revelation of God, it is all that God is, which must include a relation of God to not-God—creation—in some way, but not in time and space. Another way to put it is that all that is possible for creation is revealed in the self-positing of the Word.[30] Bulgakov is clear that he is not arguing that creation is necessary for God to be God; nor is he arguing that God's election of humanity is constitutive of the being of God. Bulgakov does argue, however, that creation is inherent to the idea of God and that it is impossible for humans to think God without thinking God eternally relating to creation in some way. For Bulgakov, understanding the Trinity as *sophia* was a necessary development of the patristic categories of *hypostasis* and *ousia*, so as to conceptualize the fulfillment of God's relations to the world in time and space, a relation inherent to the self-revelation of God's being from all eternity.

Creation is the action of the Holy Trinity. As the Logos/Word/Content of God's Wisdom, the Son is the *hypostasis* who images created being, all that God is for creation, and all that creation is meant to be for God. Content/Object/ Word, however, needs the movement of the Holy Spirit to be actualized. Creation is the realization/becoming in time/space of all that is imaged in the Logos from eternity. Creation in time and space is essentially a repetition of

30. Bulgakov, *The Lamb of God*, 101–17.

the being of God,[31] which includes the self-revelation of the Father in the Son through the Holy Spirit. (As an aside, with the notion of "repetition of God," we see some affinities with Pannenberg's thought.) World is created *Sophia*, because it images and is a movement toward the realization of all that is imaged from eternity in the Logos—what God is for creation and what creation is meant to be for God.

Why does Bulgakov refer to *Sophia* as divine-humanity? Because *Sophia* as self-revelation of God eternally images all that God is for creation and all that creation is meant to be for God.[32] Creation is ontologically distinct essence, but is divine as the image of that which is eternally imaged; it is, thus, created *Sophia*. The Logos is the heavenly man, because from eternity the Logos is the *hypostasis* that can be incarnated, or can incarnate created nature. It can do so because it is spirit, and because the hypostatization of *ousia*, which is *Sophia*, eternally images created nature as created *Sophia*. The ontological link, then, is both Spirit, which is distinct from nature and which is the realization of nature as free necessity, and Image—not energies, or *hypostasis*, or nature by themselves. Why is such an elaborate conceptualization of the Trinity necessary? So that divine-human communion occurs intrinsically and not through overpowering the created other.

It is tempting to accuse Bulgakov of simply mapping trinitarian theology onto German idealism for the sake of making the doctrine relevant. It is hard to deny this influence, especially in Bulgakov's mapping the phenomenology of created spirit onto the being of God as Absolute Spirit. We must remind ourselves, however, that Bulgakov constantly affirms that he begins with revelation, and that even this anthropology of created spirit is given in revelation. Rather than being simplistically influenced by the German idealists, one could argue that Bulgakov saw the roots of idealist notions of the phenomenology of the Spirit in the Christian trinitarian distinction between *ousia* and *hypostasis*, which itself is grounded in the revelation of God in Christ. It could be argued that Bulgakov is actually correcting the German idealists and bringing to completion the unfinished work of the patristic development of the Trinity, which would explain his critically appreciative engagement with the patristic texts. One sees here resonances with Karl Rahner's approach, who argues from the premise of the self-communication of God to a transcendental

31. Sergius Bulgakov, *The Bride of the Lamb*, trans. Boris Jakim (Grand Rapids: Eerdmans, 2002 [1939/1945]), 222.

32. Sergei Bulgakov, *Sophia—The Wisdom of God: An Outline of Sophiology*, rev. ed., trans. Patrick Thompson, O. Fielding Clarke, and Xenia Braikevitc (Hudson, NY: Lindisfarne Press, 1993 [1937]), 14.

anthropology accounting for the human person as possible recipient of a self-communication of God. Bulgakov's appropriation of the German idealist tradition is much like Rahner's use of philosophy, which, according to Karen Kilby, was more ad hoc than directly grounded in a particular system.[33] If, again like Rahner, there is a foundationalist strain in Bulgakov, in the sense that his theology is informed by what he would argue is a universal dimension to human existence, it is a foundationalism informed by the prior affirmation of the divine-human communion in Christ. If the Trinity is a revealed fact of revelation, Bulgakov believed that theology must, to use Rahner's language, justify the axiom that the immanent Trinity is the economic Trinity and vice versa, or that God's self-communication is threefold by appealing to the aspects in human experience that constitute the human experience as open to supernatural grace. Finally, it should be noted that Bulgakov's identification of nature with givenness/necessity and person/spirit with freedom will become formative for the development of twentieth-century Orthodox theology of the Trinity. One sees a similar distinction in Vladimir Lossky, who attributes it to the Cappadocian Fathers without any mention of Bulgakov's use of the distinction.

In critically assessing Bulgakov's trinitarian theology, it is hard not to notice the datedness of the application of the German idealist-like understanding of the phenomenology of Spirit to God. As I hinted at earlier, it reminds one of the early Barth's notion of God as the revealer, revealed, and the revelation; when reading it, one is tempted to simply dismiss his understanding of God's trinitarian life on the basis of God's self-revelation with a "been there, done that." The biggest problem with Bulgakov's use of the phenomenology of self-revelation of Spirit for understanding God's trinitarian life is the inconsistency it creates in his own system. First, Absolute Spirit is defined by absolute freedom, but Bulgakov subjects the absolutely free Absolute Spirit to the necessity of the logic of self-revealing Spirit. Bulgakov would argue that one cannot escape the use of necessity language when speaking of God, and I would agree with that, otherwise you get Zeus, as David Tracy once said to us in a class on the Trinity, echoing Bulgakov's reference to Mount Olympus: "Here, the Trinity in Divinity in unity, as well as in the distinction of the three concrete hypostases, must be shown not only as a divinely revealed *fact*, valid by virtue of its facticity, but also as a *principle* owing to which Divinity is not a dyad, tetrad, etc., in general not a pagan Olympus, but precisely a Trinity, exhausting itself in its fullness and self-enclosedness."[34] Bulgakov is

33. Karen Kilby, *Karl Rahner: Theology and Philosophy* (London: Routledge, 2004).

34. Bulgakov, *The Comforter*, 7.

fully aware of the danger of ending up with Zeus, which he feels he avoids with his trinitarian deduction. To argue, however, that in order for God to know Godself, God must reveal God to Godself, is still to subject God to a principle of necessity of self-revelation, that is, to a principle other than God's own being. This, together with postmodern criticism and modifications of idealist notions of the self, make this particular aspect of Bulgakov's trinitarian theology more difficult to retrieve.

The problems, however, with his so-called "trinitarian deduction" do not necessarily lead to the jettisoning of his sophiology. What Bulgakov saw most clearly was that the Christian conceptualization of God as Trinity was motivated not simply by a particular understanding of salvation, but was ultimately an attempt to account for how God *is* in such a way so as to be in communion with what is not-God, which is the real point of the Trinity. Bulgakov also saw clearly that although much important work was done by Greek and Latin Christian thinkers, more needed to be done. More specifically, he saw that the categories of *ousia*, *hypostasis*, and *energia* could not by themselves do the work of conceptualizing God's being as one of communion with the not-God. God's being is not reducible to either *ousia*, *hypostasis*, or *energia*; each by itself, though necessary for an adequate expression of God as Trinity, cannot express all that is entailed in the trinitarian being of God, which includes God's relation to the not-God. *Sophia* emerges, on my reading of Bulgakov, from the insight that perhaps a fourth term is needed in order to account God's communion with the world and the world's openness to the life of God.

I would agree with Rahner, who in his "Oneness and Threefoldness in God in Discussion with Islam" argues that the Christian doctrine of the Trinity is a radicalization of monotheism insofar as it attempts to account for how God is both transcendent and immanent to what is not-God. He makes the distinction between an abstract or theoretical monotheist and a religious monotheist. To avoid the former, the monotheist must affirm that the one God is mediated concretely in history. To this, he adds,

> It is *only* when created modes of mediation . . . in the ultimate sense are denied to him that he is really the sole God, close to us, who is present as himself in salvation history. . . . God *must* mediate to himself through himself; otherwise he remains remote in the last resort and in this remoteness is present only by the divisive multiplicity of created realities which point to God's remoteness. . . . Since these two modes of factuality of the one God in and despite

their diversity are themselves God and not something created and different from him, they must belong always and eternally to God himself as such.[35]

When it comes to the immanent Trinity, for Rahner less is more, and, as I read him, the most we can do is argue toward these hypostatic distinctions. To go beyond that is to risk introducing spatial categories into the being of God that are incoherent, like the infinite nearness and distance between the Father and the Son, or God making room for creation.[36] To argue for these hypostatic distinctions, however, is not the same as Lossky's apophatic restrictions on *theologia*; indeed, for Rahner, *theologia* is possible, but must be tempered not so much by the limits of human understanding as the criteria for intelligible speech on God. For Rahner, Christian theology can indicate why it is necessary to affirm permanent distinctions within the life of God in order to account for God's self-communication to the world, but any move beyond this endangers turning theology into mythology.

Rahner is much more in continuity with Athanasius in seeing the Trinity as the Christian attempt to make sense of how God "must" be in such a way so as to be in communion with creation. In this sense, the doctrine of the Trinity is speculative, but not in the sense that it attempts to render the intelligibility of a propositional truth; it is speculative in the sense that it is offering an account of how God "must" be so as to be in a real relation with what is not-God. Put another way, the Christian doctrine of the Trinity was constructed within the Christian story, but it is not only to Christians that it can be shown to be a reasonable and beautiful account of the God–world relation. It is also not the case that simply because the link between the doctrine of the Trinity and the grammar of divine-human communion was forged in the fourth century that such an understanding of God lacks credibility in the postmodern era. It is this link between the principle of divine-human communion and the self-differentiation of the being of God that I would argue is one of the most retrievable elements of these enduring Christian classics.

Returning to Bulgakov, *sophia* attempts to account for God's trinitarian being as communion with the not-God, but does so in a way that avoids the pitfalls of social trinitarianism. One could ask: Why not just *esse*? One could argue that Bulgakov's *sophia* has affinities with the Thomistic notion of *esse*. I would agree with that, but I also think that Bulgakov would argue that *esse*,

35. Karl Rahner, "Oneness and Threefoldness in God in Discussion with Islam," in *Theological Investigations*, vol. 18: *God and Revelation* (New York: Crossroad, 1983), 118.

36. Karl Rahner, *The Trinity*, trans. Joseph Donceel (New York: Crossroad, 1997), 100.

because arrived at philosophically, can only ground an analogy of being that makes a certain kind of knowledge possible, but not knowledge as communion. This critique applies also to the neo-Palamite expression "divine energies," popularized in contemporary Orthodox theology by Vladimir Lossky. In terms of the analogy of being, Bulgakov is closer to Balthasar in attempting to conceptualize a trinitarian understanding of being that would allow for communion, but introducing the spatial categories of "infinite nearness and infinite distance" into the trinitarian being of God would make Bulgakov uncomfortable. Here, for me, lies the real relevance and challenge of Bulgakov's notion of *sophia*: how to think the immanent Trinity in such a way that heeds the cautions of Rahner—that is, that there is little we can actually say about the immanent Trinity—but also elaborates a theology of the immanent Trinity that accounts for God's being as communion with the world, but does so without falling into the inevitable problems of a social trinitarianism. The question that Bulgakov poses to contemporary trinitarian theology is whether a category is needed beyond *ousia*, *hypostasis*, and *energia* in order to render intelligible the God–world relations revealed and realized in the person of Christ.

I want to end with a brief reflection on the late Catherine LaCugna's *God for Us*, the first book I ever reviewed.[37] If one were to bracket her work on the premodern sources, which I think is misleading, I have grown more appreciative of her Rahner-inspired claim that a theology of the immanent Trinity ultimately negates the economic Trinity. While I have grown very much to appreciate that danger, I think a theology of the immanent Trinity—*theologia*—is unavoidable, especially if one understands the point of the Trinity as the conceptualization of God as being in communion with the not-God, and wishes to avoid a theology that makes the Trinity look like Zeus. But to engage that never-ending theological challenge, Bulgakov was definitely right about one thing: it requires the acquisition of *sophia*.

---

37. Catherine LaCugna, *God for Us: The Trinity and Christian Life* (San Francisco: HarperSanFrancisco, 1991).

4

The Trinity and the World Religions

Perils and Promise

Gavin D'Costa

The doctrine of the Trinity performs many tasks in Christian theology. For instance, it allows us to name God as Father who is revealed in Jesus Christ, through the power of the Spirit, so that our God-talk can refer analogically to the divine mystery. This is most significant as we turn to the question of the Trinity and other religions. Reflection on the world religions is often divided into two specific areas. First, there is a general "theology of religions." Here various theological questions are explored, such as: What, if any, is the mode of "revelation" outside Jesus Christ? How is that revelation, if there is such, related to salvation? Do the Spirit and do the Son act within the world religions? If so, how is this to be understood? Is the kingdom of God operative outside the visible boundaries of the church? Are the Trinity, Christ, and the church necessary for salvation? These are just some of the questions that are being reflected on in Anglo-Saxon theology. The second field concerns specific questions related to particular engagements, a "theology with religions," when for example Christianity encounters Hinduism and there is a question of whether the Trinity is analogous to the *trimurti*; or in what way does the Muslim doctrine of God as taught by Al Ghazali correspond to the Christian doctrine of the one God taught by Thomas Aquinas? How does the Trinity affect the understanding of "oneness" in this specific encounter? I will mainly focus on the first area in this chapter.

In what follows I want to develop an argument in two sections.[1] First, I want to indicate how recent reflection on the religions has been impoverished when the Trinity is *not* the guiding light. I want to suggest that the Trinity actually helps secure the goals of many theologians who try to avoid trinitarian reflection. Second, I want to examine briefly some helpful trinitarian approaches and note their strengths and weaknesses. I will close with some very brief remarks.

AVOIDING THE TRINITY?

Since the liberal tradition of the nineteenth century, the Trinity is sometimes seen as a problem rather than as a resource in engaging with other religions. Why? For some, Karl Barth's trinitarian emphasis exemplifies the problems. The argument against Barth (summarized) runs as follows: if God is Trinity and the Trinity is God, then other religions can never amount to anything other than idolatry or human grasping, for none proclaim Father, Son, and Spirit. Barth's christocentric focus is also deemed problematic, as it means that there can be no authentic "faith" outside of those who expressly confess Jesus Christ as Lord. According to his critics, Barth is seen to close down interreligious dialogues rather than opening them up.[2] In reaction to this perceived "closed" circle, nontrinitarian theologies have been developed in the English-speaking world. Schematically speaking, they either emphasize one or two of the following instead: (a) the "Father," (b) the "Spirit," (c) a nondivine "Jesus" or a purely degree Christology, (d) or "the kingdom," but not in a trinitarian balance. I refer readers to a more detailed outline and critique of such thinkers in their complex diversity.[3] But to help readers of this essay, let me put a little flesh on these bones. Such summaries fail to do justice to careful reflection by the authors mentioned.

John Hick's vast corpus exemplifies a use of three of these four trajectories at different stages in his writing and in relation to different audiences—the Father, a nondivine Jesus, and the kingdom. During his early period, Hick stressed the "God of love" (the "Father") at the center of the "universe of faiths."[4] Hick argued that a loving God would not consign the majority of humankind

1. This contribution draws on some of my published paper, "The Trinity in Interreligious Dialogues," in Gilles Emery and Matthew Levering, eds., *Handbook on the Trinity* (New York: Oxford University Press, 2011), 573–86, but has been edited to address the focus of the present volume.

2. See, for instance, Paul Knitter, "Christomonism in Karl Barth's Evaluation of the Non-Christian Religions," *Neue Zeitschrift für systematische Theologie und Religionsphilosphie* 13 (1971): 99–121, http://academiccommons.columbia.edu/item/ac:146259.

3. Gavin D'Costa, "Pluralist Arguments: Prominent Tendencies and Methods," in Karl Josef Becker, Ilaria Morali, and Gavin D'Costa, eds., *Catholic Engagement with World Religions* (Maryknoll, NY: Orbis, 2010), 329–44, with a full bibliography for all writers mentioned here.

4. John Hick, *God and the Universe of Faiths* (London: Collins, 1977), 168–80.

to perdition just because they had never heard about Christianity. To bolster this argument against the obvious objection, What of the teaching of the New Testament regarding Christ?, Hick also argued that the doctrine of the incarnation should be understood "mythically," not ontologically, expressing the force of poetry and deep existential commitment by Jesus' followers. He drew the analogy of a Valentine card where traditionally the lover celebrates his or her loved one. Hick says that if he wrote to his wife, Hazel, that she is the most beautiful woman in the world, a reader some centuries later might think the claim literal (that Hazel is more beautiful than any other woman in the world at the time of writing) or an expression of Hick's devotion and love for his wife. Hick notes that the poetic language of lovers, which expresses a deep existential commitment, should not be confused with the literal claims of scientific language. This is precisely what happened with the New Testament: poetic claims were hardened into literal and thus metaphysical claims. This "mythologization" meant that the Buddha, Muhammad, the Dao, and other "mediators" (persons or key texts) could all draw people to the loving God, and thus to salvation, just as Jesus did for Christians. How might we know this? Through their fruits was Hick's answer: through the reality of the "kingdom of God" in actions of love, justice, compassion, and kindness.

Hick cuts a thoughtful path working within the lineage of liberal Protestant theology. The emphasis on works and the move away from metaphysics inevitably plays down traditional trinitarian theology. It is not that trinitarian theology has nothing to do with social and political life but, rather, that Hick's emphasis on "values" such as "love" and "justice" can be freed from their traditional trinitarian narration. The challenge to trinitarian theology of religions here is to show that Hick's specific criticisms can be met, or that they are ill-conceived.

Liberation-orientated theologians such as Aloysius Pieris, a Jesuit from Sri Lanka, and Paul Knitter, a Roman Catholic layman who is now a dual-belonger (both Catholic and Buddhist), make the "kingdom" the criterion for discerning God's activity in all religions. Like Hick, they are able to discern equally salvific traditions within more than one religion. Knitter and Pieris find this kingdom-centeredness especially helpful in dealing with nontheistic Buddhism. This soteriocentric emphasis, as Knitter calls it, is an attempt to take one step further than Hick in attending to the social and political as the prime arena where the "meaning" of God is to be found in practices. Hence, for Knitter, a Buddhist and a Catholic and a Marxist working together for the liberation of the poor and oppressed are working together for the kingdom, whereas those Catholics who believe the right doctrinal things but do not practice liberation toward their brothers and sisters and toward the earth are actually less close to God than the Buddhist in the example. Knitter and Pieris have an important point and also highlight the complex world that actually exists, for instance the relation of beliefs, practices, and the appropriation of beliefs in practices and vice versa. A trinitarian theology of religions must show that without beliefs which are primarily generated in liturgical practices, social and political practices are diminished or not fully accounted for. And any trinitarian theology of religions must also attend to the reality of suffering and poverty to convince these writers that such theology is important.

The emphasis on the Father alone leads to important questions: What is the basis for such a normative doctrine of a loving God? Do the different religions yield the same "God of love"? Is such a narration of the "God of love" acceptable to any particular religion in its attempt to privilege no one religion? Can this doctrine commend itself to orthodox trinitarian belief? And what of religions that have a normative nontheistic "divine" like Buddhism? Hick eventually had to mythologize "God," as he had to mythologize the "Son" (as well as mythologize other religion's normative truths) to try and be fair to all religions. The emphasis on the kingdom in Hick and the liberationists also generates complex questions: Can the kingdom be detached from the person of Jesus? Can it be detached from the church? And is it not ultimately just a privileging of certain values, possibly those exalted by liberal moderns, when detached from the person of Christ?[5]

I cannot argue for this fully here, but would contend that the universal fatherhood of God, the Father and Mother who loves all peoples, and the joyful acknowledgment of traces of the kingdom outside the visible boundaries of the church (and its all-too-shadowy presence within the history of the church) are both quite in keeping with orthodox trinitarian theology. Indeed, I have argued, trinitarian theology better grounds such claims in a robust Christian manner, without having the negative impact upon other religions usually attributed to it.[6]

Finally, the pneumatological emphasis has arisen in part because it seems to avoid what has been called the "christological impasse" (Amos Yong), which is seen as the roadblock upon the recognition of other revelations erected by the unique status given to the Son, Jesus Christ, in Christian theology. English-language writers like Stanley Samartha, the Protestant Indian theologian; Metropolitan George Khodr, an Orthodox theologian; and the evangelical

---

5. On this latter point see especially John Milbank, "The End of Dialogue," in Gavin D'Costa, ed., *Christian Uniqueness Reconsidered* (Maryknoll, NY: Orbis, 1990), 174–91.

6. Gavin D'Costa, *The Meeting of Religions and the Trinity* (Edinburgh: T&T Clark, 2000).

Amos Yong working in the United States, all want to argue that the Spirit is present in other religions. They employ a certain reading of Irenaeus and urge that we should see God's works being carried out by "both hands": the Son *and* the Spirit. The Barthian subordination of the Spirit to the Son, as is argued by Samartha and Yong, is thereby overturned and the great riches and depths found in other religions can be joyfully acknowledged. As with the above writers, such short summaries cannot do full justice to this rich and innovative theology.

However, questions arise here: Is the doctrine of perichoresis and the unity of the "persons" thus compromised? Can the Spirit be biblically other than the Spirit of the Son? Does this neglect of Christology universalize the Spirit in a rather Gnostic and ahistorical fashion? The most problematic question in all these four trajectories outlined above is the minimization of the atoning value of Christ's death and the transformation of the human condition through his resurrection and ascension. One might observe that this neglect is a central feature of a range of modern theological developments, which in the Roman Catholic tradition arise from a more optimistic reading of Thomas Aquinas's adage that grace perfects, not destroys, nature. This has meant that the emphasis falls on the continuity that grace has with creation and nature. In the liberal Protestant tradition, this optimistic reading of human nature has both nontheological features (a greater estimation and indebtedness to human culture) as well as theological traditions that it mines. Schleiermacher, or at least a version of him, stands as a strong "master" in this line. The more Augustinian-influenced forms of Reformation and Catholic theology have in common their deeper suspicion of human nature (with varying degrees of damage envisaged) and thus they do not normally subscribe to the trends I have spoken about. I mention this issue to show how the theology of religions is so closely related to dogmatic questions and is not a subfield of theology but arises out of dogmatic considerations. I would contend that the heart of Christian truth and the universal mission it generates is minimized by these nontrinitarian theologians. Is such a loss of salt necessary for the attainment of the common good or, rather, does it actually undermine the common good by removing the unique Christian contribution? I think the latter, but that requires extensive argument.

The Trinity as Central in the Engagement with Religions

The burden of the rest of this essay is to show how a trinitarian approach might address the worries of the critics outlined above and also provide a richer, more orthodox response to religious pluralism that actually opens more doors than it closes. However, there are also approaches that utilize trinitarian conceptualities that are problematic in perhaps utilizing other conceptualities that do not fully correspond to the mainstream tradition of trinitarian theologies. To specify what I mean by orthodox trinitarian theology, I would suggest that it conform to the following specifications: (1) it is able to account for and profess the Nicene and Apostles' creeds that are shared by all trinitarian Christian communities; (2) that the full divinity and full humanity of the Son is the anchor for explicating and confessing the full divinity of the Spirit and Father, and the ontological unity of the these three "names"; (3) and that all Christian liturgy, language, and practice should be shaped by attention to Father, Son, and Spirit. One can say this and acknowledge a vast plurality within the tradition that is accepted as part of trinitarian orthodoxy.

The two most influential trinitarian theologians of the modern period are arguably the Protestant Karl Barth (1886–1968) and the Catholic Karl Rahner (1904–1984). I must attend to them as they have so profoundly affected Anglo-Saxon writings through their extensive translation into English. This should remind us that, due to extensive translation, the notion of "Anglo-Saxon" is already saturated with non-Anglo-Saxon sources and influences.

Let me start with a mistranslation that has deeply scarred the reception of Barth. Barth attended to the question of the religions at least twice. He has been deeply misunderstood in part because of the English mistranslation of his first famous essay "The Revelation of God as the Abolition [*Aufhebung*] of Religions."[7] *Aufhebung* might equally be translated as "lifting up" or "sublation," rather than abolition. When Hegel uses the term *Aufhebung*, he emphasizes both a taking up of a concept and its being rendered anew in this process. This I think is more akin to what Barth was implying in this essay: anything worthwhile in a religion is taken up and transformed in the light of Christ, for without Christ, it is always incomplete. The early Barth was concerned to establish that revelation is trinitarian and salvific. To use the term *revelation* of anything other than Jesus/Spirit/Father dangerously invites idolatry. Barth is keen to establish the uniqueness of Christian revelation in its particular narrative form of Israel's covenant and the coming of Jesus Christ.[8]

Barth's immense strength was his firm rooting of God as Trinity and a searching and searing critique of culture and religions, including Christianity—and one might say, especially Christianity—from this vantage

---

7. Karl Barth, *Church Dogmatics* I/2 (Edinburgh: T&T Clark, 1970), §17.

8. For a full bibliography and sound defense of Barth on this issue, see Garrett Green's edition of Karl Barth, *On Religion: The Revelation of God as the Sublimation of Religion* [new translation and commentary of *Church Dogmatics*, §17] (London: Continuum, 2006), as well as Sven Ensminger, *Karl Barth's Theology as a Resource for Christian Theology of Religions* (London: Bloomsbury, 2014).

point. His relentless concern to concentrate God-language in trinitarian narrative is a font for postliberal theology and more philosophical forms of Reformation theology that can be found in contemporary Anglo-Saxon literature. For some brief examples, I would draw the reader's attention to the work of some creative and faithful uses of Barth that are well worth exploring further: see the Protestant evangelical Kevin Vanhoozer,[9] the postliberal Lutheran theologian George Lindbeck,[10] and the postliberal theology of William Placher.[11] There is also an irenic use of Barth, with a large dose of pragmatism from the Jewish theologian Peter Ochs, in the writings of David Ford, who has pioneered "scriptural theology."[12] In translation and very significant is the earlier historicist turn of the German Lutheran theologian Wolfhart Pannenberg, whose work in theology of religions has been oddly neglected.[13] Lindbeck's understanding of doctrine as grammar produces both a very open approach to other religions: learning their grammar and then mutual betterment at the grammarian exercise; and taking the heat out of the question of the salvation of non-Christians. Regarding the latter, in fidelity to the *fides ex auditu* ("faith comes from hearing'), Lindbeck posits an after-death and prejudgment chance to choose the gospel. Apart from the evangelical theologian Clark Pinnock, who seems to have learned more from the Catholic Rahner than from his Protestant Reformed resources, in my opinion Protestant *trinitarian* approaches have succumbed to fewer problems than have Catholic approaches.[14]

---

9. Kevin Vanhoozer, ed., *The Trinity in a Pluralistic Age: Theological Essays on Culture and Religion* (Grand Rapids: Eerdmans, 1996).

10. George Lindbeck, *The Nature of Doctrine: Religion and Theology in a Postliberal Age* (London: SPCK, 1984); idem, "*Fides ex auditu* and the Salvation of Non-Christians: Contemporary Catholic and Protestant Positions," in Vilmos Vajta, ed., *The Gospel and the Ambiguity of the Church* (Minneapolis: Fortress Press, 1974), 92–123.

11. See, for instance, William C. Placher, *The Domestication of Transcendence: How Modern Thinking about God Went Wrong* (Louisville: Westminster John Knox, 1996), and *Jesus the Savior: The Meaning of Jesus Christ for Christian Faith* (Louisville: Westminster John Knox, 2001).

12. See, for instance, David F. Ford, *Christian Wisdom: Desiring God and Learning in Love* (Cambridge: Cambridge University Press, 2007), with several references to Peter Ochs's publications, including *Peirce, Pragmatism, and the Logic of Scripture* (Cambridge: Cambridge University Press, 1998), and *Textual Reasonings: Jewish Philosophy and Text Study at the End of the Twentieth Century*, ed. Peter Ochs and Nancy Levene (Grand Rapids: Eerdmans, 2002).

13. Wolfhart Pannenberg, "Towards a Theology of the History of Religions," in idem, *Basic Questions in Theology: Collected Essays*, vol. 2 (Philadelphia: Fortress Press, 1971), 65–118; as well as idem, "Religious Pluralism and Conflicting Truth Claims," in Gavin D'Costa, ed., *Christian Uniqueness Reconsidered* (Maryknoll, NY: Orbis, 1990), 96–106.

The serious exception to this rule is the Protestant American theologian S. Mark Heim, who argues that the Trinity endorses the view that each religion may have a different final telos, just as there are three in the Trinity, not one.[15] His argument is so novel that it requires special attention. Heim is one of the clearest exponents of radical pluralism, which is committed to acknowledging the real plural ends of religions. Heim avoids both "pluralists" and "exclusivists," who he argues fail to properly engage with particularity and difference. The former, in arguing for the general equality of all religions, fail to engage with the self-descriptions of those religions and the different religious ends actually posited and practiced. The latter are committed simply to dismissing difference, unable to make sense of the true, good, and beautiful that is found in other religions. "Inclusivists," who seem able to affirm the value of non-Christian religions, are still problematic for Heim, for they only affirm others insomuch as they are more or less pale reflections of Christianity. Furthermore, the different ends envisaged by these religions are temporal stopping places, as possible and helpful preparatory schools for final fulfillment to be found in Christianity, or alternatively, if taken absolutely in themselves, can lead to a rejection of the fullness of trinitarian truth in the eschaton.

Heim follows in the footsteps of recent writers like Joseph A. DiNoia, O.P., Paul J. Griffiths, Francis X. Clooney, S.J., and David Burrell, C.S.C., who all want to take these religions seriously in their own terms. Heim achieves his goal in a four-step trinitarian argument. First, the self-described telos of a religion must be respected and seen as a possible "real" end, both temporally and eschatologically. If the latter aspect is denied, the religion is not taken seriously and in its own terms. Second, he asks whether these differing ends can be viewed as "real" relations with the trinitarian God confessed by Christians, for otherwise they cannot be affirmed as "real." In this respect, Heim self-consciously develops the inclusivist position—but with a twist. He is clear that such a "real" relationship cannot constitute "salvation," as the latter is reserved for the beatific vision. "Salvation" is an intra-Christian term. Using examples from many religions, Heim argues that the differing ends of these traditions can be constructively related to a trinitarian understanding of God. For the latter, Heim relies heavily on Raimundo Panikkar's *The Trinity and the Religious Experience of Man*.[16]

14. Clark H. Pinnock, *A Wideness in God's Mercy: The Finality of Jesus Christ in a World of Religions* (Grand Rapids: Zondervan, 1992).

15. S. Mark Heim, *The Depth of the Riches: A Trinitarian Theology of Religious Ends* (Grand Rapids: Eerdmans, 2001).

Heim argues that the Trinity is characterized by three types of relation.[17] The Father represents impersonal identity within which two trajectories are found. The first, the *apophatic*, is grounded in the emptiness by which each of the divine persons makes space for the other; and the second, the *unitive*, is grounded in the coinherence or complete immanence of each of the divine persons in the others. Heim locates Theravada Buddhism within the first and Advaita Vedanta within the second. The second relation, characterized by the Son, is the "iconic," which also has two aspects. One is the focus of encounter with the divine life through mediated, but not explicitly personal, categories: a law, a book, or institution. The Buddhist *dharma* or the *tao* of Taoism are examples. Heim suggests that from a "Christian perspective, it is the common purpose or will of the triune God that is apprehended under such" images.[18] The second iconic aspect focuses on God as personal being, and while law and morality feature here, they are filtered through an "I-Thou" encounter. Christianity, Islam, Judaism, and forms of Hinduism are to be found here—even though Heim makes it clear that all religions coordinate and balance all three relations in different ways. The third relation, characterized by the Spirit, transforms external relations into internal communion, mutual indwelling, perichoresis. Heim, unlike Panikkar, fails to actively employ this category in relation to other religions, but sees it as the balancing function that establishes all three persons as equality in difference. (We will examine Panikkar shortly below.)

The third step of Heim's argument is to then argue that these "real" relations help establish a double goal. Christians can affirm that other religions, in terms of their own self-description, lead to a "real" relationship with the divine reality such that difference is taken seriously. Different teloi are envisaged and they have intrinsic worth. This is radical pluralism and echoes an earlier process writer, John Cobb, who used the Trinity to argue in this manner.[19] Heim's position does not exclude that a Buddhist converting to Christianity will affirm that Buddhism acted as a *praeparatio evangelica*; rather, he retains that aspect of traditional inclusivism.

The final step of Heim's argument, which establishes its utter novelty, is his pushing the different teloi as final eschatological differences willed by God.

16. Raimundo Panikkar, *The Trinity and the Religious Experience of Man* (London: Darton, Longman & Todd, 1973).

17. Heim, *Depth of the Riches*, 181–97.

18. Ibid., 211.

19. See John B. Cobb, *Beyond Dialogue: Towards a Mutual Transformation of Christianity and Buddhism* (Philadelphia: Fortress Press, 1982).

Dante's *Divine Comedy* nicely exemplifies traditional cosmology, embodying a triple-decker universe (heaven, hell, purgatory) that collapses into a double-decker finish—the saved and the damned). Heim wants to change the map so that there are four decks that eventually collapse into three. First, there is salvation, characterized by communion through Christ with God. Second, there are "alternative religious ends, the distinctive human fulfillments of the various religious traditions. Each of these grasps some dimension of the triune life and its economic manifestations, and makes it the ground for a definitive human end."[20] Then, third, there are destinies that are not religious ends at all, where people cling definitively to created realities in place of or over against God. Finally, there is the possibility of negation, whereby nothing is idolized and creation rejected. In the end, the two latter categories collapse into one, thus making three ends. Hence, in Heim's proposal, we finally have the saved, the others in "real" relation, and the damned.

Heim's thesis closely hovers over the dividing line between pluralism and inclusivism and he raises some significant points: the importance of understanding religions in their own terms and thus taking a plurality of ends seriously; the creative riches offered in trinitarian theology to make sense of the different ends; and the potential reductionisms in exclusivism, inclusivism, and oneness pluralism. However, does Heim's proposal actually secure what he set out to do: to accept other religions in terms of their own self-description? For example, Advaita, in terms of its own self-understanding, eschatologically radically negates the category of "relation," a point that Heim does admittedly acknowledge, such that it is difficult to see the telos of Advaita being eternally preserved within a trinitarian framework. "Identity" in Sankara cannot be assimilated to immanence or coinherence within three divine persons, or at least not without a lot more argument. The point is that assimilating the final ends to aspects of the Trinity might make sense from a Christian theological viewpoint, but one cannot claim that this is *not* an assimilation and thus transformation of the final telos of that other religion. The arguments between Sankara and Ramanuja make it clear that, even within Hinduism itself, the importance of the integrity and implications of a particular telos cannot be dislodged or assimilated and be acceptable to those within that particular tradition.[21] In effect, the Buddhist who has become a Christian and sees Buddhism as a *praeparatio evangelica* might well posit the type of move Heim in part makes, but to register

---

20. Heim, *Depth of the Riches*, 272.
21. See Eric Lott, *Vedantic Approaches to God* (London: MacMillan, 1980).

that which is telos as *praeparatio evangelica* to the final telos is veering on the incoherent.

Second, I am not entirely convinced that Heim historically and theologically shows us whether and how coinherence, perichoresis, and other vital trinitarian terms function in his overall model—and whether they are capable of being employed in the highly schematic way he envisages. This is also a problem with Panikkar's work, from whom Heim draws so deeply, as we shall see below. Obviously, even were this problem attended to, my basic objection above would still be unaffected. It may be a sound conclusion to say that this form of radical trinitarian pluralism at least attempts to take religious differences seriously, but it fails to hold those differences together in any intelligible form. Another pluralist who sees this problem and suggests a slight different form of radical pluralism is the Portuguese Roman Catholic Henrique Pinto, but the Trinity plays little part in his work, or certainly not as significant a role as does Michel Foucault.[22] Let me turn now to the Roman Catholic trinitarian theologies of religion that have become important in the Anglo-Saxon literature.

Rahner's theology has been hugely influential in Roman Catholic circles since the 1960s. In *Spirit in the World*, Rahner argues that the Spirit is present to all humans *qua* humans, such that all nature is always graced nature with an orientation to God.[23] This unthematized (nonexplicit) relation to God is fully and most explicitly thematized in the God-Man, Jesus Christ. In history, it is through this revelation that we discover the reality of graced nature, which until then is never properly known. Nevertheless, all history affords the possibility of a person saying "yes" to the teleological drive of their own graced nature in acts of love, trust, and hope—without explicit confrontation with the revelation of Christ. A person can say "no" to unthematized grace in acts of despair, hatred, and evil, but there is a profound contradiction involved in sin's use of transcendental freedom to foreclose its own freedom. The outcome of Rahner's *Spirit in the World* is that all humans *qua* humans are capable of finding redemption through the Spirit in their concrete actions that teleologically orient them to Christ.

While Jesus exemplified the fullness of this "yes" of humankind to God and God to humankind, this "yes" is to be found in fragmentary form everywhere, including the religions—amidst a "no." Rahner thus coined the terms "anonymous Christian" and "anonymous Christianity," reflecting the

22. Henrique Pinto, *Foucault, Christianity and Interfaith Dialogue* (London: Routledge, 2003).

23. Karl Rahner, *Spirit in the World* (London: Sheed & Ward, 19682).

christological orientation of all grace in terms of final, not efficient, causality. The non-Christian as an anonymous Christian secretly says "yes" to Jesus when she says "yes" to hope and love. The non-Christians' religion, which cannot be divorced from their "yes," may contain elements and practices that support this "yes"—thus anonymous "Christianity."

In this configuration, Rahner's great strength is that he manages to hold together both trinitarian and ecclesial concerns, while being profoundly open to interreligious dialogues at every level (personal, social, spiritual, philosophical, and theological). Rahner also suggests a positive relation to non-Christians. Insomuch as God may be discovered in the religions, then Christians have much to learn in interreligious dialogues while still being under the demand to preach the good news to all people. Rahner suggests that the historian of religion has the job to check the validity of the anonymous Christianity thesis. Here again, he was groundbreaking in reconfiguring the history of religions within a theological reading. Rahner's achievement is considerable, as is his impact on Catholic theology of religions.

Rahner has been criticized for the chauvinism of the term "anonymous Christian," but that misses the point: the terminology is entirely intra-Christian theological reflection.[24] More important are the trinitarian problems that arise. First, Rahner's deployment of the Spirit seems to take what is traditionally the Spirit's function of upholding and sustaining creation and turns it into a redemptive grace. Or one might say that there is no clear distinction between the forms of grace such that redeeming grace is co-present with sustaining and upholding grace in a way that departs from the tradition and certainly from Scripture in a problematic manner. A very astute trinitarian criticism of Rahner's work is to be found in the writing of Edmund Hill, and Hans Urs von Balthasar presents a devastating critique of anonymous Christianity.[25] The converse side of this conflation of supernatural saving grace with nature is the minimizing, if not possible abandonment, of the atoning significance of Christ's cross. Balthasar sees Rahner as abandoning the cross, but this seems to go too far. One might say that Rahner has a higher valuation of human nature. This goes back to the earlier point I made above about the Thomist–Augustinian differences of emphasis. One should, of course, not push these into two binary

24. For further discussion, see Gavin D'Costa, *Theology and Religious Pluralism* (Oxford: Blackwell, 1986), 80–117. The vast literature since 1985 is discussed in Karen Kilby's rich defense of Rahner, *Karl Rahner: Theology and Philosophy* (London: Routledge, 2004).

25. Edmund Hill, "Karl Rahner's 'Remarks on the Dogmatic Treatise *De Trinitate* and St. Augustine'," *Augustinian Studies* 2 (1971): 67–80; Hans Urs von Balthasar, *The Moment of Christian Witness*, trans. Richard Beckley (San Francisco: Ignatius, 1994).

camps, as there are thinkers who draw both these two giants together into a more critical form of Thomism, such as Tracey Rowland. As Rowan Williams nicely puts it when contrasting Rahner with Balthasar, Rahner tends to see a world full of well-meaning humanists while Balthasar sees instead torture, violence, and institutional greed raping human dignity. In Rahner, the deep scar of original sin is minimized.[26]

Putting aside the difficulty of assessing Rahner fairly, we can also pursue the trinitarian structure of this theology by seeing that Rahner develops two economies—an invisible and an visible trinitarian action in the world—which never seem to quite come together. The invisible Trinity operates for the anonymous Christian, bringing him or her to salvation, while the visible Trinity operates for the explicit Christian, bringing him or her to salvation. But is that in fact the case? To rephrase the problem: How can the anonymous Christian enjoy the beatific vision that on Rahner's own accounting requires an explicit knowledge of the triune God without that implicit grace becoming explicit? I would like to pursue a line of questioning not usually developed in this critical debate; I can only do so briefly in what follows.

Rahner's answer to the question I have just posed is indirect. It is only explicitly addressed in his early theology of death, which was developed separately from his anonymous Christian reflections.[27] In his theology of death, the afterlife provides the place where the implicit knowledge of God matures and becomes explicit knowledge that is required for salvation. The proper implication thus is that the relationship to Christ that the non-Christian has is more accurately understood as a "potentiality" rather than an "actuality," which is what Thomas Aquinas teaches when he discusses this question.[28] Rahner conflates potentiality with actuality precisely because he has conflated nature with supernatural saving grace. The universality of the Spirit's action has in Rahner almost overcome the particularity of Christ's action. This also led Rahner to read the *Dogmatic Constitution on the Church*, §16, as the Catholic Church's major move from salvation pessimism to salvation optimism—a reading that Ralph Martin rightly criticizes.[29] Martin also argues that Rahner's theology had a catastrophic impact on the theology of missions.[30]

26. Rowan Williams, "Balthasar and Rahner," in John Riches, ed., *The Analogy of Beauty* (Edinburgh: T&T Clark, 1986), 11–34.

27. Karl Rahner, *Theology of Death* (London: Darton, Longman & Todd, 1965).

28. Thomas Aquinas, *Summa Theologica* III, q.8, a.3, ad.1; this is in fact the passage cited in the Second Vatican Council's *Dogmatic Constitution on the Church*, §16.

29. Ralph Martin, *Will Many Be Saved? What Vatican II Actually Teaches and Its Implications for the New Evangelization* (Grand Rapids: Eerdmans, 2012), 7–24.

Let me now follow Rahner's impact on two trinitarian Catholic theologians who have been extensively translated into English and who are deeply influenced by Rahner, but go beyond him: the Belgian Jesuit Jacques Dupuis (1923–2004) and the Indian-Spanish priest Raimundo Panikkar (1918–2010). I do not have time to treat the American Jesuit Roger Haight, who has developed a position not unlike that of John Hick, while still retaining more traditional trinitarian and christological language.[31]

Dupuis develops Rahner's position to make three bold new trinitarian moves. First, he explains the presence of Christ in the non-Christian's inner life and religion in terms of a distinction between the *logos asarkos* and *logos ensarkos*, the first being the nonincarnate saving action of the Word, the second being the incarnate saving action in the particularity of the incarnate Word, Jesus Christ.[32] This is not unlike the anonymous and explicit Christ, but it digs into the tradition to give conceptuality to the reality. Second, in parallel, Dupuis extends the economy of the Holy Spirit beyond the actions of the incarnate Word (*ensarkos*) to explain the legitimacy of non-Christian religions. The Spirit blows where it will and when it blows it brings people toward that salvation which is always from Christ, hidden or known. Dupuis builds this pneumatological part of his project by drawing heavily on the teachings of Pope John Paul II, who constantly turned to this theme in his writing. Third, Dupuis detaches the action of the Trinity from the visible sign of the church so that while salvation for the non-Christian always happens through the grace of Christ in the power of his Spirit, it does not require any ecclesial mediation or visible relationship to the church and also does not require non-Christians to become Christians. Here Dupuis is drawing to its conclusion what he sees as the un-worked-out implicit teachings of Vatican II and the postconciliar magisterium on this matter. Dupuis is a careful and cautious theologian with bold proposals. He sees his own work as dissolving the clear lines between "inclusivism" (associated with Rahner) and "pluralism" (of which he is very critical when in the form of Hick or Knitter). He advances what he sees as an inclusivist pluralism.

On trinitarian grounds, all three moves have been criticized by the Congregation for the Doctrine of the Faith (hereafter CDF).[33] I should indicate that the CDF eventually made it clear that while Dupuis was not guilty of

---

30. Ibid., 93–129.

31. Roger Haight, *Jesus the Symbol of God* (Maryknoll, NY: Orbis, 1999), as well as *The Future of Christology* (London: Continuum, 2005), esp. chs. 5 and 7.

32. Jacques Dupuis, *Toward a Christian Theology of Religious Pluralism* (Maryknoll, NY: Orbis, 1997), 297–300.

crossing the line of orthodoxy, his work can be interpreted in this fashion.[34] But the three criticisms are instructive, even if it is not clear whether Dupuis falls foul of these problems. In my own reading of Dupuis, his work is problematic in these respects, but that would need to be shown in extensive detail. First, christologically Dupuis implies that there can be a "separation between the Word and Jesus, or between the Word's salvific activity and that of Jesus, [or] that there is a salvific activity of the Word as such in his divinity, independent of the humanity of the incarnate Word" (Notification, §2). This parallels Rahner's explicit and implicit christological distinction. One can see that this is one resolution of the question addressed in Vatican II: Can a person who is invincibly ignorant of the gospel and who follows his or her conscience and that which is good, true, and holy in his or her religion be lost? The answer given at the Council was "No, they are not necessarily lost because they die as non-Christians." This does raise the question, then, of how they can be saved without any explicit knowledge of Christ. Dupuis's answer is an attempt to address this problem to which there are no formal magisterial teachings giving a clear answer. However, the CDF's response might be seen as teaching that this answer falls into a problem in that it creates a new christological difficulty to overcome a genuinely difficult question.

Second, pneumatologically Dupuis implies that "the salvific action of the Holy Spirit extends beyond the one universal salvific economy of the Incarnate Word" (Notification, §6). Rahner never does this. Dupuis self-consciously does move toward what he calls an "inclusive pluralism." Rahner stopped short at "inclusivism." Dupuis uses the Spirit to relate salvation wherever it happens to the Christ-event, which is not explicitly known. *Gaudium et spes* §22 seems to imply such a possibility but the CDF points out the difficulty of disconnecting the one concrete salvific economy of Christ with the actions of the Spirit.[35] Again, one can see Dupuis trying to attend to a problem that is real, but the response sees the danger in Spirit Christologies and pneumatologies that I outlined above in regard to these Spirit solutions.

33. *Notification on the Book 'Toward a Christian Theology of Religious Pluralism' by Father Jacques Dupuis, SJ* (Vatican City: Libreria Editrice Vaticana, 2001).

34. For some helpful texts that throw further light on the Dupuis "case," see William R. Burrows, *Jacques Dupuis Faces the Inquisition: Two Essays by Jacques Dupuis on* Dominus Iesus *and the Roman Investigation of His Work* (Eugene, OR: Pickwick, 2010). See also Terrence Merrigan's judicious and balanced analysis of Dupuis's work, in "Exploring the Frontiers: Jacques Dupuis and the Movement 'Toward a Christian Theology of Religious Pluralism'," *Louvain Studies* 23 (1998): 338–59.

35. For the Vatican documents, see Norman Tanner, ed., *Decrees of the Ecumenical Councils*, vol. 2: *Trent to Vatican II* (London/Washington, DC: Sheed & Ward/Georgetown University Press, 1990).

The third issue is ecclesiological. While it is right "to maintain that the Holy Spirit accomplishes salvation in non-Christians also through those elements of truth and goodness present" in them, it is not legitimate to "hold that these religions, considered as such, are ways of salvation . . . because they contains omissions, insufficiencies and errors regarding fundamental truths about God, man and the world" (Notification, §8). Again, Rahner stops short of Dupuis's move, although his term "legitimate religion," drawn from Israel before the coming of Christ and analogically applied to other religions, in fact leads to Dupuis's conclusion. However, Rahner argued that a "legitimate religion" becomes "illegitimate" for the person who has heard the gospel and rejected it, but not for other adherents of that religion. Dupuis abandons this notion, but partly because it is so difficult to apply. Yet he is also clear that those who are invincibly ignorant of the gospel do belong to religions in good faith and it is through that belonging, rather than despite it, that they are saved by God's grace mediated in part through those traditions. It is important to note that the CDF in no way denies the reality of God's saving presence in elements of the world religions and in persons themselves and in the reality of the Holy Spirit's presence. In the document *Dominus Iesus* it returns to this theme and introduces a new conceptuality that helps the debate.[36] In §21 it says:

> Certainly, the various religious traditions contain and offer religious elements which come from God, and which are part of what "the Spirit brings about in human hearts and in the history of peoples, in cultures, and religions." Indeed, some prayers and rituals of the other religions may assume a role of preparation for the Gospel, in that they are occasions or pedagogical helps in which the human heart is prompted to be open to the action of God. One cannot attribute to these, however, a divine origin or an *ex opere operato* salvific efficacy, which is proper to the Christian sacraments. Furthermore, it cannot be overlooked that other rituals, insofar as they depend on superstitions or other errors (cf. 1 Cor. 10:20-21), constitute an obstacle to salvation.

In relation to the ecclesiological issue, it might be argued that, for Catholic ecclesiology, the Trinity is the foundation of the church and the visible sign of God's activity. In this sense, redemption, if it happens through God, must be connected with the church as it is the objective and *ex opere operato* visible means of salvation. This tentative alternative requires a lot more argument and

---

36. *Dominus Iesus* (Vatican City: Liberia Editrice Vaticana, 2000).

it needs to address the questions that Dupuis has legitimately raised. What is at stake is the best trinitarian way that the realities of other religions might be explicated, both maintaining the necessity of the church for salvation (also required by *Dominus Iesus* §20) and doing full justice to the true, good, and holy elements found within the religions. This exploration is still in its infancy.

Dupuis's writings are important for pushing forward the trinitarian agenda. The same might be said of Panikkar, who in his early work replicated Rahner's position, but in his later work made bold steps forward.[37] I think many of his later steps (christological, pneumatological, and ecclesiological) are akin to Dupuis. (Interestingly, Dupuis criticizes Panikkar's Christology and later thinking for precisely the reasons that the CDF criticizes Dupuis's work).[38]

Panikkar develops what he calls a vision of a "cosmotheandric reality," whereby the "modalities" of the Father, Son, and Spirit are mutually corrective pointers toward the divine mystery. The Father represents the apophatic truth that the divine is utterly other, such that nothing can be properly said of "it" and silence is the purest way of responding to this unfathomable mystery. Allied to this path is the way of mysticism and asceticism, which strip down the pretensions of the self in the light of the "nothingness" of the divine. This brings about a deep self-surrender or self-forgetfulness, and thus a profound compassion, love, and service. He sees various strands of apophatic mysticism within Christianity, and most profoundly within Theravada Buddhism and Advaita Hinduism. However, for Panikkar there is always a danger of indifference to the world in this mystical path. The Son is an icon compared to the utter mystery of the Father that is beyond all forms. The "Son" represents the path of devotion and personalism, the ecstasy of love and joy, mercy and forgiveness, personal reconciliation and humanity. Indeed, Panikkar reads the *kenosis* of Christ, his self-emptying, in terms of the *sunyata* and *nirvana* of Buddhism. He also sees theistic Hinduism within this iconic spirituality. If the danger of the Father's path was worldly indifference, the danger of the Son's path is anthropocentrism, making the human the measure of all things, or in its divine form, assuming God to be a "person" writ large. Third, the Spirit represents the unseen mediator, which is only seen in its powerful effects. This path is also associated with power and charism, and Panikkar relates this to the Shaivite Sakti tradition in Hinduism and Tantric Buddhist traditions that map the deep powers within the human in which the divine resides, the *kundalini*.

37. Raimundo Panikkar, *The Unknown Christ of Hinduism* (London: Darton, Longman and Todd, 1964; see esp. the 2d ed., 1981), as well as idem, *The Trinity and the Religious Experience of Man: Icon-Person-Mystery* (Maryknoll, NY: Orbis, 1973).

38. See Dupuis, *Toward a Christian Theology*, 151–52.

The danger of this path is that of idolizing works or rites. Panikkar is content to allow the reality of each tradition to fructify and transform each other, while recognizing that none has the whole truth and all have some truth, a truth that is pluriform, not unitary. Religions are thus complementary paths to the cosmotheandric reality.

Panikkar's approach is especially helpful for his vast erudition and intimate knowledge of the Eastern traditions and for his trinitarian appreciation of many aspects of the world's religions. There is much to appreciate and affirm in his work, a task well undertaken by Rowan Williams.[39] However, there are problems with Panikkar. In my view, it would be better that the cosmotheandric reality be construed as an analogical resonance to the mystery of the Trinity, as *vestigia Trinitatis*. This would usefully provide points of contact for respectful exploration and dialogues. However, for Panikkar there is almost an inversion of the *vestigia* tradition, for he seems to want to say that Christianity itself has vestiges of the cosmotheandric reality that are far greater and deeper than disclosed in the Christian revelation. The symbolic triadic structure subordinates the historical particular narrative of revelation. It is certainly true that Christian revelation cannot be equated with the fullness of God's mystery as if nothing more of God can be said, known, or worshiped. However, it is held that the revelation given in the Trinity *is* that of God's very self, who we will come to know face to face only in heaven.

I have critically examined this small selection of trinitarian theologians to show that many of the problems identified by nontrinitarian theologians are being attended to within a trinitarian theology. Respect for others, learning from the religions, as well as working together for the common good are all richly facilitated within a trinitarian orientation. None of the trinitarian theologians I have discussed actually attend to the sociopolitical realm in any detail as do the liberationists, but neither are they guilty of any closing off of attention to that area. It might be said that the focus has been more on the doctrinal elements within trinitarian thought rather than the liturgical and political. That the latter are important and require attention is not in question. And in this respect, a trinitarian orientation might also call for a deep critique of both other religions and Christianity itself when they or it stifle the common good or extinguish the "lights" within sectors of their own tradition. This is a theoretically, politically, and socially complicated issue, but necessary from a theological standpoint. I have drawn attention to critical aspects of these

---

39. Rowan Williams, "Trinity and Pluralism," in Gavin D'Costa, ed., *Christian Uniqueness Reconsidered* (Maryknoll, NY: Orbis, 1990), 3–15.

theologies not to minimize their important contributions, but to alert the reader to many unresolved issues once the trinitarian path is walked.[40]

Concluding Tentative Remarks

I want to suggest that five mysteries of the faith—the Trinity: Spirit, Son, Father; the church; and the kingdom—need to be constantly held *together* and in *tension* to properly reflect theologically upon interreligious dialogues. The first are central and they generate the second two. When these five are held together they open all sorts of rich avenues along which to develop a Christian engagement with the religions. Using shorthand, one might say the following: To forget the Son is to erase the scandal of particularity. To forget the Spirit is to erase the universal outreach of the Son's work. To forget the Father is to forget the unitive purpose of the triune revelation—drawing human community into a communion of love and forgiveness. To forget the church is to erase the visible sign of trinitarian glory in the liturgy and the liturgy's power in transforming creation. To forget the kingdom is to erase the justice and peace inaugurated in Christ's person that might transform the earth into heaven. I have only begun to touch upon many complex questions and there are lots of disputed questions in this field.

40. There are many other theologians who might have been profitably discussed at greater length in this section such as Colin Gunton and Clark Pinnock. For a very useful and extensive survey of trinitarian theologies of religion, see Veli-Matti Kärkkäinen, *Trinity and Religious Pluralism: The Doctrine of the Trinity in Christian Theology of Religions* (Aldershot, UK: Ashgate, 2004).

5

Colin Gunton on the Trinity and the Divine Attributes

Marc Vial

The aim of this essay is not to offer a general presentation of the theology of Colin E. Gunton, who was born in 1941 and was a prominent theologian until his untimely death in 2003. Such an overview can be read elsewhere.[1] As I was working on the theme of God's almightiness, assuming that the treatment of this question should be grounded in a trinitarian theology, I discovered Gunton's last book, *Act and Being*, the precise purpose of which is to bring to the fore the resources an account of God's trinitarian being and act offer for a specifically Christian approach to the divine attributes.[2] This essay is mainly devoted to an analysis of some of the claims Gunton makes in *Act and Being*. First, however, let us begin with a brief exposition of some of the major elements of Gunton's trinitarian theology in general.

GUNTON'S TRINITARIAN THEOLOGY: SOME GUIDELINES

In 2003, the year of Gunton's death, a collection of his essays on the Trinity was published, the subtitle of which refers to a passage from *Act and Being*:[3] *Toward a Fully Trinitarian Theology*.[4] The word *fully* deserves scrutiny. Although not in an

---

1. See Christoph Schwöbel, "The Shape of Colin Gunton's Theology: On the Way Towards a Fully Trinitarian Theology," in Lincoln Harvey, ed., *The Theology of Colin Gunton* (London: T&T Clark, 2010), 182–208.

2. Colin Gunton, *Act and Being: Towards a Theology of the Divine Attributes* (Grand Rapids: Eerdmans, 2002).

3. Ibid., 104.

4. Colin Gunton, *Father, Son and Holy Spirit: Essays toward a Fully Trinitarian Theology* (London: T&T Clark, 2003).

exclusive way, it is intended, if I am not mistaken, to emphasize the distinctive character of the Holy Spirit's being and work, a character which, according to Gunton, the Western theological tradition has neglected. The presentation of Gunton's understanding of the third person of the Trinity will allow me to sketch other aspects of his trinitarian theology. This first part will be based on two of Gunton's writings: *The Promise of Trinitarian Theology*, in which the main elements of Gunton's trinitarian theology are already present,[5] and a synthetic article, "God the Holy Spirit."[6]

Gunton stresses the Holy Spirit's distinctive character by using the expression coined by Basil of Caesarea: "perfecting cause."[7] The Spirit is the one whose specific act is to perfect: it brings to perfection the creation (that is, everything which is not God) as well as the love that God is. This very simple statement leads us to think that the emphasis on the specificity of the Holy Spirit's person and work has important consequences for the way Gunton conceives the economic Trinity (the relationship the three persons have with the world) as well as the eternal or immanent Trinity (the relationship the three persons have with one another). Let us begin by considering the economic Trinity. Following Barth, Gunton contends that we cannot have any access to the knowledge of God's *being* except by considering God's *acting*. We will return to this point later. For now, let us turn to the specific act of the Holy Spirit in and for the world.

Here is the main thesis: the Holy Spirit is the *perfecting cause* of the creation, for its proper activity consists in leading everything which is not God into communion with God, that is, leading creation to its destination.[8] The Spirit is therefore the one who enables human beings to correspond to what God has in mind in God's creative purpose. Gunton insists on the fact that the Spirit's activity is not limited to a simple restoration. The Spirit's acting consists less in enabling human beings to return to their supralapsarian condition than in perfecting them, in allowing them to coincide with their telos: to coincide with what God wants *for them* to be. To put it in other words, the Spirit's activity is better understood in *eschatological* terms rather than in protological ones.[9] This eschatological dimension of the Spirit's acting is fundamental in Gunton's

---

5. Christoph Schwöbel has noted this in "The Shape," 198.

6. Colin Gunton, *The Promise of Trinitarian Theology* (Edinburgh: T&T Clark, 1991); and "God the Holy Spirit: Augustine and His Successors," in idem, *Theology Through the Theologians: Selected Essays (1972–1995)* (Edinburgh: T&T Clark, 1996), 105–28.

7. Colin Gunton, "Being and Concept: Concluding Theological Aspects," in *The Promise*, 168. "The Perfecting Cause" is also the title of the fourth section of "God the Holy Spirit."

8. Gunton, "God the Holy Spirit," 120.

thought and, according to him, it is precisely this eschatological dimension that the New Testament emphasizes.[10] One must be cautious here and see that this dimension refers to an eschatological *dynamic*, that is, a process that does not "jump" over history, but which is at work in time. Gunton writes: "In the economy it is the action of the Spirit not simply to relate the individual to God, but to realise in time the conditions of the age to come."[11] The best manifestation of this state of affairs is Christ's resurrection: "the resurrection of Jesus Christ from the dead serves as a model for the possibilities for the transformation of matter in general."[12] What has been realized *in the Son* is the model of what will be realized *for and in the whole creation*. The Holy Spirit is precisely the agent of such a realization. Although not *separated* from the Son's activity, the Spirit's act is nevertheless *distinct* from it: the Son is the *raison d'être* of everything that is, whereas the Spirit is the one whose acting leads everything that is toward its telos, namely its being in the Son in which everything has been created.

Such a doctrine seems very classical indeed, insofar as the Spirit is conceived as the principle thanks to which creatures (especially human creatures) are allowed to be participants in the work accomplished by the Son. However, it is Gunton's contention that the Spirit's action is also the condition of the creating and redemptive activity effected by the Father in the Son. The Spirit's activity is indeed constitutive of the Son's act, in that it makes it possible for the man of Nazareth to be the Son he is, allowing the Son's humanity to be the perfect expression of the Father's will. We see here, according to Gunton, what it means for the Holy Spirit to be the *perfecting cause*: it means that he makes it possible for the man of Nazareth, who shares the common human condition and who is *really human*, to fully be *God's* unique Son, whose humanity as such is the mode of being the second person of the Trinity is from all eternity destined to be. In Gunton's mind, only such a pneumatology, which thinks the Spirit's relation to Jesus not as a permanent presence, but as an act operated by a person toward another person, allows us really to think the full humanity of the Son.[13]

---

9. Ibid., 127: "the Spirit is . . . the one who perfects creation by realising the communion of persons and the transformation of matter. Here, we can indeed speak of 'return'; but of a process by which that which was in the beginning is not so much restored to a former integrity as returned perfected to the Father through the Son and by the Spirit—an eschatological rather than a protological return, if we may so speak."

10. Ibid., 119–20.

11. Colin Gunton, "Augustine, the Trinity and the Theological Crisis of the West," in *The Promise*, 50.

12. Gunton, "God the Holy Spirit," 120.

The designation of the Holy Spirit as perfecting cause, first considered from the standpoint of its activity *in history*, is also at work in Gunton's treatment of God's *eternity*, that is, of the immanent Trinity. Here is his thesis: the Spirit does not only perfect creation, leading it to its telos; the Spirit also perfects the Father's and Son's mutual love, contributing in a specific way to the communion of love that God is. Such an assertion is highly polemical, in that it challenges what Gunton considers as a weakening, traceable to Augustine, of the Western trinitarian tradition. To analyze this accusation in every detail and to evaluate it would go beyond the scope of this essay.[14] It will be sufficient to say that Gunton's judgment on Augustine concerns the designation of the Holy Spirit as *vinculum caritatis*, the bond of love that unites the Father and the Son. To put it shortly, it seems to our author that such a designation is problematic from the standpoint of the economic Trinity as well as from the standpoint of the immanent Trinity. It fails to take into account the specific act of the Holy Spirit in the economy, and it also fails to express the depth of love in Godself. These two aspects are related: it is precisely because it presents the Holy Spirit as the bond of love uniting exclusively the Father and the Son that it fails to allow, according to Gunton, for the integration of any entity which is not God into the fellowship of the Father and the Son. But such an integration is precisely made possible by a more adequate understanding of the Holy Spirit. Relying on insights from Richard of Saint-Victor's *De trinitate*, Gunton asserts that the perfection of love consists in what the Victorine master called *condilectio*, which exceeds simple mutual love in that it opens this love to a third.[15] This is precisely the role of the Holy Spirit in the eternity of the divine life: perfecting the love of the Father and the Son by opening it to that which differs from them, namely the creature. Gunton writes:

13. Ibid., 115–16.

14. For Gunton's judgment on Augustine, see his "Augustine," in *The Promise*, 31–57.

15. Richard of Saint Victor, *La trinité* III,19, ed. Gaston Salet (Paris: Cerf, 1999), 208–10: "Quando unus alteri amorem impedit et solus solum diligit, dilectio est, sed condilectio non est. Quando duo se mutuo diligunt, et summi desiderii affectum invicem impendunt et istius in illum, illius vero in istum affectus discurrit et quasi in diversa tendit, utrobique quidem dilectio est, sed condilectio non est. Condilectio autem jure dicitur, ubi a duobus tertius concorditer diligitur, socialiter amatur et duorum affectus tertii amoris incendio in unum conflatur. Ex his itaque patet quod in ipsa divinitate condilectio locum non haberet, si duobus tantum consistentibus tertia persona deesset. Non enim hic de qualicumque, sed de summa condilectione loquimur et qualem creatura a Creatore nunquam meretur, nunquam digna invenitur." Gunton refers to this passage in several places: "The Concept of the Person: The One, the Three and the Many," in *The Promise*, 92; "Being and Concept," 175n.2; "God the Holy Spirit," 126–27. For an English translation, see Ruben Angelici, *Richard of Saint Victor on the Trinity: English Translation and Commentary* (Eugene, OR: Cascade, 2001).

> The perfection of the divine love is revealed by the fact that it is neither self-love nor the merely reciprocal love of two for each other, but a love intrinsically oriented to community. The Holy Spirit is then indeed the dynamic of the divine love, but one that seeks to involve the other in the movement of giving and receiving that is the Trinity: that is, *to perfect the love of Father and Son by moving it beyond itself*. Corresponding to the eschatological movement of the Spirit *ad extra* there is within the divine eternity one who perfects the love of God as love in community. To be God is to be intrinsically related to the other in communion, and the Spirit is the one who enables this communion to be.[16]

The Holy Spirit is thus the agent through which God's love is completed, as far as it is *constitutively*—that is, from all eternity—open to what is not God. Hence creation and redemption are nothing but the outward manifestations, in time, of the internal and eternal divine reality. Similarly, the Holy Spirit is *constitutive of God's being itself*, which must be understood as communal love, creating communion because resulting from communion. Contrasting in this regard with Zizioulas, who, faithful to the idea of "monarchy," asserts that the Father is the Trinity's cause, Gunton contends that the Son and the Spirit are also such causes, though differently: the Son is constitutive of God's being insofar as he responds to his begetting by the Father with his obedience and love at work in the incarnation and passion, whereas, by opening the love of the Father and the Son outwardly, the Holy Spirit is constitutive of God's being as God's *being-as-love*.[17] Such a claim is coherent with a more general trinitarian thesis Gunton owes to Zizioulas's reading of the Cappadocian Fathers: giving up Barth's understanding of the three as *modes of being* as well as Rahner's designation of them as *modes of existence* or *subsistence*, Gunton asserts that God's being must be conceived as a communion of *persons* whose relations are such that each person receives its being from the other two, and therefore is (and is itself) only through its relation with the others.[18] Gunton's trinitarian theology comes thus under the so-called perichoretic model, whose aim is to bring down any contradiction between divine unity and Trinity by pointing out that, though no person *is the other*, no person is *without the other*, so that

---

16. Gunton, "God the Holy Spirit," 127.
17. Gunton, "Being and Concept," 165.
18. Gunton, "The Concept of the Person," 96.

the action of the three are fundamentally the same one, although exercised in a specific way.

THE DIVINE ATTRIBUTE OF ALMIGHTINESS AND TRINITARIAN THEOLOGY

Let us now turn to the problem of the divine attributes and the trinitarian resolution Gunton offers. The main question I would like to address is this: To what extent does a trinitarian theology improve a theology of divine attributes? To put it more precisely: To what extent does an account of the three divine persons allow a specifically Christian approach of the attributes problem, from the point of view of the attributive process itself (the process by which it is possible to attribute to God some qualities or perfections) and as far as the content of these predicates is concerned?

It seems to me that Gunton's position can be reduced, for a general characterization, to a thesis expressed in *Act and Being*: "attribute is best understood in terms of action, in God's case the action in which God is who he is."[19] The following lines can be read as a commentary of this statement.

Let us begin with an analysis of the term *attribute*. It is well known that Barth was very doubtful as to the legitimacy of this term, preferring to speak of "perfections" (*Vollkommenheiten*), which is less formal or general and thus more suitable for God.[20] Although Gunton is convinced by the reasons given by Barth to justify such a substitution, he nevertheless continues to use the more traditional term *attribute*. Assuredly, this last term could lead us to consider the process by which we are able to know God (and therefore our own capacities, considered in themselves) rather than God's being itself and the act by which God enables us to know God. However this ("logical") term *attribute* can, according to Gunton, rightfully be used for one reason and on one condition. The reason consists in the fact that it resorts to a common use; the condition is that by "attributes" we mean the proprieties of God's being that *God* has expressed and by which God expresses Godself.[21] (It could perhaps be helpful to distinguish between "attribute" and "perfection," meaning by "attribute" the conceptual or "logical" correspondent of one of God's ways of being, as it is revealed by God.) However that may be, it seems to me that it is possible to speak of Gunton's understanding of "attribute" by using the phrase "God's

---

19. Gunton, *Act and Being*, 108.

20. Karl Barth, *Die kirchliche Dogmatik* II/1, 362 (§29); *CD* II/1 (Edinburgh: T&T Clark, 1957), 322.

21. Gunton, *Act and Being*, 9: ". . . because it accords well with familiar usage, I shall maintain the traditional langage of the attributes, hoping to keep in mind that we are concerned only with what God grants us to attribute to him on the basis of what he has shown us."

perfection in act." If I am not mistaken (but I must confess that I have not read his entire *œuvre*), Gunton does not make use of such a definition. I do, however, think that such a characterization is not unfaithful to his thought, since he calls the power and wisdom of God divine "attributes in action."[22]

This statement leads us to the second part of our commentary: the concept of divine action. We are now tackling Gunton's main thesis about the divine attributes: God's being itself is knowable, but it is only knowable on the basis of God's action in and for the world. This statement supposes another, prior claim: God's cognoscibility. By challenging what he calls "the predominance of the negative," Gunton challenges a traditional chapter of the Christian tradition, namely, the tradition of negative theology. In a certain sense, the reason why the negative tradition fails, according to him, is the same as the reason why Barth is critical of the term *attribute*: it focuses on the human mind's capacities to the detriment of the possibilities that God gives the human by making Godself known. Thus, concerning negative theology and its claim that we can only say what God is not, Gunton contends that "what might appear to be a proper human modesty before the divine can turn into the supreme blasphemy of denying revelation."[23]

To evaluate to what extent Gunton does justice to the apophatic tradition would exceed the scope of this essay; I will instead analyze Gunton's basic affirmation, namely that it is through God's action that God's being is knowable. This statement must be explained in two respects, the first concerning its noetic character, the second its ontic basis. Both are contained *in nuce* in the title of Gunton's book on the divine attributes: *Act and Being*. The precedence of the term *act* refers to the noetic precedence of act over being, that is, to the fact that an account of God's action in and for the world is required to determine God's being. The knowledge of God's being, or the knowledge of the kind of God that God is, or the kind of God that God decided to be, ensues from what God has accomplished for the world and what God continues to accomplish. A biblical "proof" of such a state of affairs can be found (according to Gunton, who follows a major trend in contemporary exegesis) in Exodus 3:14, the classical biblical locus, for both Judaism and Christianity, of God's nomination. Contrary to the contention made by numerous patristic and medieval theologians, Gunton asserts that the revelation of the Name refers neither to "being" abstractly conceived nor to divine aseity understood at the same abstract level. It certainly refers to God's being, but the form itself of

---

22. Ibid., 153.
23. Ibid., 36.

God's self-nomination, and first of all the grammatical form of the future ("I shall be who I shall be"), refers to the fact that God's being will be revealed by what God will do.[24] In this regard, our theologian can without any problem welcome the traditional affirmation according to which we can know God only through God's effects. The fact is, however, that Gunton does not understand such a thesis in a traditional way, as grounding and warranting an exercise in natural theology. For by "effect" he means precisely creation, reconciliation, and redemption—in other words, the divine acts constitutive of the economy.[25]

As far as its noetic aspect is concerned, Gunton's main statement is as follows: only the account of God's creative and redemptive acts allows us to be precise about the way God has decided to be God, that is, the way in which God expresses God's perfection (we, on the other hand, need a plurality of concepts to grasp the various aspects of God's being: God's perfections)—in act. Considering the basis of this affirmation will give us the opportunity to determine the meaning of the conjunction "and" in the title *Act and Being*. The main contention is: the divine actions constitutive of the economy reveal (in a strong sense) God's being, since, when performing such actions, God exercises God's divinity and thus *is* who God is. What God does is grounded in the being God is.[26] And so it would perhaps not be unreasonable to assert that God's economic doing constitutes a modality of God's being. The divine acts are here understood not as imperfect reflections of the divine being (effects infinitely removed from their cause), but as the very *expression* of God's being: in these creating and redemptive works, God expresses Godself *as God*.

The influence of Barth is noticeable here, as well as Eberhard Jüngel's reading of Barth: God is God in coming to the world, and first of all in letting the world come to being. Contrary to Hans Jonas, who, in *The Concept of God after Auschwitz*, sees as the condition of the creation of the world God's self-renunciation to Godself (or at least God's renunciation to some of God's prerogatives), Jüngel contends that God *corresponds* to Godself in creating.[27] And in his polemical book on justification, Jüngel asserts that the act

24. Ibid., 10–11.

25. Ibid., 112.

26. Ibid., 97: "That is the order of knowing: we know God (by his ostensive self-definition) from and in his acts. We know *who* God is from what he does. The other aspect of our response to the same divine self-presentation in time is that the order of being grounds the order of knowing, so that what God does in time is shown to be a function of what he is in eternity."

27. Hans Jonas, *Der Gottesbegriff nach Auschwitz. Eine jüdische Stimme* (Berlin: Suhrkamp, 1987), 15–17; Eng. trans.: "The Concept of God after Auschwitz: A Jewish Voice," *The Journal of Religion* 67 (1987): 4–5. See Eberhard Jüngel, "Gottes ursprüngliches Anfangen als schöpferische Selbstbegrenzung. Ein

of justification is nothing but the expression, in act, of God's justice.[28] What is the case for justice is also the case for the other divine attributes, and in this respect Gunton's reading of Jüngel is consonant with the doctrine developed in *Act and Being*: the divine acts constitutive of the economy give access to God's attributes, since the "attributes" (as we call them) are nothing but God's perfections *in act*, that is, God's perfection as *realized* in the economy.[29] Jüngel unfolds this thesis in a trinitarian way. The same is true of Gunton, but with the specific accents of his own trinitarian theology. Its most general formulation runs like this:

> In sum God's being is known in and through his action, his triune act. God's action is triune in the sense that it is the action of Father, Son and Spirit, whose *opera ad extra* are inseparable from one another, though they are distributed, so to speak, between the three persons: the Father being the originating source of action, which he performs through the Son's involvement in the created world and the Spirit's perfecting of created things in anticipation of and on the Last Day.[30]

To see what is at stake in such a thesis and its main consequences, I will consider one divine attribute in particular: God's almightiness.

Following Christoph Schwöbel, Gunton distinguishes between the two kinds of attributes classically considered by the Christian theological tradition: the attributes we might call "personal," since the concepts that correspond to them are elaborated from an account of God as personal agent (mercy, justice, fidelity, etc.), and the predicates that traditionally ensue from a more "metaphysical" consideration of God's being (the negative attributes such as infinity, impassibility, or immutability, etc., and the attributes we might call "absolute," like aseity, omniscience, and almightiness).[31] Like Barth and Jüngel,

---

Beitrag zum Gespräch mit Hans Jonas über den 'Gottesbegriff nach Auschwitz'" (1986), in *Wertlose Wahrheit. Zur Identität und Relevanz des christlichen Glaubens. Theologische Erörterungen III* (Tübingen: Mohr Siebeck, 2003), 154.

28. Eberhard Jüngel, *Das Evangelium von der Rechtfertigung des Gottlosen als Zentrum des christlichen Glaubens. Eine theologische Studie in ökumenischer Absicht* (Tübingen: Mohr Siebeck, 1998), 63–64; Eng. trans.: *Justification—The Heart of the Christian Faith: A Theological Study with an Ecumenical Purpose*, trans. Jeffrey F. Cayzer (London: T&T Clark, 2001), 75–77.

29. Colin Gunton, "The Being and Attributes of God: Eberhard Jüngel's Dispute with the Classical Philosophical Tradition," in *Theology Through the Theologians*, 85.

30. Gunton, *Act and Being*, 113.

31. Christoph Schwöbel, *God: Action and Revelation* (Kampen: Kok Pharos, 1992); Gunton, "The Being and Attributes of God," 71–72; idem, *Act and Being*, 21–22.

Gunton does not want to relinquish attributes such as impassibility and almightiness; what he rejects are not the "metaphysical" attributes as such, but the classical metaphysical process by which these concepts are elaborated. Here the way in which Jüngel treats almightiness is emblematic and seems to guide Gunton's approach. Assuredly, like Barth, the German theologian rises up against any conception of almightiness that would reduce it to an abstract lordship (an arbitrary power without any limit except the limit constituted by the principle of noncontradiction): such a conception would be an abstraction, in that it would disregard the precise way God has chosen to exercise God's lordship, a way that has been revealed on the cross.[32] According to Jüngel, conceiving almightiness as *potentia Dei absoluta* fails more precisely in that it leads to a concept elaborated by leaving aside the concept of love which corresponds to the way God *is* God.[33] I shall not enter here in details, wondering, for instance, if Jüngel does perfect justice to the way the theologians of the past, especially the Middle Ages, conceived God's almightiness. More important is Jüngel's reasoning: it does not consist in keeping only the biblical predicates, such as love, while giving up the so-called metaphysical ones, such as almightiness, but, like Barth, Jüngel reflects on the former in the light of the latter.[34] Only such an approach is able to avoid a "metaphysical" conception of attributes such as almightiness. Referring to Jüngel, Gunton writes: "Thus the traditional attributes of self-determination, omnipotence and transcendence are now construed on the basis of a theology of gracious personal action rather than on metaphysical necessity, and are accordingly transformed in their meaning."[35] This is also the case in Gunton's own theology: far from having to negate that God is almighty, one must consider *to what extent* God can receive such an attribute, and *why* it is necessary to attribute to God this predicate if one does not want to give up thinking about God as such.

I begin with the second question: Why ought we continue to say that God is almighty? Since Gunton, like Jüngel, relates God's almightiness to God's love, he sees God's power as the very condition of God's exercise of love. Gunton defines indeed, in general terms, God's almightiness as "the guarantee

---

32. Eberhard Jüngel, *Gott als Geheimnis der Welt. Zur Begründung der Theologie des Gekreuzigten im Streit zwischen Theismus und Atheismus* (Tübingen: Mohr Siebeck, 1977, 2010), 26–27; Eng. trans.: *God as the Mystery of the World: On the Foundation of the Theology of the Crucified One in the Dispute between Theism and Atheism*, trans. Darrell L. Guder (Edinburgh: T&T Clark, 1983), 21–22.

33. Jüngel, *Gott als Geheimnis*, 432; *God as the Mystery*, 316.

34. Gunton, *Act and Being*, 100.

35. Gunton, "The Being and the Attributes", 81.

that what God began in creation he will complete."[36] As far as creation is concerned, almightiness appears thus as the condition, for the communion of love which God is, to posit into being an otherness to which, as we have seen at the beginning of this paper, the Trinity is originally open. But almightiness is also the condition for everything that is not God (and even the godless) to be integrated in God's communion. If it is necessary to acknowledge Jüngel's position, according to which any almightiness conceived without reference to love would not be convenient to God, it is also necessary to add that any love which would not be all-powerful would not be God's love, since it would lack the conditions of God's creative and redemptive character—the very conditions of its effectiveness.

To what extent, then, is God almighty? No wonder that, in Gunton's thought, the content of the concept of almightiness ensues from the consideration of the triune actions of God, and especially the activity proper to each person of the Trinity in the Easter event. It is here, indeed, that God's power *is* at work, and that, in the eyes of faith, it is *seen* in act.[37] It essentially appears as the Father's redemptive action as it is mediated by the proper activity of the two other persons. The Son's proper act reveals the *form* and *content* of the Father's redemptive work. The form of this *action* seems at the first glance paradoxical, since it appears as a *passion*: the cross is the theater of the Son's suffering and subjection to the annihilating powers. Nevertheless, Christ's passion is not the opposite of the Father's almighty action, but the condition of its very exercise: it manifests that the redemptive action consists in God's actual encounter with the annihilating powers, an encounter that is realized in the Son and in full communion with the Father's redemptive project. Against any staurology which, like Moltmann's, sees in the event of the cross the *locus* of the separation between Father and Son, Gunton discerns in it, on the contrary, the expression of their real fellowship, since the suffering of the Son, *incarnandus* from all eternity, is nothing but the form of his assent to the redemptive project, a project whose aim is to overcome evil, sin, and death, not by annihilating them as it were from outside, but by assuming them in order to liberate creation of them.[38] God is almighty in that God is able to enter—and actually enters—nothingness without being annihilated by it. The Holy Spirit's proper

---

36. Gunton, *Act and Being*, 133.

37. I summarize this in ibid., 125–32.

38. See ibid., 126–27: ". . . the cross is the passion of the Son, but *as such* and in complete unity with the omnipotent redemptive action of the Father. It is, to use Paul's characterization, the power and wisdom of God. It is the power of God in action because it is the means by which God meets evil on its own ground and defeats it without using its methods; it is divine wisdom in action because it is the only

action consists in perfecting the work accomplished by the Son, and first of all to make it possible. It is thanks to the Spirit's activity that the *man* of Nazareth becomes "obedient to the point of death" (Phil. 2:8), thus corresponding actually to the Son of God he is, that is, the one who has been destined to take flesh and to meet human beings, who are sinners, in the depth of their condition. It is also thanks to the Spirit that Jesus' suffering has a redemptive value, since what has been realized in the Son—his resurrection from the death, due to the activity of the Spirit, according to Gunton—is nothing but the anticipation of the completion of creation, which will also ensue from the Spirit's work. God is almighty since the Son's triumph over the negative powers has an eschatological character and constitutes the prolepsis of their complete defeat to come.[39]

CONCLUSION

Perhaps one should go further than Gunton and develop in a more detailed way a theology of the divine attributes, in particular of God's almightiness. As far as the economy is concerned, one could, for example, assert that, if God can enter evil, sin, and death without being annihilated by them, God's almightiness consists precisely in the fact that from now on evil, sin, and death have been deprived of any separating power: God is almighty not only because God has annihilated their power in God's Son or because their complete annihilation will occur when God will be all in all, but also because, even if evil, sin, and death have not yet been annihilated, their separating power already has been. And as far as God's being is concerned, perhaps one could relate God's almightiness and the immanent Trinity in such a way that we could discern the condition of God's power in the very relationships the persons of the Trinity have one with the others: are not the persons linked together in such a way that not even the Son's entering into death and sin is able to break these relationships? The fact remains, nevertheless, that Gunton intended to further develop his theology of the divine attributes,[40] an aim his untimely death unfortunately impeded.

The fact remains also that, if he did not have time to develop a full treatise of God's attributes, Gunton nevertheless offered something like prolegomena, some fundamental insights helping us to get out of the trouble in which the contemporary discourse about God's almightiness finds itself. As is well known,

exercise of power that is proportionate to the need and condition of the sinner and successful in bringing about its end."

39. Ibid., 130: "The Spirit is the one who enables Jesus' suffering to be redemptive, to make it of *eschatological* significance, and therefore truly the Father's sovereign action. That is to say, the suffering of the Son on the cross takes place only for the sake of the eschatological defeat of suffering."

40. Ibid., vii.

a major trend—in francophone Christian theology, at least—speaks in favor of giving up this attribute. Many reasons are alleged to justify such a position. However, it seems to me that these reasons can be reduced to these two: (1) the understanding of almightiness as the divine capacity to intervene in history in order to rectify it; and (2) the inscription of the discourse about almightiness in the problematic of evil, and even in a theodicy. These premises lead naturally to a conclusion: if by "almightiness" one means God's capacity to prevent evil from happening, since evil's proliferation is a fact, it is therefore impossible to continue to speak about an almighty God. But such a conclusion is not necessary if one thinks that the original *locus* for the discourse about God's power is not theodicy but trinitarian theology. A trinitarian understanding of the Easter event allows us, indeed, to assert that the victory over sin and evil is a victory over their separating power. The nucleus of such a specific Christian understanding of God's almightiness lies in the Pauline affirmation according to which "neither death nor life, nor angels nor rulers, nor things present nor things to come, nor powers, nor height nor depth, nor anything else in all creation, will be able to separate us from the love of God in Christ Jesus our Lord" (Rom. 8:38-39). Undoubtedly, such a concept of almightiness differs from the concept of a pure capacity, adopted since the end of the Middle Ages, and which consists, according to recent historians, in an oblivion of the biblical and patristic notion of *pantocratoria*.[41] And, assuredly, such a concept leaves open the question of evil. Perhaps the confession of God's almightiness will necessarily have an aporetic dimension, since its exercise in the present (of) history remains problematic.[42] The fact is, nevertheless, that a trinitarian approach of God, here only sketched, allows us to reopen this question.

---

41. Jean-Pierre Batut, *Pantocrator. 'Dieu le Père tout-puissant' dans la théologie prénicéenne* (Paris: Institut d'Études Augustiniennes, 2009).

42. See Eberhard Jüngel, "'Meine Theologie'—kurz gefasst" (1985), in *Wertlose Wahrheit*, 14; Eng. trans.: "'My Theology'—A Short Summary," in idem, *Theological Essays II*, trans. Arnold Neufeldt-Fast and John B. Webster (Edinburgh: T&T Clark, 1995), 18.

6

God's "Liveliness" in Robert W. Jenson's Trinitarian Thought

Christophe Chalamet

ROBERT W. JENSON AND THEOLOGICAL EXISTENCE

Robert W. Jenson is a major figure in anglophone contemporary theology. Whether one agrees with him or not, ignoring him is not an option. Born in 1930 in Eau Claire, Wisconsin, to a Lutheran family, he embarked on the study of theology at Luther College, in Decorah, Iowa, in 1947, before going to Luther Seminary in 1951, returning to Luther College in 1955 as an instructor in religion and philosophy (1955–1957). He then traveled to the University of Heidelberg in order to pursue his studies at the doctoral level. Mentored by Peter Brunner, Jenson studied Karl Barth's doctrine of election and became acquainted with a young *Privatdozent* named Wolfhart Pannenberg. "My agreement with Pannenberg dates from then and is fundamental," Jenson wrote in 2007.[1] Another important collaboration began in Heidelberg, with Carl Braaten, with whom he would eventually publish an ecumenical journal and many edited volumes. Members of the jury for his doctoral examinations were the distinguished scholars Edmund Schlink, Gerhard von Rad, Hans von Campenhausen, and Günter Bornkamm.[2] Thanks to Bornkamm, Jenson took part in a daylong seminar given by Martin Heidegger. Several years later he joined a study group with Hans-Georg Gadamer. Upon the completion of his doctoral degree in 1959, having successfully submitted his dissertation, which he had written in part in Basel,

---

1. Robert W. Jenson, "A Theological Autobiography, To Date," *Dialog* 46, no. 1 (2007): 46–54, at 49. I rely in great part on this article for this biographical section.

2. Ibid., 49.

and which had received the stamp of approval from Barth himself, Jenson returned to the United States. His dissertation was published in 1963.[3]

From the early 1960s on, he taught at Luther College, where some of his colleagues sought to get rid of him because of what they took to be liberal views on historical-critical methods of exegesis and on evolution. He did not share their fear of such approaches. When it turned out Jenson would retain his position, several colleagues from the religion and biology departments resigned *en bloc*. After several years at the University of Oxford (1966–1968), where he discovered Anglicanism, Jenson began teaching at the Lutheran Theological Seminary in Gettysburg, Pennsylvania. In 1968, he became involved in the bilateral official dialogue between Lutherans and Episcopalians and then, a bit later, the dialogue between Lutherans and Roman Catholics (George Lindbeck was part of this, too). Twenty years later, in 1988, returning from a year at the Center for Ecumenical Studies in Strasbourg, Jenson continued his teaching career at St. Olaf College, in Northfield, Minnesota. He founded *Pro Ecclesia*, a theological journal with an ecumenical vision, and eventually began to work on his *Systematic Theology*, which appeared in two volumes, in 1997 and 1999.[4] In 1998, after ten years at St. Olaf, he was about to retire from teaching when Wallace Alston, the director of the Center of Theological Inquiry (CTI) on the grounds of Princeton Theological Seminary, invited him to join the CTI. Jenson accepted and became "Senior Scholar of Research," a position he kept for seven years, advising resident scholars at the Center.

There is no doubt that Jenson has contributed (and continues to contribute!) to the trinitarian renewal of the past decades in the anglophone world. In what follows I seek to present and evaluate certain aspects of his thought that seem particularly decisive in his overall theology. Much more could be said of Jenson's trinitarian theology; indeed, his entire theology is centered on God's trinitarian life.[5]

3. Robert W. Jenson, *Alpha and Omega: A Study in the Theology of Karl Barth* (New York: Thomas Nelson, 1963).

4. Robert W. Jenson, *Systematic Theology*, vol. 1: *The Triune God* (New York: Oxford University Press, 1997); vol. 2: *The Works of God* (New York: Oxford University Press, 1999). Hereafter *ST* I and *ST* II.

5. I was unable to read Timo Tavast's dissertation, titled *Ajassa identifioituva Jumala: Robert W. Jensonin Triniteettioppi* ("God who Identifies Godself in Time: Robert W. Jenson's Trinitarian Doctrine," University of Joensuu [Finland], 2006). But one may read, from the same author, "The Identification of the Triune God: Robert W. Jenson's Approach to the Doctrine of the Trinity," in *Dialog: A Journal of Theology* 51, no. 2 (2012): 155–63; and "Challenging the Modalism of the West: Jenson on the Trinity," *Pro Ecclesia* 19, no. 4 (2010): 355–68.

The first volume of Jenson's *Systematic Theology* is divided into three main sections: after the "prolegomena," one finds a part on the triune "identity" and another on the triune "character." What does Jenson do in these three sections? One way to answer that question could be the following: Jenson seeks to speak of God's "liveliness."[6] Jenson fights what he takes to be two grave errors: first, the idea that there is the trinitarian God and, behind that God, the "One" God or simply "the One." His other intent is to destroy any static understanding of God. Here, the role of the Holy Spirit is crucial. Let us take a closer look at these two sets of claims.

THE TRIUNE GOD AND THE "ONE"

Jenson often writes that God is one being in three identities who share a history. God is not a reality beyond the history of these three identities. God is personal, through and through. Human language about God is not simply anthropomorphic and therefore inadequate. Here is the identity of God as witnessed by Scripture: a personal being in three distinct identities. Following several major figures in twentieth-century theology, especially Barth and Rahner, Jenson prefers not to talk of three "persons." It is better to speak of three "identities" (*ST* I:106). But that does not mean God is not "personal." Here is a key claim, and one that signals a departure with regard to Pannenberg, who has distanced himself from personalist language in his own doctrine of God (*ST* I:117).

Theology, in (late) modernity even more than before, cannot presume that its interlocutors have much acquaintance with God-talk. It is therefore problematic to think that theology should focus on the *beneficia*, according to Jenson. There lies an error shared by Bultmann and certain liberal theologies of

---

6. David Bentley Hart has briefly touched upon this aspect of Jenson's theology in "The Lively God of Robert Jenson," in *First Things* 156 (October 2005): 28–34; available at http://www.firstthings.com/article/2007/01/the-lively-god-of-robert-jenson-4. These pages are much more relevant to the theme of the present paper than Hart's treatment (in the various senses of the term) of Jenson in *The Beauty of the Infinite: The Aesthetics of the Christian Truth* (Grand Rapids: Eerdmans, 2003), 160–66, in which Hart focuses on the way Jenson interprets and appropriates Rahner's axiom on the immanent and the economic Trinity. According to Hart, Jenson "is simply one of the most provocative, ingenious, and formidable proponents of a certain kind of Trinitarianism writing today," and his work is "enormously important" ("The Lively God"). Hart's disagreement with Jenson, which is about as deep as his admiration, has to do with Jenson's proximity with Rahner's axiom, and also with Jenson's rejection of the doctrine of the *logos asarkos* and of traditional understandings of divine impassibility and immutability.

the nineteenth and twentieth centuries, which rely on the well-known sentence from the first edition of Philip Melanchthon's *Loci communes*.[7]

The question of God's being and God's identity thus comes to the fore. But, once again, it would not be sound to subordinate that question of God's identity as triune under the questions of being or the reality of "the One." That is precisely Augustine's severe "misstep" (*ST* I:113), under the influence of Platonism: a God who is metaphysically "simple," in whom no real difference but also no real movement can exist or take place (*ST* I:111–13; *ST* II:301).

But does not the idea of a "monarchy" of the Father contribute to the same problem, ultimately, since it posits the Father which by himself constitutes deity, "and so again excluding the Son and the Spirit from full deity" (*ST* I:116)? Jenson prefers to speak of a "mutuality" between the three divine identities, rather than using the term *monarchy*. His affinity with the Cappadocians is clear, when he suggests that there is no divinity above or beyond the triune God. And yet he is reluctant to envision a monarchy of the Father, because of the risk of a return of a sort of simple monad, a "One" beyond God the Father, Son, and Spirit. There is no pure essence beyond the triune identity, nor any divine being above divine action. Such claims seem vital to me, in trinitarian discourse.

God Is and Has a History

The other aspect Jenson particularly—and rightly—emphasizes is what he calls God's "liveliness." One may wonder whether Jenson does it in the best way. But let us begin by listening to what Jenson says.

Jenson is very vehement in his critique of the theological tradition, alive and well today as it was yesterday, which conceives of God as "immutable," "immobile," whose past is in no way different from God's future, of a God who is cut off from any temporality, and who is thus simply and purely a-temporal.[8]

---

7. "Philip Melanchthon's maxim, that to know God is to know his benefits, can hold only where the *identity* of the God to be known is antecedently secure. In modern context, it is plainly false and has been a disaster for the church." Jenson, *ST* I:51n.68. Here is Melanchthon's sentence: "Nam ex his proprie Christus cognoscitur, siquidem hoc est Christum cognoscere beneficia eius cognoscere, non, quod isti docent, eius naturas, modos incarnationis contueri." *Melanchthon's Werke* II/1, ed. Hans Engelland and Robert Stupperich (Gütersloh: Mohn, 1978), 20.

8. ". . . the biblical God's eternity is not the simple contradiction of time. What he transcends is not the having of beginnings and goals and reconciliations, but any personal limitations in having them" (*ST* I:217). Atemporality means the end of the divine vitality (*ST* II:301). Karl Barth already wrote this: "Even the eternal *God* does not live without time. He is supremely temporal. For his eternity is authentic temporality, and therefore the source of all time". *Church Dogmatics* III/2, trans. Geoffrey Bromiley (Edinburgh: T&T Clark, 1960), 437. "His immutability is not a holy immobility and rigidity, a divine

God's eternity, in the scriptural witness, far from simply contradicting temporality, represents God's "temporal infinity" (*ST* I:217).[9] To be sure, divine temporality is radically different from ours since it transcends "distension" or temporal "succession."

One of Jensons's main targets here is Vladimir Lossky, from whom God's reality is "alien to all becoming, all process, all beginning."[10] Where does this understanding of God, which Jenson calls an "aberration" (*ST* I:152), come from? Certainly not from the biblical narrative. This is a theological "disaster," writes Jenson, for God is here "frozen" (*ST* I:152). It relies on a Greek interpretation of "being," where "to be is to remain as one began" or "to persist" (*ST* I:159). Aristotle's and Plato's God is the God of "stillness," whereas, for Jenson, "[t]o be God is always to be open to and always to open a future, transgressing all past-imposed conditions."[11] God's identity is a "way."[12]

The event par excellence that signals newness in God and for God is Jesus' resurrection: ". . . the events in Jerusalem and on Golgotha are themselves inner-triune events . . ." (*ST* I:191). Such a sentence is yet another testimony to the influence of Hegel on several major Western theologians in the 1960s and 1970s (Pannenberg, Jüngel, and Moltmann) who developed their theologies in more or less critical dialogue with Barth. The surprising thing about Jenson's theology is that, for a theologian who is so interested in God who is not "frozen," who is history, one finds very little engagement with the works of

death, but the constancy of His faithfulness to Himself continually reaffirming itself in freedom" (*Church Dogmatics* IV/1, 561).

9. See Jenson, *Alpha and Omega*, 61: "According to Barth, God is not timeless but rather the Lord of time. The time which He has in His eternal aliveness is the possibility and model of created time." Or: "He is not timeless in the sense that He is bereft of time. He *has* time" (ibid., 74). Wolfhart Pannenberg welcomes the expression "temporal infinity," but qualifies it in the following way: ". . . it is not enough to say that 'God's deity is temporal infinity. . . . His deity not only is continuing without end but also means wholeness of life." Pannenberg, "Eternity, Time, and the Trinitarian God," in Colin E. Gunton, ed., *Trinity, Time, and Church: A Response to the Theology of Robert W. Jenson* (Grand Rapids: Eerdmans, 2000), 64.

10. *ST* I:152. Jenson quotes Vladimir Lossky, *À l'image et à la ressemblance de Dieu* (Paris: Aubier-Montaigne, 1967), 78; Eng. trans.: *In the Image and Likeness of God*, ed. John H. Erickson and Thomas E. Bird (Crestwood, NY: Saint Vladimir's Seminary Press, 1974, 2001).

11. See also II:146, where Jenson mentions the "perhaps only two possible deities": "the gods whose transcendence is the fixity of the past and the security we seek in it and the God whose transcendence is the unmanageability of his futurity."

12. See the title of ch. 4 of *Systematic Theology*, vol. 1: "The Way of God's Identity" (63–74). David B. Hart says it well (see above, n. 6): "Jenson's central claim is that God is the event of what happens between the Father and Jesus, as enabled by and lifted up in the Spirit."

Eberhard Jüngel, whose powerful little book on "God's being in becoming" would represent, one would think, an indispensable dialogue partner, especially coming from someone like Jenson for whom, like Jüngel, Barth had so deep an impact. But one looks in vain, in Jenson's two volumes of his *Systematic Theology*, for any reference to Jüngel's creative "paraphrase" of Barth, even though Jüngel, right from the first pages of his book, writes about the *Lebendigkeit Gottes*, which he conceives as a trinitarian *Lebendigkeit*. Right from the first paragraph, Jüngel wishes to avoid a possible misunderstanding of the title of the book, which is not about a "God who becomes" (a "werdenden Gott") but about God "whose being is in becoming" ("der Gott, dessen Sein im Werden ist").[13] God is not on God's way to being God, God is not "realizing" or fully actualizing God's being over time. But God's being "has its ontological place in becoming."[14] There is no part of God's being that is not historical. For Jüngel, the claim that God's being is in becoming seeks to think about God in a "consistent historical" way.[15]

There is "event" in God. The central event, for Jenson, is the resurrection (much more than the incarnation, as in Schleiermacher, or the cross, as in many Lutherans, including Jüngel). "The great occurrence of dramatic causality is the Resurrection. That the Son once slain would rise is, after the fact, an eternal certainty, but it was not beforehand, and also not for God" (*ST* I:160). The resurrection represents a disruption not only for human beings, but for God as well. It is new for God, too. It is a contingent event that eternally determines who Jesus is, as well as the triune identity of God.[16] In Jenson's trinitarian

13. Eberhard Jüngel, *Gottes Sein ist im Werden. Verantwortliche Rede vom Sein Gottes bei Karl Barth. Eine Paraphrase* (Tübingen, Mohr, 1966), iii ("Lebendigkeit Gottes"; "Vom 'werdenden Gott' ist *nicht* die Rede") and iv ("in Trinitarischer Lebendigkeit"); Eng. trans.: *God's Being Is in Becoming: The Trinitarian Being of God in the Theology of Karl Barth; A Paraphrase*, trans. John Webster (Edinburgh: T&T Clark, 2001). Jenson shares with Jüngel (it is a Barthian legacy) a fascinating critique of apophaticism (see Marc Vial's essay in the present volume for a similar intention in Gunton's theology) as well as a "dynamic" understanding of God's being. But Jenson is a very different kind of Lutheran theologian than Jüngel. Jenson is deeply committed to ecumenical theology, to the catholicity of Christian theology, whereas Jüngel is more focused on his Lutheran tradition, read through Barthian lenses (and vice versa: Barth read and corrected from a Lutheran standpoint, as can be seen esp. in Jüngel's recent monograph on justification, *Das Evangelium von der Rechtfertigung des Gottlosen als Zentrum des christlichen Glaubens. Eine theologische Studie in ökumenischer Absicht* (Tübingen: Mohr Siebeck, 1998, 1999); Eng. trans.: *Justification—The Heart of the Christian Faith: A Theological Study with an Ecumenical Purpose*, trans. Jeffrey Cayzer (Edinburgh: T&T Clark, 2001).

14. *Gottes Sein ist im Werden*, 92; *God's Being Is in Becoming*, 94.

15. *Gottes Sein ist im Werden*, 106 (". . . Gottes Sein konsequent geschichtlich zu denken"); *God's Being Is in Becoming*, 107 (". . . thinking of God's being in a thoroughly historical way").

theology, the Spirit makes "all things new" (Rev. 21:5), not only on earth but also in and for God. Jenson has taken great care not to follow Barth's somewhat limited account of the Holy Spirit. One does not wonder "where the Spirit went" in Jenson's mature work.[17]

THE SPIRIT AS SOURCE OF DIVINE "VITALITY"

God's "liveliness" is intimately related, in Jenson's thought, to the action of the Holy Spirit. But how does the Spirit "vitalize" God? In three distinct ways, it seems to me:

1. First, insofar as the Spirit "*is* the End of all God's ways."[18] Pannenberg's shadow is especially obvious when Jenson writes: "The Spirit is the Liveliness of the divine life because he is the Power of the divine future. . . . He is the Love into which all things at the last be brought, who is thus the fulfillment not only of created life but of the divine life" (*ST* I:157). "The Spirit . . . is in himself the perfection, the liveliness, of the divine life" (*ST* I:159). The Spirit's "being" is itself "anticipation" of God's telos (*ST* I:191).

2. Second, the Spirit "links" the Father and the Son in the midst of the Father's abandonment of the Son at Golgotha. Jenson rejects what he detects in Augustine's and Barth's theologies, namely, at the end of the day, a sort of "I-Thou Trinity," which is closer to a bi-nity than a Trinity. The Spirit in the Augustinian tradition is too often conceived as the relation itself between two persons, and not as a real *partner* in that communion (*ST* I:155). And yet Jenson uses the terminology of the *vinculum* ("link") when he reflects on the abandoning of the crucified: the Spirit is "the bond of triune love also in abandonment."[19]

---

16. Tavast, "Challenging the Modalism of the West," 362.

17. Robert W. Jenson, "You Wonder Where the Spirit Went," *Pro Ecclesia* 2 (1993): 296–304.

18. "Of course we have already many times noted and said where in fact the Spirit stands: at the end of God's ways because he *is* the End of all God's ways" (*ST* I:157). Jenson also writes about the Spirit as the "goal" of God's ways (*ST* I:161).

19. ". . . the Spirit who will raise Jesus had come in advance . . . and 'rested' on him from the moment of his dedication to this death, to be the bond of triune love also in abandonment" (*ST* I:191).

3. As we saw above, the Spirit enlivens the divine life and brings it to its perfection. But not only to its goal! Since his first book, *Alpha and Omega*, Jenson, in Barth's footsteps, has sought to embrace divine temporality in all its breadth, keeping together the origin and the end as well as everything in between. The Spirit anticipates the ends of God's ways, as we saw, but the Spirit also "frees" the Father and the Son, so that they love each other. The event, or the living communion, which God's being is, begins with the liberation of which the Spirit is the subject and the Father and Son its objects. Jenson thus proposes a sort of story of the Father and the Son's liberation by the Spirit toward love. Jenson offers numerous variations on the theme of the freeing of the Father and the Son by the Spirit.[20] Now, this is a very strange kind of liberation theology—a liberation of God through the Spirit, through which the Father becomes "paternal" by engendering the Son. The Spirit seems to be triggering something within the Father, who then becomes who he is, namely the Father of the Son, the Father from which the Spirit proceeds. If one wonders how the Spirit can be simultaneously the source of the Father's paternity and the outcome of a procession which originates in the Father, Jenson replies that "the Spirit so proceeds from the Father as himself to be the possibility of such processions, his own and the Son's" (*ST* I:158).[21] The Spirit effects

---

20. "He [the Spirit] is another who in his own intention liberates the Father and the Son to love each other" (*ST* I:156). ". . . the Spirit liberates God the Father from himself, to be in fact fatherly, to be the actual *arche* of deity. . . . the Spirit liberates the Father for the Son and the Son from and for the Father; the Son is begotten and liberated, and so reconciles the Father with the future his Spirit is. . . . The Spirit is the one who liberates the Father and Son for each other, and whose liberation is the gift of himself" (*ST* I:161). "The Spirit is *Spiritus Creator* as he frees the Father from retaining all being with himself, and so frees what the Father initiates from being the mere emanation it would have been were the Father God by himself" (*ST* II:26). David Bentley Hart ("The Lively God") regards this way of talking about the Spirit as a "rather daring formulation." I share that reaction.

21. In his interpretation of the *filioque*, Jenson, who seeks a *via media* between Oriental and Latin theologies, relies in part on Palamas: "The Spirit does not derive his being from the Son, but does derive his energy from the Son. . . . it is Christ who gives the Spirit to Israel and the church, that very Spirit who does *not* derive his being otherwise than from the Father . . ." (*ST* I:159). This seems to me to be quite close to the Eastern position, in that the Spirit derives from the Father alone with regard to *theologia* (God's immanent being), while deriving from the Father and the Son with regard to *oikonomia* (God's act *ad extra*). And yet Jenson defends the *filioque* a few pages earlier, following Barth's main argument, namely that there is no gap between the immanent and the economic Trinity, that what is true *ad extra* is already true *ad intra*: "The *filioque* reads this giving into God himself, and just therefore must be

something both prior and subsequently, apparently, to what is a double proceeding rather than an engendering *and* a proceeding.

Before I turn to an analysis and evaluation of these claims, I wish to note that Jenson refers to John Zizioulas, who had already written about the work of Spirit as a liberating work. If the specificity of the Son has to do with the fact that he becomes history by assuming human flesh, the Spirit's work resides in the liberation of the Son and the divine economy of any servitude to history: God's work in Jesus is not confined to the past.[22] As can be seen, the difference between Jenson and Zizioulas on this matter has to do with the object of the Spirit's liberating work: for Jenson, it is mainly the Father who is liberated (sometimes it is both the Father and the Son); for Zizioulas, it is the Son, in relation to history.

EVALUATION

What can we make of all that? Is it sound and profitable (to use Calvin's favored term) in Christian theology to seek to understand how God "becomes" triune? The theological tradition has often believed it is, even if it has not been able to say much beyond the distinction between "engendering" and "proceeding." I am not convinced of the necessity to reflect on the way God "becomes" triune. The debate, these past thirteen years or so, among a number of Barth's anglophone readers, over the question of the (logical, not chronological) priority of God's decision in relation to God's triune being, has shown at least one thing, namely that those who are animated by good intentions and who wish to rid theology of speculation (defined here as God-talk that abstracts from Jesus Christ) do not necessarily reach their goal: speculation returns through the back door.[23]

---

maintained. . . . For it is the very function of Trinitarian propositions to say that the relations that appear in the biblical narrative between Father, Son, and Spirit are the truth about God himself" (*ST* I:150). Barth states his rule in this way: ". . . we have consistently followed the rule, which we regard as basic, that statements about the divine modes of being 'antecedently in themselves' cannot be different in content from those that are to be made about their reality in revelation." *Church Dogmatics* I/1 (1932), 479; *Kirchliche Dogmatik* I/1, 503. It seems possible to view such a claim as a precursor of Rahner's axiom.

22. John Zizioulas, *Being as Communion: Studies in Personhood and the Church* (Crestwood, NY: St. Vladimir's Seminary Press, 1985), 130. Jenson draws on Zizioulas when he writes: ". . . had there been no Pentecost, had Jesus risen into the eschatological future while we were simply left behind, he would still be for us an item of mere memory, imprisoned in history. That it is not so is the church-founding work of the Spirit . . ." (*ST* II:181).

23. On this debate among readers of Barth, see Michael T. Dempsey, ed., *Trinity and Election in Contemporary Theology* (Grand Rapids: Eerdmans, 2011).

Without falling into the traps of a narrow biblicism, as if systematic or constructive theology was simply supposed to restate the content of the Scriptures and avoid any nonbiblical category, should we not raise the question of the relation between Jenson's proposal on the Father's (and the Son's) liberation by the Spirit, on the one hand, and, on the other hand, the liberation, in the biblical narrative, of a particular people from bondage, the liberation from the bondages of sin and death, in two stories of a victory of life over death? Despite Jenson's intention to correlate God's being to these two liberating events, which stand at the center of the two Testaments, it seems to me that he deviates too much from this story of liberation in *our* human history. I applaud Jenson's interest in the "liveliness" of God, against any "petrification" of God that obfuscates God's life, but I remain unconvinced by his talk of the Spirit's liberating work with regard to the Father (and the Son). Gunton's talk of a "perfecting" of the divine love by the Spirit is much more adequate, it seems to me.[24]

Perhaps, despite his best intention, here and there Jenson has a tendency to focus on the divine identity to the point where God's act *ad extra* seems to fade away. His way of organizing his *Systematic Theology* in two parts, the first volume on the triune God, the second on the works of God *ad extra*, signals a problem.[25] Certainly, one can't say everything simultaneously. But is it not the case that God's works *ad extra* are fully thematized too late? Jenson is critical of the third- and fourth-century Fathers who limited the interpretation of the Logos to protology, but is it not the case that Jenson ends up speculating on how the triune God came to be triune?[26]

What should we think of the implication, in Jenson's trinitarian theology, that the Father has no vitality except through the Spirit? The Father, not the Spirit, is *fons divinitatis* in this theology. But the Spirit seems to be the *fons vitae* of the divine triad, as if the Father were inanimate without the Spirit. And so

24. See, in the present volume, Marc Vial's contribution (ch. 5, above).

25. See above, n. 4. Jenson is aware of the problem, when he writes: "It must be admitted that the distinction between these matters and those chosen to be covered in volume 1 is at some points tenuous . . ." (*ST* II:v). Tavast rightly summarizes an important aspect of Jenson's thought: "The economic Trinity is not only economic or part of our history, but first and foremost the economy of salvation is part of the Triune God's own history which constitutes God's immanent life as the real Trinitarian God" (Tavast, "Challenging the Modalism of the West," 358). If Tavast is correct in his description of Jenson's thought, shouldn't then "the economy of salvation" be fully integrated in this history of the triune God *right from the start* (rather than in a second volume)?

26. *ST* I:108.

the Spirit seems to have a "quality" that is wholly other from the Father and the Son, as if the Spirit were the (only?) living and vivifying reality in God.

Whoever speaks of "liberation" means liberation "by" something, "from" and "for" something. One sees why the Spirit is liberating the Father: the Father is freed to engender the Son. But "from" what is the Father liberated or in need of liberation? One finds the beginning of an answer on this question of liberation "from" and "toward" something when Jenson writes about the Son's liberation by the Spirit: the Son is freed "from" the Father, "for" the Father (*ST* I:161). This raises further questions: Was the Son in some way "captive" of the Father, and thus in need of liberation from the Father? What is the point or purpose of such theological speculation? Is this kind of talk required when one wishes to speak of God's "liveliness"?

Even if Jenson treats God's triune being in volume 1 and God's works *ad extra* in volume 2, he does not separate these two themes, as would be expected from someone who criticizes the doctrine of the *logos asarkos* and who appropriates Rahner's axiom.[27] But does he adequately correlate his talk of God's liberating God with the liberating work of God in the world? In volume 2 of his *Systematic Theology*, Jenson writes about the community's participation, in the Spirit, in the liberation the Spirit enacts in the Father and the Son (*ST* II:107–108, 173). He writes that the "liberation of Jesus is accomplished not only by the Resurrection but also by the Spirit's liberation of a community to receive and be his actuality within the present time of this age" (*ST* II:181). One discerns here a very interesting, but underdeveloped, analogy between God's "liveliness" and the liveliness of the human person and communities, for any individual person, any community "has and is a spirit" (*ST* II:181).

Concluding Remarks

Jenson's intent to think God as the living God, as the God of Scripture who is communion of life in God's very being, is praiseworthy. His overall project, which seeks to raise the question of God's identity as witnessed by Scripture, and which answers the question in a trinitarian way, is worthy of admiration. But one may wonder if his way of talking about God's liveliness is the best one, for Jenson seems to be thinking of a Father and a Son who are not at all lively,

---

27. *ST* I:139–142. On the question of the *logos asarkos*, Jenson has evolved: he approves of it in 1963 in *Alpha and Omega*, 166–67 (not without caution and nuances, for he sees the connection between this topic and the idea of a *Deus absconditus* beyond revelation). About Rahner's axiom, Jenson writes unambiguously: "I was on Karl Rahner's side before I ever heard of him" ("A Theological Autobiography," 47).

until they are freed by the Spirit's vivifying act. The Spirit seems to be the reality that triggers God's triunity. Then only does the Father become who the Father is.

7

Social Trinity

Theological Doctrine as a Foundation for Metaphysics

Mathias Hassenfratz-Coffinet

This essay focuses on the theme of the Trinity, conceived metaphysically, in Joseph Bracken's thought. Bracken is among the people who, when thinking about God, are not interested in debates about nature, essence, or substance. A key influence on his thought is Alfred North Whitehead's metaphysics, which is a metaphysics of events in which reality is dynamic.

A. N. Whitehead (1861–1947), the father of process philosophy, elaborated his philosophical system as an attempt to redefine reality so as to understand the existence and interaction of all the elements of the universe in a framework informed by modern science, especially mathematics and physics. Process theologians, including Bracken, rely on this framework and this interpretation of the world. I will begin with a short historical presentation of Bracken's theological context, before turning to the specificities of his trinitarian thought.

Process theology was theistic, in its beginnings, without a robust Christology, and quite anti-trinitarian. That was still the case of Charles Hartshorne, Whitehead's disciple, a pioneering figure in the theological offshoot of process thought. Faithful to Whitehead's philosophical language, he argued for a dipolar, rather than trinitarian, conception of God. Several theologians, such as Schubert M. Ogden, John B. Cobb, and David R. Griffin, have produced important works on Christology since the 1970s, which began to free process theology of pure theism.[1] Griffin did not clarify his position

---

1. Schubert M. Ogden, *The Point of Christology* (San Francisco: Harper & Row, 1982); John B. Cobb, *Christ in a Pluralistic Age* (Philadelphia: Westminster, 1975); David R. Griffin, *A Process Christology* (Philadelphia: Westminster, 1973).

on the Trinity in his 1973 dissertation, but it obviously was not a matter of great importance to him at the time. In more recent publications, however, especially in the collective volume (co-edited by Bracken) *Trinity in Process* (1997), as well as in *Searching for an Adequate God* (2000), Griffin affirms trinitarian discourse, under certain conditions.[2] In his own contribution to *Trinity in Process*, Cobb argues for the importance of trinitarian discourse, while explaining that his interest for this doctrine grew very late in his career, in 1994, and that a binitarian—rather than trinitarian—formulation might be more helpful.[3] True to its name, process theology has thus evolved significantly in regard to trinitarian thought: the first generation, with Hartshorne, was distrustful. The subsequent generation, with Cobb and Griffin, has slowly but surely begun to open that door.

Let us now turn to Joseph Bracken's interpretation of the Trinity. Born in 1930, he is a Jesuit theologian and belongs to the small number of process theologians who are Roman Catholics. He received his doctorate from Freiburg University (Germany) in 1968 and taught theology for many years at Xavier University, in Cincinnati, Ohio, where he is now professor emeritus. He has spent the main part of his academic career trying to articulate process philosophy and trinitarian thought. His central aim has been to reinterpet the doctrine of the Trinity using process categories and its cosmology.

According to process theologians, language is grounded in metaphysics. All linguistic statements necessarily rely on a specific understanding of reality.[4] In his book *The One in the Many* (2001), Bracken seeks to show that even Jacques Derrida is, consciously or unconsciously, more a metaphysician than Derrida himself would admit.[5] That is one of process theologians' important claims, namely that metaphysics shapes the preunderstanding of any theological or philosophical statement as a generally nonexplicit and unconscious *norma normans*. It is a prism through which we apprehend reality. Hence, any

---

2. "Given this distinction . . . we can entertain the possibility that the manifold reasons that have brought Trinitarianism into disrepute may have resulted less from the idea that God is threefold than from the form this idea took in a supernaturalistic context." David R. Griffin, "A Naturalistic Trinity," in Joseph Bracken and Marjorie Suchocki, eds., *Trinity in Process: A Relational Theology of God* (New York: Continuum, 1997), 25.

3. John B. Cobb, "Relativization of the Trinity," in ibid., 21–22.

4. Alfred North Whitehead, *Process and Reality: An Essay in Cosmology*, ed. David R. Griffin and Sherburne Donald (New York: Free Press, 1985 [1929]), 11. See also idem, *Religion in the Making* (Cambridge: Cambridge University Press, 1930 [1926]), 78–79.

5. Joseph Bracken, *The One in the Many: A Contemporary Reconstruction of the God-World Relationship* (Grand Rapids: Eerdmans, 2001), 89.

theological or philosophical statement is, consciously or unconsciously, grounded in metaphysics. The process theologians's commitment to Whitehead is thus, for them, a sign of methodological rigor. To say that Bracken's trinitarian interpretation relies on metaphysics is, then, close to being pleonastic.

Bracken's aim is to consider the consonance of reason and revelation, rather than subordinate revelation to reason, as he believes most process theologians do when they seek to understand God only through metaphysics, without acknowledging that metaphysics may need to undergo certain modifications in order to become consistent with revelation.[6] Bracken thus begins with the Trinity as absolute certainty about the being of God, before revising Whitehead's system. My goal is to analyze Bracken's revision of Whitehead's system in relation to the theme of the Trinity, and to evaluate these modifications with an eye toward the coherence of Bracken's scheme and his aim.

GOD AS SOUL OF THE WORLD

In process theology, the relation between God and the world is typically interpreted in a hierarchical way. A society is made up of smaller events that have certain interrelations linking them, thus forming a unity that is greater than the sum of its parts, precisely thanks to these relations. A human being is a society of cells, a cell is a society of molecules, a molecule is a society of atoms, an atom is a society of even smaller elements, and so forth. In such complex and hierarchical societies, a centralization of power takes place, as well as the emanation of a single entity that becomes the "presiding" occasion: in an animal or a human, for instance, consciousness, through the brain, makes a decision, and other components obey.[7] The presiding entity, or consciousness, gathers data, so that the pain of a wound to the foot becomes the president's pain; pleasure, wherever it may come from, becomes the monarch's pleasure. The power or dominance of the president over the body is great, but not absolute. He will undoubtedly do everything for the good of all of his components, since he himself experiences their pleasure and their pain. It is often with this

---

6. Joseph Bracken, "Review of David Ray Griffin, *Whitehead's Radically Different Postmodern Philosophy: An Argument for Its Contemporary Relevance*," http://ndpr.nd.edu/news/23029-whitehead-s-radically-different-postmodern-philosophy-an-argument-for-its-contemporary-relevance/. Bracken writes: "This is why in my own rethinking of Whitehead's metaphysics I presumed from the start that his metaphysical categories needed revision in order to accommodate Christian belief in God as Trinity."

7. Whitehead, *Process and Reality*, 109, *passim*. The term *monarch* is also often used to designate the dominant entity of a society.

illustration of God as soul of the world that process theology describes the relation between God and the world. Bracken, however, suggests a different approach, one focused on the Trinity.

A Social Interpretation of God

Bracken sees in the Trinity a society in which certain interrelations pertain and which, through a free and gracious decision, shares this interrelation with the world. Since a society is shaped by interrelations that constitute it, each member of the society is ontologically subordinated to it, and at the same time each member is able to modify the structure or the character of that society, since the latter is constituted by this interrelation, and since each member is an agent in these interrelations.[8] There is, then, no domination by God who would be the "president" but, rather, a communion in the trinitarian society.

God is above all a society, the principle of the world's existence, rather than a kind of emanation as the "soul of the world." For most process theologians, God and the world exist in a relation of intimate interdependence, to the point where one cannot talk of God's self-sufficiency, since God, as the soul of the world, would be nothing without the world. The matter is quite different in Bracken's trinitarian interpretation. For him, this interdependence is looser: there is an interdependence; there is no divine aseity; God is affected by the world, but God does not depend on the world in order to exist, since God exists through the inner-trinitarian communion that God shares with the world. The world, however, depends on God for its existence. There is an asymmetrical interdependence.

The Trinity grounds the claim of creation's dependence, which includes humanity's dependence, on God. Through these relations, which are made possible by the trinitarian communion, the whole is a unity that is greater than the sum of its parts. In a similar way, a human being is greater than the sum of its material components, even without an exterior and independent addition such as a substantial soul, as in body-soul dualisms. We can also broaden the consequences and apply them to society, or a mini-society such as a couple: in their relationship and complementarity, a couple is more than two individuals, but forms a unity that exceeds them. The same is true of a stone: it is greater than the sum of its parts, which form a unity because of their relations, even if these relations are absolutely unconscious and can be seen as a specific combination of minerals. Such a society of minerals, which form a stone, draws its existence from creation's communion in the Trinity.

8. Bracken, *One in the Many*, 138–39.

Thinking that way about the interrelation between minerals that make up a stone is anything but anecdotal, in Bracken's opinion, for all of creation depends on God for its existence.

How the Trinitarian Communion Functions

Let us now turn to the ways in which this communion functions. First, the Father decides which ideal vision of the world to propose for each being in the world, which design for creation: what each creature has to do. In Whiteheadian terms, in proximity to the Platonist world of ideas, God's primordial act offers each worldly entity the initial aim by organizing the world of values.[9] This totally universal world of values is set up by God so that it may fit the immediate particularity of the world: each entity needs this world of values at every moment in order to come into existence by producing, from this proposition of organization or this initial aim, the synthesis of its internal and external relations. Without it, the event of existence could not take place.

Second, the Son decides to make the experience of the world his own experience, to share this experience. Process theologians are panentheists: the experience of the world is lived by God without any assimilation of God by the world. We can see this as perfect empathy, total compassion; the joy and suffering of the world are shared by God at the highest level. This experience is similar to what we indicated above about the "president," but without the centralization of power. According to Bracken, this sharing of the experience of the world is the specific role of the Son. Whereas the Father gives something unconditioned, which the world will only partially make concrete, the Son acknowledges this incomplete concretization and integrates it into the divine experience of the world, so that the Father's design, at the following moment, may fit the world as it is rather than fit an abstract world. Without the Son, the Father would be completely detached from the world. In Whiteheadian terms, it is the consequent action of God.

Finally, the Spirit actualizes the experience received by the Son in order to enable the Father to permanently propose a new vision of the world, a vision that is consistent with what the world has actualized on the basis of its own free will. The Spirit actualizes what the Father simply proposed. It thus unites the Father and the Son; it is the relation between the Father and the Son. In Whiteheadian terms, the Spirit is the author of the superjective nature of God.[10]

9. On God's primordial nature, see Whitehead, *Process and Reality*, 7, *passim*. And for God's consequent nature, see ibid., 12, *passim*.

10. Ibid., 87.

Bracken considers the Father as the "subsistent principle" that offers the world a possibility of existence. We must make clear that the Father's "project" is not only a project about something to be done: it is a project of existence, it is about incarnating a certain value. It is a project about something to be done only insofar as, in such an event-based system, existence itself is an act. Being angry, or perceiving anger in someone else, is an act, just as perceiving distress rather than meanness in a heated argument is an act. Being is an act. God acts by proposing a certain act of existence that the creature will more or less actualize. The Son, as "subsistent principle of provisional or current actuality of the world of creation,"[11] will share in this experience. He acknowledges the difference between project and realization. Then the Spirit, as "subsistent principle of ultimate actuality within the creation,"[12] will ensure that the Father takes account of it as the Father proposes the new design in the following instant. This way of understanding God's act is clearly Whiteheadian, but this threefold division of the act is Bracken's own original addition. For Whitehead, there is only one act of interaction with the world, an act renewed by God in each moment. We may call Whitehead's interpretation "bi-polar" in the sense of the giving and, in return, the sharing of the world's experience, in this way of splitting the interaction in two: action and reaction. But this division is purely theoretical, since any action is an interaction that we can compare with Newton's second law: if I push on the table, the table pushes back on my hand; it cannot be otherwise, even though one may want to dissect this interaction in a purely theoretical way. Bracken, therefore, emphasizes the fact that the world is related to God through the relations between the persons of the Trinity and not just through a single person. The three persons of the Trinity, simultaneously and in one movement, work for and with the world.

If the Father is the act of God and the Son the reaction, the Spirit is the synthesis that makes a unity possible. One may interpret the act by using the example of the projection of a movie at a speed of twenty-four images per second. The change of images, which is absolutely imperceptible, is the process of coming-to-the-world; but only the images themselves are seen, not the change of images. The superjective nature relates to the picture itself; God's primordial nature, for Bracken, namely the Father's act, is similar to the light on the screen, a light perceived by our eye; the consequent nature of God, or the Son's action, is similar to the perception, by the movie itself, of the viewer of the movie, in order to adjust the next image according to the way in which the movie is being perceived, thus creating a sort of evolving movie that adapts

11. Bracken, "Panentheism from a Process Perspective," in *Trinity in Process*, 102.
12. Ibid.

itself to the viewer, who therefore takes part in the evolving movie, since she influences its unfolding. But the unfolding of the movie cannot be reduced to the interaction with the viewers, for there is also an internal process of synthesis: a personal appropriation and a free reaction with regard to the received data; the next image is not determined, but only influenced, by the viewers' reaction. The Spirit determines this synthesis.

GOD OUTSIDE THE WORLD

The fact that, in Bracken's interpretation of God, God does not depend on the world and stands outside of the concrete world, as opposed to most process theologians who follow Whitehead closely, raises questions. Bracken writes about the relation between God and the world in terms of transcendence and immanence, vertical and horizontal, but these categories are foreign to Whitehead, for whom God and the world belong to the same category: the concrete world.[13] For Whitehead, God is the universal bond with the world of ideas, which God organizes in order to shape the particular project of existence God has in mind for creation. The world of ideas and the concrete world transcend each other. It is not the case that one of the two is transcendent, while the other is immanent. There are not two worlds, of which one is superior to the other. Instead, the two qualify each other. Transcending, in Whitehead's thought, means "going beyond," "going through," rather than "going above" or "on top." Just as the design and the meaning of a master's painting is not limited to the painting itself, and yet the design is not more important than the painting itself, each is qualified by the other, and does not exist without the other. This use of terms foreign to Whitehead is telling. It is related to Bracken's way of displacing God outside the world and to the asymmetrical dependence Bracken sees between God and the world.

Despite the proximity of Whitehead's system to Platonist ideas, it differs from them in one important respect: ultimate reality is not linked with the world of ideas, but with the concrete world in which the world of ideas embodies itself. A mystical escape outside the world would therefore be completely devoid of interest.

Bracken modifies and reinterprets the system. His emphasis on the ultimate *locus* of reality seems to have been displaced, as his interpretation of the

---

13. "The combination of the two [i.e., the ideas of God as 'unmoved mover' and as 'eminently real'] into the doctrine of an aboriginal, eminently real, transcendent creator, at whose fiat the world came into being, and whose imposed will it obeys, is the fallacy which has infused tragedy into the histories of Christianity and of Mahometanism." Whitehead, *Process and Reality*, 342.

importance of matter shows. Matter is only what supports events and their relations. In the divine communion, there is no need of matter.[14] This idea, that it is possible to separate being from its constituting material aspect by conceiving matter simply as a support, is a very strange thing to behold, coming from a process theologian. It reintroduces a sort of substantial soul, which can be saved (saved in the sense of a computer "backup"), when it is in fact the product of relations between its components and its history in acts.[15] But, according to Bracken, though the soul springs up from the society (in the Whiteheadian sense of the word), it can be extracted and saved by God, in God.

Bracken is thus far more idealistic than Whitehead. The concrete world loses some of its importance. The creation is grounded in the Trinity, but the Trinity alone is eternal; through communion with it, there is eternal life. Surely, since creation is grounded in God, it has a certain importance. But its importance is much relativized, when compared to the "classical" Whiteheadian system.

Bracken seeks to prevent the criticism that his proposal, with its social construal of the Trinity, leans toward tritheism.[16] It would indeed be a mistake to accuse him of tritheism, for the problem may in fact be the opposite: either modalism, as we find it in other process theologians (Bracken is convinced he has not fallen into that trap either), or a problem of internal consistency. By positing the Father, the Son, and the Spirit as three conscious and distinct, yet intimately related, entities; by attributing one role to the Father, another role to the Son, and yet another one to the Spirit, there is a risk to lose sight of God's unique act. It no longer is a unified act by a unique entity. We may dissect an act, but not the subject of the act as subject. To give an illustration: if we say that one part of one's brain has received information, that another part has analyzed that data and sent it further, and that a third part has responded to the data and led to a reaction, we forget one essential thing, namely that it is a unique subject who did all of that. By subordinating the unity of an entity under its

14. Joseph A. Bracken, *Society and Spirit: A Trinitarian Cosmology* (Cranbury-London-Mississauga: Associated University Press, 1991), 141.

15. Bracken follows (while modifying) Marjorie Suchocki's idea of subjective immortality (ibid., 142, referring to Marjorie Suchocki, *The End of Evil: Process Eschatology in Historical Context* [New York: State University of New York Press, 1988], 81). According to Anna Case-Winters, subjective immortality "resonates with understandings of judgement that assume a purgatorial purpose" ("Endings and Ends," in Joseph A. Bracken, ed., *A World Without End: Christian Eschatology from a Process Perspective* [Grand Rapids: Eerdmans, 2005], 189). But nowhere does Suchocki claim that matter is only a medium for another reality which transcends it, and nowhere does she write about purgatory.

16. Joseph A. Bracken, *The Triune Symbol* (Lanham, MD: University Press of America, 1985), 24–25. Cobb, for instance, accuses Bracken of tritheism: "Relativization of the Trinity," in *Trinity in Process*, 5.

multiplicity, one would lose sight of the relations which, for process theologians (Bracken included), manifest the fact that a whole is more than the sum of its parts. It is a subject who perceives, analyzes, and reacts, just as it is God who proposes, experiments, and analyzes before proposing again. Dividing the act, or locating which act takes place in which part of the brain, may be interesting theoretically, as we deepen our understanding, but we should not lose sight of the unity of the subject.

Similarly, in the Whiteheadian system, recognizing several aspects in God is one thing, but seeing several distinct entities in God leads to a significant problem. One is indeed confronted with the classical problem of the necessity of having an entity we call "God," and which would be three simultaneously. Here Bracken uses the term *Godhead*.[17] And indeed, at the metaphysical level, since they are one being, something must exist that makes them a unit: a single entity that emanates from this society, possessing a unique will, which forms what we could name "conscience," "soul"—a God above the Trinity, since the idea of a division of one act into three distinct and conscious authors cannot find a place within the Whiteheadian system. In order to clarify his intention and avoid that problem, Bracken calls on a metaphysical specificity of God, against the fundamental principle of process theology, according to which God must not be an exception to, but rather an exemplification of, the metaphysical system.[18] Consequently, through their perfections, the persons of the Trinity perfectly unite their thoughts, their acts, their wills, and their consciousnesses.[19] The distinction of persons thus depends on their interrelations and on the fact that they constitute a community.

Whereas process theologians claim that, as a consequence of their system, it becomes possible to give an intelligible and reasonable account of faith, this interpretation of God as tripersonal society, rather than as one entity, reopens the problem of its intelligibility. A vision of the world, or a metaphysical system, is elaborated, starting with what we take to be real. It is a speculative generalization about reality, which bases itself on what we deem to be real. The rest is mere hypotheses and logical deductions that stem from these premises. Ultimately, the whole has to be consistent with, and true to, our experience of the world. Religious experience, or religious intuition, having shaped the formulation of a doctrine, is part of that experience of the world. It is not

17. Bracken, *Society and Spirit*, 126.

18. Whitehead, *Process and Reality*, 343.

19. Bracken, *Society and Spirit*, 130. ". . . while as distinct persons they possess separate consciousnesses, nevertheless they together form a single shared consciousness which is perfect in all respects and which thus corresponds exactly to their communitarian reality as one God" (Bracken, *Triune Symbol*, 24–25).

doctrine itself, because doctrine is just a provisional formulation, a partial truth that depends on the system and culture in which it was elaborated.[20] And so, using a doctrine, which comes from a particular vision of the world, as a foundation for another vision of the world has an impact on the whole consistency of the metaphysical system. Bracken modifies the system in a manner that is probably more significant than he imagined: the importance of the concrete world is modified. The same is true of the concrete world's relation to the world of values, a relation that is no longer one of mutual qualifying (as in Whitehead's thought), since one is higher than the other. The world of values is not just beyond, but higher than the concrete world; there is a relation of unilateral sharing from the one to the other, which becomes a gift and thus ceases really to be a sharing. The type of relation between God with the world is thus deeply modified. God no longer belongs in the universe in the same way as the rest of the world belongs in it, since God is transcendent and no longer immanent. God no longer is the immanent yet universal entity that serves as the bond with the world of ideas. God is an exception. God no longer depends on the world, even if the world depends on God.[21]

Using preelaborated doctrines as a way to ground a metaphysics from which other doctrines may be reinterpreted—using doctrines as a hermeneutical basis, so to speak—may lead to problems of consistency or internal coherence, since these doctrines come from other metaphysical viewpoints. Bracken's interpretation of the Trinity may seem forced, not quite a natural fit. His idea of trinitarian communion is very interesting, but the fact that he mentions three distinct and conscious entities in fact reopens the "classical" problems of logic and consistency: the risk of tritheism, and the question of the author of God's acts—that is, the question whether it is the Father, the Son, or the Spirit who is the author of such and such act. Is it Godself, without any further determination, who makes decisions?

In addition, grounding all of creation in the trinitarian communion and the asymmetric interdependence of God and the world, a move that drives God outside the concrete world in a transcendent realm, the existence of

20. "Religions commit suicide when they find their inspirations in their dogmas. The inspiration of religion lies in the history of religion. By this I mean that it is to be found in the primary expressions of the intuitions of the finest types of religious lives. The sources of religious belief are always growing, though some supreme expressions may lie in the past. Records of these sources are not formulae. They elicit in us intuitive response which pierces beyond dogma" (Whitehead, *Religion in the Making*, 129).

21. Bracken's positions contrasts with Whitehead's thought: "It's as true to say that the World is immanent in God, as that God is immanent in the World. It's as true to say that God transcends the World, as that the World transcends God. It's as true to say that God creates the World, as that the World creates God" (Whitehead, *Process and Reality*, 348).

which we cannot really fathom, creates problems in a metaphysic built on the fixed principle that Whitehead calls the "ontological principle": "This general principle will be termed the ontological principle. It is the principle that everything is positively somewhere in actuality."[22] There is, then, a sort of conflict of several metaphysics, whereas on other topics, such as God's creative action, or God's action in the world, or the idea that creation exists through communion with God rather than as a consequence of a powerful act, Bracken is really helpful when he interprets the quality of God's relationship with the world, namely as a relation of power or of sharing. We can also question the fact that Bracken uses a doctrine in order to ground his metaphysics, instead of beginning from both metaphysics and doctrine in order to think doctrine using metaphysics, adapting metaphysics whenever needed. He criticizes process theologians for subordinating revelation to reason and argues that his own goal is to consider them as consonant. It seems to me, however, that he tends to fall into the trap of subordinating reason to revelation, thereby injuring the consistency of the scheme. A strictly systematic and less philosophical study would have begun with the doctrine of the Trinity, Scripture, and the history of doctrine, before embarking on this metaphysical work. It seems to me that a hermeneutical reflection on revelation is missing, and this lacuna does not favor a real consonance between reason and revelation, beyond any subordination of one versus the other.

Bracken's aim, in his trinitarian proposal, is twofold: he seeks to justify the faith of believers who interpret God's act in the world in a trinitarian way.[23] He then emphasizes the idea of society in an atomistic scheme, in order to bring to the fore the relations between entities. This allows him to replace the idea of a "Father," understood as a Lord who creates and dominates by strong power, with the idea of a communion in which creation partakes. The focus no longer is on the type, or the role, of each individual, but on communion and everyone's contribution to the common good.[24] A social interpretation of the Trinity, rather than a monarchical conception of God, would support, according to Bracken, a retrieval of important insights coming from marginalized minorities' theologies (black, Hispanic, feminist, etc.) within an objective framework for an open discussion.[25]

22. Ibid., 40.

23. Bracken, *Trinity in Process*, 109.

24. Bracken, *One in the Many*, 44.

25. Ibid., 45. Bracken refers to the equality of the persons in the trinitarian communion (against the domination of a monarch) as well as to the interrelations between persons in the Trinity in a democratic fashion; democracy is a Whiteheadian term; see Whitehead, *Process and Reality*, 108. It is a law level of

Bracken's aim is twofold in his trinitarian proposal. The problem is that each picture has drawbacks. If we keep only the idea of communion, we lose that of authority, of protection, in favor of communitarian egalitarianism, which can also means protection, but not in the same way. In the group's protection, it is the power of the sum of the components, including our own, which protects, not the power of an Other. We are ourselves an instance of power. If God is no more king, we have a share of that power. We lose the idea of respect and subordination:[26] we do not respect a brother, an equal, in the same way than we respect a Father or a master. By avoiding submission to God as a lord, we take the risk never again to submit ourselves or, more exactly, to submit ourselves permanently before other instances, which are worldly. Any change of picture affects the original meaning; we add and we subtract, for better or for worse.

Bracken's attempt to overcome atomism is excellent, it seems to me. He brings to the forefront the interpretation of the whole, against the atomistic tendencies of most process theologians. But by starting from a doctrine in order to revise Whitehead's metaphysics, Bracken modifies its foundations, shaking the whole building. He should perhaps simply have displaced one aspect of Whitehead's philosophy, since Whitehead himself called his scheme the "philosophy of organism" precisely in order to underline the interdependence of everything with regard to everything.[27] I should add that prehensions (that is, "interactions") constitute in his scheme a "category of existence" in its own right.[28] This shows the fundamental importance of relations in his scheme of events. Had Bracken begun with a less atomistic interpretation of Whitehead's scheme, he could have focused first on the interpretation of the Trinity as a way to express God's relation to the world (i.e., the economic Trinity), and only secondly on God's being in Godself (i.e., the immanent Trinity). The Trinity would then only be a doctrine one formulates using the categories of metaphysics, simultaneously modifying metaphysics, since God's act would be, without it, interpreted in a "dipolar" way. But it

organization, an egality of the members of a society. For example, a stone has no center of control, whereas most animals have this kind of central organ: the brain. The democratic way of interacting makes alterity possible, whereas monarchy suggests the idea of a unique life, and consequently an intrinsic intolerance. But if the communion (rather than being, gender, and power) of the divine persons is emphasized, then the manly, power-hungry, glorious dimensions fade away. One may then incorporate the criticisms that these theologies (black, Hispanic, feminist, etc.) raise in order to reshape theology.

26. Whitehead uses this term in a positive manner. See Whitehead, *Process and Reality*, 337.

27. Whitehead, *Process and Reality*, 59, *passim*.

28. "Category of Existence" no. 2, in Whitehead, *Process and Reality*, 22.

could be that this proposition, too, may be seen as subordinating revelation under reason, without reaching a consonance between the two; one could argue that here the *norma normans* is metaphysics. Walking on a ridge always is a challenge.

List of Contributors

Christophe Chalamet is professor of theology at the University of Geneva. His work has focused on dialectical theologians, modern Protestant thinkers, and the Social Gospel within francophone Protestantism.

Gavin D'Costa is professor in Catholic theology at the University of Bristol. He has published several books that focus on a Christian theology of religions in a Trinitarian perspective.

A graduate of the University of Strasbourg, *Mathias Hassenfratz-Coffinet* is a doctoral student at the University of Geneva, where he is writing a dissertation on hope in a Process perspective.

Karen Kilby is the Bede chair of Catholic theology at Durham University. She previously taught at the University of Nottingham. She has published acclaimed books on Karl Rahner and Hans Urs von Balthasar, and has authored an influential critique of social Trinitarianism.

Aristotle Papanikolaou is Archbishop Demetrios Professor in Orthodox Theology and Culture at Fordham University. In addition to numerous studies on recent and contemporary Trinitarian theology in the Eastern/Orthodox tradition, he has published a book on Vladimir Lossky and John Zizioulas and, more recently, *The Mystical as Political: Democracy and Non-Radical Orthodoxy* (University of Notre Dame Press, 2012).

Christoph Schwöbel is professor of systematic theology at the University of Tübingen. He has published widely on Trinitarian theology and other key topics in Christian theology. Among his recent books is *Gott im Gespräch. Theologische Studien zur Gegenwartsdeutung* (Mohr, 2011).

Marc Vial teaches systematic theology at the Protestant Theological Faculty of the University of Strasbourg. He has published a book as well as numerous articles on medieval theology, Reformation theology, and contemporary Protestant theology. Among the topics he has written about in recent years is the idea of God's almightiness.

Index

Albertus Magnus, 36
Alberus, Eramus, 47
Alexander of Hales, 36
Al Ghazali, 107
Alston, Wallace, 142
Anselm of Canterbury, 36, 59
Aquinas, Thomas, 5, 26, 34, 36, 42,
44–46, 48, 58, 60, 88, 107, 111, 119
Aristotle, 57–58, 65, 145
Asendorf, Ulrich, 46
Athanasius, 104
Augustine of Hippo, 1, 5, 7, 15, 24, 36,
37, 42–43, 48, 90, 130, 144, 147
Augustus (Emperor), 65
Ayres, Lewis, 43, 76

Bacon, Hannah, 8
Balthasar, Hans Urs von, 81, 97, 105,
118–19
Barnes, Michel René, 37, 43, 76
Barth, Karl, 3–6, 13, 35, 76, 97, 102,
108, 112–13, 128, 131–36, 141–49
Basil of Caesarea, 7, 26–27, 31, 62, 128
Batut, Jean-Pierre, 139
Boethius, 33
Boff, Leonardo, 6, 86
Bonaventure, 36
Bornkamm, Günter, 141
Braaten, Carl, 141
Bracken, Joseph A., 153–64
Brower, Jeffrey E., 57
Brunner, Peter, 141
Bulgakov, Sergius, 87, 95–105
Bultmann, Rudolf, 143
Burrell, David, 114
Burrows, William R., 121
Butin, Philip W., 62

Calvin, John, 62, 149
Campenhausen, Hans von, 141
Carras, Costa, 12
Case-Winters, Anna, 160
Clooney, Francis X., 114
Coakley, Sarah, 6, 76
Cobb, John B., 115, 153–54
Congar, Yves, 4, 37
Constantine, 65
Cordes, Paul Josef, 49
Craig, William L., 55
Cunningham, Mary B., 97

Dante, 116
D'Costa, G., 8, 108, 110, 118
DeHart, Paul J., 2
de Régnon, Théodore, 36–37, 42
Derrida, Jacques, 73, 154
Di Noia, Joseph A., 114
Dorner, Isaak August, 3
Dupuis, Jacques, 51, 120–23
Dionysius (Pseudo-), 36, 80

Eckstein, Hans-Joachim, 40
Elert, Werner, 46
Emery, Gilles, 44, 45
Ensminger, Sven, 112
Eusebius of Caesarea, 65
Evdokimov, Paul, 96

Faber, Johannes, 47
Feenstra, Ronald J., 55
Florovsky, Georges, 90, 96–98
Ford, David F., 113
Foucault, Michel, 117
Fyodorov, Nicolai F., 64

Gadamer, Hans-Georg, 141
Geach, Peter, 56
Geffert, Bryn, *96*
Green, Garrett, *112*
Gregory Nazianzen, *26–27*, 66
Gregory of Nyssa, 7, 27, 60
Grenz, Stanley J., *12*
Griffin, David R., 153–54
Griffiths, Paul J., 114
Groppe, Elizabeth T., *5*
Gunton, Colin E., 7, 36–37, *59*, *60*, *64*, 76, *125*, 127–38, *146*
Gutiérrez, Gustavo, 98

Hahn, Ferdinand, *40*
Haight, Roger, 120
Harnack, Adolf von, 3, 77
Hart, David Bentley, *59*, *143*, *145*, *148*
Hartshorne, Charles, 153–54
Hassenfratz, M., 8
Hegel, Georg Wilhelm Friedrich, 2–3, 112
Hegemon, Petrus, 47
Heidegger, Martin, 141
Heim, S. Mark, 114–17
Helmer, Christine, *46*, 47
Hennessy, Kristin, *37*
Hick, John, *73*, 108–10, 120–21
Hill, Edmund, 118
Holmes, Stephen R., *37*, 76
Hurtado, Larry W., *40*
Husbands, Mark, *64*

Inwagen, Peter van, 56–57
Irenaeus of Lyon, 111

Jenson, Robert W., 7, 16, *17*, 37, 59, *79*, 141–51
John Paul II, 120
John of Damascus, 96
Johnson, Elizabeth A., 36, 79, 98
Jonas, Hans, 134

Jüngel, Eberhard, *3*, 4, *37*, 134–36, *139*, 145–46

Kärkkäinen, Veli-Matti, *51*, *125*
Kant, Immanuel, 1–2
Kasper, Walter, 37, *49*
Khodr, George, 110
Kilby, Karen, 6, 75, 102, *118*
Knitter, Paul, *108*, 109–110, 121
Knuutila, Simo, *47*
Kripke, Saul, *30*

LaCugna, Catherine M., 5, 105
Leftow, Brian, 55–56
Leibniz, Gottfried Wilhelm, 56
Leiner, Martin, *3*
Lenin, 98
Levin, Christoph, *41*
Lindbeck, George, 113, 142
Lombard, Peter, *36*, 44
Lossky, Vladimir, 87–90, 93–94, 96–98, 102, 104–5, 145
Lott, Eric, *116*
Lundberg, Matthew D., 7
Luther, Martin, 30, 46–47

Major, Georg, 47
Martin, Ralph, 120
McCall, Thomas H., 55, 59–60
Melanchthon, Philip, 144
Merrigan, Terrence, *121*
Milbank, John, *110*
Min, Anselm K., 45
Molnar, Paul D., 4
Moltmann, Jürgen, 4, 6, *37*, 59–60, 86, 98, 137, 145
Moreland, James P., 55
Morris, Thomas V., *54*

Newton, 158
Nietzsche, Friedrich, 90

Ochs, Peter, 113

Ogden, Schubert M., 153
Ott, Heinrich, 35

Palamas, Gregory, *5*
Panikkar, Raimundo, 115, 117, 120, 123–24
Pannenberg, Wolfhart, 4, 98, 101, 113, 141, 145, 147
Papanikolaou, A., 8, *94*, *98*
Pelikan, Jaroslav, *80*
Peterson, Erik, 65–66
Phan, Peter C., 35
Pieris, Aloysius, 109–10
Pinnock, Clark H., 113, *114*, *125*
Pinto, Henrique, 117
Placher, William, 113
Plantinga, Alvin, 33
Plantinga, Cornelius, 55
Plantinga, Richard J., 7
Plato, 145
Polkinghorne, John, 62

Ratzinger, Joseph, 36, *49*
Rahner, Karl, 3–6, 10, 13, 44, 76, 101–5, 112–13, 117–23, 143, 151
Rea, Michael C., *55*, 57
Richard of St. Victor, *36*, 130
Rowlands, Tracey, 119

Saarinen, Risto, *47*, *49*
Samartha, Stanley, 110–11
Schleiermacher, Friedrich D. E., 2, 61, 111, 146
Schlink, Edmund, 141
Schmaus, Michael, *36*
Schmitt, Carl, 65
Schwöbel, Christoph, 7, *9*, *16*, *33*, *38*, *42*, *46–48*, *64*, *127–28*, 135

Seitz, Christopher, *40*
Smith, Timothy L., *45*
Sobrino, Jon, 83
Solov'ev, Vladimir, 96, 98
Soulen, Kendall R., 73, 78–81
Stăniloae, Dumitru, 87, 94–96
Suchocki, Marjorie, *160*
Swinburne, Richard, *54*, 55

Tanner, Kathryn, 64, *65*, 66, *68*, 74–75
Tavast, Timo, *142*, *150*
Te Velde, Rudi, *34*
Theokritoff, Elizabeth, *97*
Tholuck, August, 2–3
Thompson, Thomas R., 7
Torrance, James B., 12
Tracy, David, *93*, 102

Vanhoozer, Kevin, 113
Volf, Miroslav, 6, 36, 64, 66
von Rad, Gerhard, 141

Wainwright, Arthur W., *39*
Wainwright, Geoffrey, *51*
Whitehead, Alfred North, 153, 155, 157–64
Wiles, Maurice, *73*
Williams, Rowan, 43, 119, 124
Williams, Stephen N., *64*
Wisse, Maarten, 44
Wittgenstein, Ludwig, *27*

Yong, Amos, *52*, 110–11
Young, Frances, 39

Zizioulas, John, *4*, 13–16, 36–37, 48, 87, 90–97, 131, 149

CPSIA information can be obtained at www.ICGtesting.com
Printed in the USA
LVOW12s0107310514

387941LV00006B/7/P